THRIVING IN AN
ALL-BOYS CLUB

THRIVING IN AN ALL-BOYS CLUB

Female Police and Their Fight for Equality

Cara Rabe-Hemp

ROWMAN & LITTLEFIELD

Lanham • Boulder • New York • London

Published by Rowman & Littlefield
A wholly owned subsidiary of The Rowman & Littlefield Publishing Group, Inc.
4501 Forbes Boulevard, Suite 200, Lanham, Maryland 20706
www.rowman.com

Unit A, Whitacre Mews, 26-34 Stannary Street, London SE11 4AB

British Library Cataloguing in Publication Information Available

Library of Congress Cataloging-in-Publication Data
Names: Rabe-Hemp, Cara E., author.
Title: Thriving in an all-boys club : female police and their fight for
  equality / Cara Rabe-Hemp.
Description: Lanham : Rowman & Littlefield, [2018] | Includes bibliographical
  references and index.
Identifiers: LCCN 2017020388 (print) | LCCN 2017035118 (ebook) | ISBN
  9781442274303 (electronic) | ISBN 9781442274297 (cloth : alk. paper)
Subjects: LCSH: Policewomen—United States. | Police administration—United
  States. | Sex discrimination against women—United States.
Classification: LCC HV8023 (ebook) | LCC HV8023 .R325 2018 (print) | DDC
  363.2082/0973—dc23
LC record available at https://lccn.loc.gov/2017020388

Printed in the United States of America

Contents

Preface

I N M ARCH 2015, INVESTIGATIVE REPORTER Diane Diamond published a piece on her blog titled "More Female Police Officers, Please!" On her blog, she argued that hiring more female police officers might be a solution to the increasing violence occurring between police and young men of color. She pointed out that female police officers have strong conflict-resolution skills, which come in handy while policing the streets. She also argued that women do not have the same need as men to be macho when disrespected. Her comments hit a nerve, especially with men working in law enforcement:

> Diane. I am a public safety employee. I am speaking from experience. Female police officers can have a positive effect on the public by using natural assets of compassion and nurturing. However, the majority of female officers become nothing more than a liability when the stuff hits the fan. That is the REALITY. Because our culture dictates political correctness, we have female officers. This doesn't make females any less than males, just physically and emotionally impaired in comparison.
>
> Even the women that DO WANT to be cops do not always have the physical capacity to do the job (110lb woman in a hand-to-hand brawl with a 240lb addict in a PCP-induced rage? Don't think that's gonna end well for her).[1]

How do women overcome the attitudes expressed by cynics that women cannot handle the physical challenges of policing? This book provides the answer to this question and much more. It is an insider's view into one of the most debated issues surrounding female police officers—their ability to find acceptance in the "all-boys club" of policing. Since the Civil Rights Act of 1972 opened the door to patrol for women and made it illegal to utilize gender as a barrier to employment, female police officers have struggled to gain equality. At fifty-eight thousand female police officers, women make up 13 percent of police officers in the United States, making it one of the few existing male-dominated industries left (others include tower operators [4 percent], bus mechanics [1 percent], automotive service technicians [1 percent], and brick and concrete masons [1 percent]).[2] Their stories of success and acceptance into American police agencies reveal the workday of the brave women who wear the police uniform.

As a professor of criminal justice, I have been interviewing female police officers since 2007. To date, I have interviewed almost sixty female officers, representing all ranks (from recruit to chief), geographic locales, tenures (years of service), and police organizations (municipal, county, state, and federal). In 2007, I met Heather Noell, a lieutenant with a state police agency who had twenty-five years of police experience. She joined policing in 1981, the fifth women ever hired by her agency. I asked Noell if anything had impeded her almost twenty-five-year police career. Noell replied, "I think one thing that has impeded me the most is that police work is still a little bit of a boy's club, and I'm not a boy." That really stuck with me. I left the interview wondering if all women integrate as Heather did: feeling outside the police culture looking in, despite her impending retirement at the high rank of lieutenant.

What I have learned is that women's acceptance in policing is complex and their experiences are diverse, although there are common themes like resistance and harassment by colleagues, the glass ceiling in promotion, and gender-specific obstacles related to pregnancy and childcare. However, despite the struggles that women face to survive in the "all-boys club"[3] of policing, not only do women survive, but most also thrive in this almost exclusively male occupation. Their stories are positive and heartening. In writing this book, I tried to give their voices a forum in which to be heard while maintaining their anonymity. (The names of the women in this book have been changed to protect their identities.) Their stories are based on interviews and are exact accounts of what they said. Other stories in this book come from historical narratives, and some were snatched from the headlines of the national news media. These women have publicly told their stories, so in these cases the names/identities have not been changed for the book.

Most of what we know about women police comes from women like Heather Noell, who began policing in the early 1980s. Because of the physical and psychological demands of policing, many departments allow for retirement after twenty-five or thirty years of service—some even sooner. For this reason, women who entered policing in the 1980s, one of the largest hiring classes of women ever, were rapidly leaving the profession by 2010. I interviewed them first. A few years later, I began to interview the subsequent cohorts of women who joined policing in the 1990s and 2000s. Much less is known about these women. Far from the first, the women who joined policing in the 1990s and early 2000s reside in a culture of policing that has seen many changes in the past twenty years, including the adoption of community policing in their agencies, the strengthening of sexual harassment and affirmative action laws, and the continued recruitment and retention of female officers. All of these factors have influenced their experiences and abilities to negotiate their roles in police agencies' cultures.

For this reason, the book follows the entrance of women into policing chronologically, pointing out the relevant police and societal issues that influenced women police in each era. Dividing the book into distinct eras highlights the progress and gains women have made in policing as well as the generational differences in their lived experiences. First, the introduction, "The History of Women in Policing: Matrons to Patrol Officers," sketches a brief history of women in American law enforcement, including a review of the revolutionary changes facing policing that eventually opened the door to patrol for women. Although women have been active in police work as prison matrons since the 1800s, it was not until the late 1970s, when female officers began working in patrol, that the debate about the abilities of women in policing began. The debate centered on the female officer's ability to maintain the authority and strength necessary for the police role. This provided a backdrop for the continued resistance to women in the policing culture, including daily harassment, discrimination, and disrespect. This is the starting point for the experiences of women featured in this text.

The book's three sections—"Female Police Officers of the 1980s: Title Niners," "Female Police Officers of the 1990s: Crime Fighters or Communication Experts," and "Female Officers of the 2000s: Career Minded and College Educated"—capture the experiences of modern policewomen. Women who were hired as police officers in the 1980s were the first generation to be impacted by Title IX and the Civil Rights Act of 1972, both of which strove to increase opportunities for women. In many jurisdictions, these women were the first women ever employed by their agencies. Women officers in this era fought the widespread assumption that police were male, which they were constantly reminded of in their routine encounters with citizens and colleagues alike. Women featured in this section all broke barriers in their departments, whether it was as the first female officer, the first woman to make rank, or the first to be selected as the academy class president. Being the first had its drawbacks, as sexism and harassment were common and blatant, starting at the police training academy and continuing throughout their field training experiences and beyond. Their experiences were fueled by the continued debate over whether women could physically handle the dangerous environment in which police operated. Through their acts of courage and leadership, these women became successful role models for future generations of women police.

Daunted by the high-profile brutality cases of Rodney King and Abner Louima, the 1990s saw an unprecedented hiring trend in policing as departments attempted to become more representative of the communities they policed. Women, along with other underrepresented groups, entered policing en masse and faced the daunting task of representing the changing face of policing. By the 1990s, women were not facing the same obstacles in hiring but instead faced the new challenges of promotion and integration into the "all-boys club."[4] In the 1990s, policing was undergoing a revolution, as community policing, which relied more on communication skills and problem solving, was becoming the police modality of choice. In this section, "Female Police Officers of the 1990s: Crime Fighters or Communication Experts," I argue that this seemed a perfect fit for women, who were thought of as more natural communicators and consensus seekers.

Finally, in the section "Female Police Officers of the 2000s: Career Minded and College Educated," we see the presence of women officers changing police organizations and shaping policies; departments are now creating light-duty assignments and family-leave policies. Today, female officers hold high ranks in police agencies and achieve new "firsts," including breaking into stereotypically masculine assignments, such as SWAT (Special Weapons and Tactics) teams and CSI (Crime Scene Investigation). Often unaware of the struggles of previous generations, equality is assumed for this generation of women police. This generation's struggle is about finding a work and life balance, as police families are more the norm than ever, and finding a niche in the still highly masculine world of policing.

The conclusion of the book, "The Current Status of Women Police and Future Directions," provides some ideas about what the future holds for women entering policing today. As police agencies across the nation face a legitimacy crisis, accompanied by community demand for a "new breed" of police officers embodying interpersonal communication, problem solving, and service to community members, there is mounting evidence that female officers police differently from men. They are often more committed to public service, better at calming police-citizen interactions, and more likely to provide comfort to crime victims than their male peers are. These strengths likely stem from female officers' style of policing, which relies less on physical force. In fact, some scholars argue that if enough women enter policing, a tipping point will be reached and male colleagues may adopt women's approaches.

However, this may just be a throwback to earlier ideas about the proper place of women as caregivers and social workers, rather than crime fighters.

This book would not be possible without the encouragement and support of many other people. I would like to thank Ralph Weisheit, distinguished professor; Jackie Schneider, chair of criminal justice; and Dawn Beichner, professor, all of Illinois State University, for encouraging me during the course of this research. I want to show my gratitude to Amie Schuck, at the University of Illinois at Chicago, for believing that gender was a worthy area of dissertation study and for her review of the manuscript. It is much improved based on her suggestions. Many thanks to my husband, Jason, and my children, Lorne and Lena, for their love, support, and patience. Finally, thank you, Mom, for instilling in me the love of writing. I especially want to thank the brave women police who shared their stories with me. I hope I have done justice to their amazing careers. It is my hope that their achievements and contributions to law enforcement will inspire the next generation to follow the path blazed by women who not only survived but also thrived in the all-boys club.

Introduction

The History of Women in Policing

Matrons to Patrol Officers

W OMEN HAVE PLAYED AN INTEGRAL ROLE in police work since the late 1800s, employed in three different roles—matrons, policewomen, and police officers. Starting in the late 1800s, women were utilized as police matrons with duties limited to housing women and children in police stations, playing a motherly role to those in their care. For example, in 1892 prison matron McCarthy joined the Eldridge Street Police Station in New York City. She was "not at all the robust type of woman one would expect to see in charge of the prison at one of the worst precincts in town."[1] Instead, she was described as "small and soft-spoken," which gave her an "air of delicacy at odds with her surroundings."[2] Her sixteenth anniversary at the station was celebrated in a 1908 article in the *New York Times*. She told several stories about people she came in contact with that week, including a "crazy old" woman who had fled from her daughter and son-in-law, only to be returned; a tramp she had cared for previously several times who had died earlier that week; and drama involved in getting two starving Jewish siblings to eat and drink food that was not kosher but was all she had. Most compelling, she was concerned about the rate at which the women under her care were dying, some by their own hands.

She described a night in her professional life:

> Only the other night the Gerry Society and a young Austrian woman made things lively. The Gerry Society made a raid and sent in seventeen children fourteen boys, and three girls. I had the children in here. Next thing in comes a policeman with a woman who'd been trying to kill herself in the streets. He says

to search her watch her extra careful. Now, how was I, with seventeen Gerry Societies in my room, to watch anyone out here extra careful? Sure enough, the first trip I made to her cell, I hear her groan. She was trying to choke herself. We got her out, the doorman and me, and worked over her. When she came to I said, "You poor soul, what are you after killing yourself for?" "My man don't love me anymore. He wants me to go away. I don't care for my life. I think I die sure in a few weeks." "Arrah then, if you'll be dying so soon anyway, why do you be trying to kill yourself here and making me such a lot of trouble," said I and got her a cup of tea.[3]

This firsthand account of a night in the life of a prison matron shows why they were described as motherly. The Gerry Society was the common name for the New York Society for the Prevention of Cruelty to Children, which was founded in 1874 as the first child protection agency. It does not say in the article why the seventeen children she mentioned were at her station, as the Gerry Society had far-reaching powers to ensure the safety of children, including protecting children from sweatshops and factories, physical and sexual abuse, as well as living in immoral houses like drug dens and houses of prostitution. What is clear from her story is that she had her hands full, guarding female inmates and protecting the young people under her watch.

Twenty years later in 1911 and across the United States, an article in the *Los Angeles Times* featured the exploits of the most famous, and likely the first, policewoman, Alice Stebbins Wells, nicknamed "Policewoman Badge #1." In the article, Wells described an immoral play titled *The Girl in the Taxi* playing at the Mason Opera House that she wanted to stop from being shown. Of the play, Wells had this to say: "It is entirely too sensuous and is opposed to good morals and I shall take steps to prevent its further appearance, as I cannot conscientiously permit a play on the boards that is not in accord with good morals."[4] Based on her efforts, Los Angeles County prosecutor Eddie Guy shut the play down, signaling that Wells's recommendation was taken seriously.

Wells saw her job not as a crime fighter but as a social worker dedicated to ending the delinquency of young women and children and the slipping sexual propriety in society. This included defending child labor laws, policing promiscuity in and around military camps as well as dance halls and theaters, and preventing girls from falling into the white slave trade. Thus, the role of policewomen (1910–1960) was limited like their matron forerunners. However, by the end of the 1960s, women across the nation were recognizing that their skills could be useful on patrol. Empowered by the women's movement, they fought for the right to be police officers rather than policewomen. Wells claimed: "I am a police officer. . . . I am sure that the time will soon come when women will be frequently appointed on the police force of every city in the country for there is a certain work to be done that only they can do."[5] Women had unique capabilities, and for that reason alone they were necessary to policing.

In 1968, Betty Blankenship, age thirty-four, and Elizabeth Coffal Robinson, twenty-six, made history by being the first two women to patrol the city streets of Indianapolis, Indiana, equal to their male counterparts. In car number 47, dressed in their blue jackets, skirts, and high heels, with their guns in their purses, they went where no policewoman had ever gone before. While at the academy, the women met a sergeant instructor by the name of Winston Churchill, a memorable name, who after many long conversations had said that if he were ever in charge, he would consider allowing women to patrol. When Churchill became police chief, Blankenship and Coffal reminded him of his promise, and he fought for the opportunity in his Indianapolis department. Now all eyes focused on what would happen in Indianapolis. Would the female officers in car number 47 have the strength and authority necessary to do the dangerous job of street patrol? Would citizens accept them? Of their historic moment, Robinson said, "We knew we were making history but the size and scope of what we were doing didn't really occur to us until years later. At the moment, we just wanted to show that we could do the same nitty-gritty work that the men did."[6] Of course, as they later admitted, acceptance as full-fledged police officers did not come right away. Instead, Blankenship and Robinson continued to respond to calls for service to free up the policemen for their "more important" law enforcement duties.

More significant than patrolling the dangerous streets of Indianapolis, what Blankenship and Robinson and other policewomen of the 1970s did was abandon the historic role that women had adopted up to this point in history as specialists in caretaking and social work; they demanded to be treated as crime fighters like their male counterparts. Unlike early policewomen, female officers who entered policing during this time were not drawn to policing simply out of a wish to be of service, but because of the potential for career opportunities, which included advancement and job security. Previously, women were usually placed in segregated women's bureaus that offered a level of specialization as social workers. It provided security, but also isolation from patrol and crime-fighting tasks. As the transition from policewomen to police officers began in the 1960s–1970s, female officers attempted to transition to more general police duties, and this is when the magnitude of the segregation into women's bureaus was realized. To become full-fledged police, women needed to reject these sex-typed specialist roles and become generalists. This chapter celebrates the almost 125 years of service that women performed in policing as matrons and policewomen before breaking into patrol. (For a list of accomplishments, see the timeline on the next page.) This group of women

Women in Policing Timeline

1892 •Matron McCarthy joins the Eldridge Street Police Station, New York, as a prison matron.

1908 •Lola Baldwin (from Oregon) is the first woman to have the power to conduct arrests.

1910 •Alice Wells (from Los Angeles) is the first woman police officer.

1912 •Isabella Goodwin (from New York) becomes the first female detective after going undercover to catch a ring of taxicab thieves.

1915 •International Association of Policewoman (IAP) is founded by Alice Wells.

1916 •Georgia Ann Robinson becomes the first African American female police officer employed by the LAPD.

1918 •Mary Sullivan (of the NYPD) is the first female homicide detective.

1935 •First female-specific uniforms are created by Commissioner Lewis Valentine (in New York).

1956 •International Association of Woman Police (IAWP) is founded.

1957 •First TV show starring a female police role is *Decoy Police Woman*.

1960 •First female officers work undercover in drug and prostitution stings.

1961 •Supreme Court case *Shpritzer v. Lang* allows women to take promotional exams.

1968 •Elizabeth Robinson and Betty Bankenship (of Indianapolis) are the first woman patrol officers (assigned to car 47).

1969 •President Nixon's Executive Order 11478 allows women to become special agents.

1972 •Title VII Civil Rights Act is implemented, outlawing discrimination based on gender in public agencies.

1974 •Gail Cobb (of Washington, DC) is the first women shot and killed in the line of duty.

1985 •Penny Harrington (of Portland) is the first female chief.

1990 •National Association of Woman Law Enforcement Executives (NAWLEE) is created.

1994 •Beverly Harvard (from Atlanta) is the first female black chief.

1995 •National Center for Woman Policing (NCWP) is created.

1999 •Woman in Federal Law Enforcement (WIFLE) is founded.

overcame a unique set of obstacles to earn the recognition of the men in the "all-boys club."

Women as Prison Matrons: Protectors of Women's Virtues

Starting before the Civil War, reformers were adamant that women, not men, should supervise the growing number of imprisoned women and young girls in the United States. This created the first major professional role for women in the criminal justice system, the prison matron. The prison matron's roles in protecting the virtues of young women coincided nicely with the period's societal values. Keep in mind that during the Victorian era, which commonly refers to Queen Victoria's reign from 1837 to 1901, it was considered indecent for a young man to view too much of a woman's ankle! Women were cautioned in etiquette books not to use both hands to lift their skirts when crossing the street because it was risqué. Needless to say, guarding women prisoners, which involved seeing women in various stages of undress, was controversial. Powerful political groups, such as the League of Women Voters and General Federation of Women's Club, as well as civic and social hygiene associations such as the National Young Women and the Women's Christian Temperance Movement, played strong roles in the expansion of women's work into prisons, reformatories, and jails. They argued that female prison matrons were necessary to protect women's decency. As Estelle Freedman points out in her text, *Their Sisters' Keepers: Women's Prison Reform in America, 1830–1930*, prison matrons solved a variety of problems. First, the decency issue: female prisoners, especially intoxicated ones, behaved indecently by Victorian standards. Comments from the Women's Christian Temperance Union supporters made this point: "These women . . . may . . . disrobe themselves and stand at their cell doors. Every honest woman *must* demand that her happy sister shall be protected at all times by a woman official."[7] This brings up the second major issue that matrons solved: the issue of sex abuse. There were increasingly public stories of male guards and police taking liberties with the female inmates. In 1869 in New Jersey sex abuse was verified when a black woman who had been imprisoned for years gave birth to a mulatto (i.e., mixed race) child fathered by one of the prison guards.[8] One of the most horrific cases of sex abuse was carried out in Jeffersonville, Indiana, where female inmates were prostituted by the guards and prison officials. The allegations were released to the media and even made it to the Indiana House of Representatives:

> Very grave charges were presented to the committee against officers and guards formerly in charge of the prison, of drunkenness, and treatment of prisoners, prostitution of female convicts, and demoralization generally. Although the parties charged were no longer connected with the institution and were beyond removal or impeachment, yet, the committee, to satisfy themselves in regard to these alleged abuses and outrages upon humanity, law and order, caused Witnesses to be brought before them to testify concerning the same. Loth as the committee was to believe, the evidence compelled the conviction that many of these charges were true, though not to the extent alleged in the exaggerated report which has found its way into the newspapers.[9]

Finally, it was believed that matrons were necessary for the reformation of female prisons. After their tour of US prisons, experts Enoch Wines and Theodore W. Dwight shared their hope that prison matrons would have a motherly effect on the women under their care. "Fallen women," a term used to describe women who had "lost their innocence," as well as the grace of God, were believed to be "ignorant and neglected," making them easy prey to the "temptations caused by waste and extravagance."[10]

Due to the efforts of these groups, New York City appointed six matrons for the supervision of women and children in 1845, marking the first known instances of women in police work. It was hard work. The February 16, 1908, *New York Times* headline reads, "Police Matron's Job Is Not a Sinecure— What with Preventing Suicides and Lodging Vagrants Her Life's a Busy One."[11] The article describes the workday of Matron McCarthy, a prison matron with New York City's Eldridge police station, complete with young immigrant children, homeless old women, and mentally ill inmates. Matron McCarthy was hired after New York passed the Police Matrons Bill, following decades of ceaseless lobbying by civic and suffragette groups. It required that police matrons be on duty at night when women were arrested and that matrons conduct searches of women. Between 1880 and 1886 thirteen major cities followed, including Chicago, Boston, and St. Louis.[12] These early prison matrons, like Matron McCarthy, were mostly of working-class and immigrant backgrounds and earned approximately $1,000 a year.

Policewomen: The Social Workers

It was not until 1893 in Chicago that a woman was given the rank of "policeman." Marie Owens, a widow with five children to feed, went to work at the Chicago Health Department, tasked with enforcing child labor laws. In 1889, the city of Chicago passed an ordinance prohibiting the employment of children under fourteen years old, except in extraordinary circumstances. To ensure the enforcement of the ordinance, the city hired five women as sanitary inspectors. Their job was to monitor the working conditions in stores, factories, and tenements. Marie Owens was so successful as a sanitary inspector that her efforts caught the attention of the well-known juvenile reformer and newly appointed Chicago chief of police, Major Robert Wilson McClaughry, who hired Owens to do the same work for the city.[13]

Her hiring was not unusual for the time, as it was beginning to be common practice for police departments to hire women as prison matrons.[14] What was unusual was that Marie Owens was hired at the rank of detective sergeant and was given the power of arrest, although her arrest powers were limited to child labor law violations. Her exploits became well known in the press and her regard grew. In an article she wrote for the July 28, 1901, issue of the *Chicago Daily Tribune*, Owens described her early days on the job:

> The sights to be seen in the slums today can in no way compare with those of ten years ago and the suffering due to the inability of the older members of the family to work is, indeed, pitiable. Children were found working in factories all over the city, the frail little things in many cases being under 7. The pittance of 75 cents or $1 a week, however, helped to buy food for a sick mother, though it was at the cost of health and education. When the work was first begun a woman wearing a police sergeant's star was a novelty. Manufacturers in some cases were not inclined to admit me to their workshops, but armed with the strong arm of the law and the will to do good I soon found that in most cases the merchants met me half way and rendered me great assistance. As a result, the children were gradually thinned out, and the employers became accustomed to asking for affidavits required by law before work was given to children. Mothers had to depose as to the children's ages, and with these papers, the latter were enabled to get employment in the larger factories and stores.[15]

Owens retired in 1923 after thirty-two years of service with the Chicago Police Department. Her supervisor had this to say about her: "Give me men like she is a woman and we will have the model detective bureau in the whole world."[16]

Another influential forerunner, Lola Baldwin, was hired in Portland, Oregon, to protect women who attended the Lewis and Clark Exposition, held in 1905 to celebrate the centennial of the Lewis and Clark expedition. More than 1.5 million people passed through the halls of the exposition, learning about scientific and technological advances, such as moving picture shows, motorized blimps maneuvering in the sky, a transcontinental auto race, and even the power of electric lighting. Fueled by concerns about the so-called white slave trade, civic leaders supported the hiring of women escorts for the Traveler's Aid Society to protect the large number of single and often rural women who would visit their cities. There were concerns that young American girls would be procured as prostitutes and shipped to foreign nations, sensationally dubbed the white slave trade. In addition, they felt that the large numbers of unattached lumbermen, miners, and laborers attracted to the cities by such expositions could create undesirable influences among visiting women.[17] Baldwin headed a special force of social workers who were given quasi police powers during the exposition. The "quasi" part was due to their powers being limited to women and children, although they worked with policemen in cases that involved men. On April 1, 1908, three years after the opening of the Exposition, the city of Portland made Baldwin's position a permanent one, the "Superintendent of the Women's Auxiliary to the Police Department for the Protection of Girls," Police Star No. 33.[18]

Despite the influence of these early female police officers, the appointment of Alice Stebbins Wells to the Los Angeles Police Department on September 12, 1910, is recognized as the beginning of women's formal entry into policing.[19] Wells was the first woman to be hired as a *policewoman* and given the power of arrest. Technically, Marie Owens and Lola Baldwin were hired as *policemen*, but there is still debate among experts about who deserves credit as the first.

Wells was a deeply religious woman who saw immorality and crime as the same problem based on her many years as a social worker and theology student. "I don't want to make arrests," declared Wells. "I want to keep people from needing to be arrested, especially young people."[20] Wells, like other early policewomen, was religious, college educated, United States born, Progressive, and upper middle class. She saw police work as an opportunity to provide service to her community. The duties of early policewomen were much more complicated than that of the early matrons and varied greatly from city to city, but all centered on coping with the social conditions in large urban areas that contributed to the delinquency of children and young girls.

The policewoman role coincided with increasing societal concern with preserving sexual propriety. Young girls who dressed immodestly, used foul language, smoked, and drank were at risk for promiscuity. Policewomen were tasked with preventing girls at risk from becoming "fallen women." To prevent this fall, policewomen were responsible for the return of runaway girls to their homes, the warning of young girls about the dangers of walking alone, the suppression of dance hall evils, petty gambling in stores frequented by children, and the sale of liquor to minors.[21] Dance halls, movie theaters, skating rinks, and amusement parks were of particular concern to policewomen because they allowed for unchaperoned social mingling among young people. A March 1911 issue of *Good Housekeeping* about Alice Stebbins Wells emphasized the importance of monitoring these hotbeds of impropriety:

> She has found that there is scarcely a penny arcade whose pictures are not suggestive of evil. . . . Her duty in visiting picture shows is to see that no minors are admitted except in the company of a parent or legal guardian and that no pictures are displayed at the entrance showing deeds of violent acts or questionable morality.[22]

The fear was that young single women could easily be lured into behavior with dire consequences. For example, a young girl who worked as a typist during the day, having a few hours of freedom at night, might attend a dance hall. There she might (unwittingly) be plied with alcohol and then taken to a place conducive to promiscuous behavior, such as a nearby room or car. Her promiscuity would then lead to disease and self-hate. Some cities went as far as outlawing certain types of dances and then fining dance hall managers for permitting them. Dances like the "turkey trot," "moonlight waltz," and "bunny hug" were all prohibited in Portland, Oregon, in 1912.[23]

Despite their categorization as early policewomen, neither the women who performed these duties nor the departments that hired them wanted them known as police officers. Instead, most saw their roles similarly to Mary Hamilton, New York City's first woman police officer, who wrote in *Policewoman: Her Service and Ideals* that the role of women police was similar to that of a mother in a home.[24] Generally, male officers were not threatened by the female presence in the department as long as their functions were specifically limited to issues dealing with women and children. In situations that involved children and women, male officers were greatly relieved to have assistance. Plus, it freed up the male officers for "real" police duties, like crime fighting. According to these pioneering policewomen and their upper-middle-class advocates, policemen were best for certain duties and policewomen others. After Wells was assigned to her duties, the Los Angeles Police Department issued a directive to male officers: "No young girl can be questioned by a male officer. Such work is delegated solely to policewomen, who by their womanly sympathy and intuition are able to gain the confidence of their younger sisters."[25] Los Angeles was not alone. Most cities had sex-specific duties for male and female officers.

In her tenure as America's first sworn policewoman, Wells toured the country fighting for the hiring of more female officers. She delivered 136 lectures in seventy-three cities. By 1915, seventy women were earning police salaries in twenty-six different US cities. In 1915, the International Association of Policewomen was created at the National Conference of Charities and Corrections. Alice Stebbins Wells had secured a place on the program to speak about the creation of an organization dedicated to the compilation and dissemination of information regarding female police officers. The speech was well received, and the International Association of Policewomen was born. The organization quickly grew with members from twenty-two states and Canada.

The specialization of women police as caregivers and social workers influenced their placement in the organization. Should they be in the same unit as male officers, but with different specializations from the men, or should they have their own unit, women only? Who would lead the units? There were three common practices. One option was to put all policewomen in one bureau or unit in the police department and have them supervised by a male officer. Another option was to integrate them into different precincts (i.e., geographical areas in a large city) again supervised by the male officer in charge of the precinct. O. W. Wilson, a forerunner in the police profession-alization movement and police chief in Chicago, suggested the advantages of integrating women into already existing precincts, rather than isolating them in their own bureau:

> I would not wish to be considered facetious when I say that it would be a pity for these charming and talented ladies to isolate themselves from an integrated police organization in which they can contribute so much to department morale and dignity in addition to carrying out their function in close cooperation with other units of the department.[26]

Finally, departments could create a women's bureau with a female director who would be in charge of the activities of that division. Women's bureau directors would report directly to the police chief of the city or town. This was the most popular idea, as the newly formed International Association of Policewomen supported this option. St. Louis; Washington, DC; Indianapolis; and New York all adopted this model. Later, in the 1970s, when women tried to break into patrol work, the segregation of women into specialized bureaus provided an obstacle to their integration. After thirty years of service, Alice Wells retired in 1940 and died in 1957. A reproduction of her uniform, along with her badge, policewoman's badge number 1, is on display at the Los Angeles Police Historical Society Museum.

Wartime: Guards of Morality

The United States' entry into World War I led to an increase in the number of women performing police functions. To understand how war duties affected the number of policewomen, in 1917, thirty cities had a total of 125 policewomen. Only one year later there were almost 200 female officers.[27] The first survey of record on the subject of women police officers was conducted by the president of the newly formed International Association of Policewomen in 1919–1920. In the cities responding, most reported salaries for female officers or matrons at $1,000–$1,500 a year, and only about half required a civil service exam for appointment as policewomen.[28] In the civil service process, individuals are hired on the basis of professional merit, demonstrated through competitive examinations. The examinations provide for a fair process where all potential candidates have the same chance of being hired. It also suggests that the position was competitive. The starting salary for policewomen was very close to a first-year male patrol officer's starting salary, and it was high in comparison to other jobs women could expect to find during this time period, as employment opportunities for women during the 1920s were severely limited.

Many cities surveyed did not differentiate between the terms *prison matron* and *policewoman*. Sometimes these terms were used interchangeably. In other words, policewomen were doing guard work and matrons were doing police work. The same political and civic groups who lobbied for police matrons in the late 1800s, such as the Women's Christian Temperance Movement and League of Women Voters, began to lobby for expanded roles for women, including full police duties. However, there was a strong belief that women were not cut out for the physical challenges of policing. August Vollmer, a leader in the police professionalization movement, published an article on March 15, 1930, titled "Meet the Lady Cop," in which he championed the increased use of women police, arguing that if a policewoman had need of a weapon or force, she could always "call a man officer to her assistance; after all, you have to leave a little leeway for the male impulse to protect the weaker sex, even in a police department."[29] Even supporters of the idea of women police like Vollmer did not see them as capable of full police duties.

Not surprisingly, despite their increased numbers, women's roles continued to be limited in policing. While female auxiliary police were hired due to wartime manpower shortages, their roles were limited to inspecting dance halls and nightclubs and maintaining female morality and community peace. During World War I, the secretary of war created a military program called the "American plan" along with a civilian version, "The People's War," intended to teach enlisted men and the general public the dangers of promiscuity and venereal diseases. The American plan included sex education and venereal disease prevention for all military recruits, including a film titled *Fit to Fight*, which told the story of five soldiers and their encounter with several prostitutes and the resulting disease and shame that followed. The concern for the moral welfare of military personnel and civilians did not stop there. Laws were passed in 1917 creating prostitution-free zones within a five-mile radius of all military camps and mandating the closure of the remaining red-light districts.

Policewomen played an important role in the civilian social hygiene program, the People's War. In an effort to fight the "emotionalism which was sweeping the country and making a hero of every man in uniform," female officers engaged in "protective work" for girls.[30] The goal of this protective work was to maintain the moral purity of young girls living near the military camps and also to control prostitution and venereal diseases. In fact, Lola Baldwin, one of the most famous policewomen of the time, nicknamed "Portland's Municipal Mother," served as a federal law enforcement officer for the Committee on Protective Work for Women and Girls from 1917 to 1920. This was a unique opportunity for women at the federal level of law enforcement. Women would not be hired into the more common agencies, such as the Federal Bureau of Investigation and the Secret Service, until the late 1970s.

By 1930 there were six hundred policewomen nationwide. During the 1930s, the police professionalism movement dominated the occupation of policing. The progressive reformers publicized law enforcement as the primary goal of a modern department. Order maintenance, service issues, and administrative duties, normally assigned to women, were ridiculed and belittled. Some policewomen even encouraged the idea that women were specialists in caregiving and social work and should be segregated from "real" police work. In 1936, Detroit's deputy commissioner of police, Eleanor L. Hutzel, said, "The work which women can do will always be minor as compared with what men can do."[31] The idea that women police were best suited to deal with women and children remained conventional wisdom up until the 1970s in many departments.

Women's police presence resurfaced again during World War II, but women who joined the ranks during this time continued to serve even after the men returned home, unlike other male-dominated occupations women assumed during the war, made popular by the iconic Rosie the Riveter. This was likely because their limited role provided security for the almost 850 women who joined policing from 1940 to 1950. Public interest in female officers increased too. For example, in 1941, *Good Housekeeping* profiled a Washington, DC, police officer in the article "Good Housekeeping Found Out What a Policewoman Does." The article featured the variety of police calls a policewoman in Washington, DC, would respond to, including a hit-and-run incident involving a child; deserted wives who needed help locating their husbands; investigating "disorderly dance halls, alcoholic wives and daughters, crying babies, crooked fortunetellers, cruelty to children"; and persuading women who had been arrested to pose for their mug shot photo.[32] The heavily photographed exposé featured women as primarily dealing with women's issues, but with guns! The article cautioned readers, "Policewomen learn to shoot a pistol at arm's length during their three months' training course and are crack shots when graduated."[33] The ability of women police to carry guns in the line of duty was not always favorably portrayed. A few years later, in 1949, the *Saturday Evening Post* featured New York City policewomen in a story titled "Some Cops Have Lovely Legs."[34] Illustrating the article was a picture of a policewoman applying makeup. In the article, the author tells a comical (and likely untrue) story about two female rookie cops' exploits in arresting a tailor who had been sexually harassing his cashiers. After erroneously pointing the wrong end of the gun at themselves and their desk sergeant, the story concludes with him sending them to get coffee until they can get their emotions under control. In sum, the image of female officers from New York City portrayed in the (obviously inaccurate) article was that they were beautiful and unusual, but incapable of being real police officers.

Paving the Way to Patrol

The 1950s brought a different type of woman into policing: young, middle-class, military veteran, and civil servant careerists.[35] Unlike their upper-middle-class, feminist forerunners, these women were overwhelmingly middle class, high school educated, and comparable to the men with whom they served. Most no longer were motivated by the ideals of social work and prevention that early policewomen adhered to. Instead, they wanted to do law enforcement and crime fighting. These policing careerists joined the police department to take advantage of new career opportunities. Like their male counterparts, they were concerned with upward mobility in the department and their own professional development.

Despite the increased number of female officers, there were still many obstacles to them being fully integrated into police organizations. As you recall, early policewomen were segregated into specialized women's bureaus. Female officers had achieved high ranks in women's bureaus, but within those bureaus could not move into other areas of policing, such as patrol. The officers were faced with the decision to give up either security within the women's bureaus or the ability to move into other bureaus in the department. In 1956, the International Association of Policewomen was reestablished, changing its name to the International Association of Women Police (IAWP). The organization had dwindled in numbers following the death of its longtime president (1919–1932), Mina Van Winkle. The "new" organization took on a mission different from their early police sisters: to fully integrate women into police departments rather than into women's bureaus.[36] At the same time, female police officers across the nation began to demand promotional opportunities similar to those of their male counterparts. This is apparent in the definition of a policewoman passed at the International Association of Chiefs of Police held in 1966:

> A policewoman is a sworn peace officer, empowered to enforce all of the laws and ordinances of the jurisdiction and to detect and arrest violators, and is appointed for the increased moral protection of women and minors and for the prevention of delinquency among such women and minors, and for such other police duties as can best be performed by a woman. Like the policeman, the policewoman is subject to the rules, regulations, and disciplinary procedures of the department and is entitled to the same rights, salary, privileges, and opportunities.[37]

Some departments simply did not allow women to take promotional examinations.[38] That was the case in New York City until Felicia Shpritzer (nicknamed "Lt. Nerve"), a twenty-year veteran of the New York City Police Department, sued the chairman of the Civil Service Commission because the commission turned down her application to take the sergeants exam.[39] In her 1959 plea, "A Case for the Promotion of Policewomen in the City of New York," Shpritzer argued for the right of women to be promoted:

> That women are an important part of the New York City or any large police department has been proved by the constant increase in their numbers since the first matron was appointed. That women can perform police functions beyond matron duty and the care of lost children has been shown by the ever-widening scope of their duties and activities, their assignment to more and more of the bureaus and squads previously all-male in character, and their receiving designations of the several grades of detective. That women are capable of performing their work with courage and efficiency on a par with the male members of the Department has been shown repeatedly by acts of bravery and outstanding police service for which they have received both public and departmental recognition. That women are capable of being executives has been demonstrated in many police organizations, including New York's which has had two women deputy commissioners, as well as four directors of the Bureau of Policewomen since it was established as the Women's Bureau in 1924. Allowing the women the same chances to advance as the men—a procedure accepted in almost every phase of civil service—carries out the philosophy of good personnel administration.[40]

Her plea was not enough to convince the Civil Service Commission. Joined by her friend, Gertrude Schimmel (nicknamed "Inspector Brains"), they fought for two years through three different court cases before they were allowed to take the promotional exam. Schimmel went on to be the first woman deputy inspector in the New York City Police Department. Their fight became one of the most famous cases in the history of women police. More important, the court's decision in this lawsuit was an indicator of a shift in thinking and employment practices during the 1960s and 1970s.

Patrol: Women's Fight for Equality

Revolutionary changes in policing began in the 1960s and 1970s. These changes applied considerable pressure from the federal government to local police departments to broaden the opportunities for women in policing. First, legal changes made it illegal to deny a woman an equal opportunity in a police career. In 1972, Congress amended Title VII of the 1964 Civil Rights Act, making it illegal for both private and public employers to have discriminative employment practices based on gender. Title VII of the 1964 Civil Rights Act specifically forbids employers to "omit, segregate, or classify his employees in a way which would deprive or tend to deprive any individual of employment opportunities . . . because of such individual's sex."[41] The 1972 amendments extended coverage of the act to public employees, including police officers.

A year later, the court's decision in *Griggs v. Duke Power Company* confirmed that a plaintiff in a discrimination suit need not prove the employer was discriminatory in intent and that it was the employer's responsibility to prove ability was directly related to a job task. If a job requirement disproportionately disqualified a group or class, the employer had to prove that ability was "reasonably necessary to the normal operation of that particular business or enterprise," called a bona fide occupational qualification.[42] This forced police agencies to examine their entry qualifications to ensure they were necessary to police work. During the 1970s the qualifications for entering police work often included height and weight requirements. Many departments required that new officers be at least five feet, seven inches in height and of proportionate weight. This rule excluded 95 percent of women in society. After height and weight requirements were abolished, many departments began to require some form of physical fitness testing. For example, the Toledo Police Department adopted a test that included (1) fifteen push-ups, (2) twenty-five sit-ups, (3) a six-foot standing broad jump, and (4) a twenty-five-second obstacle course. These requirements were also struck down because it was unclear to the courts how these physical fitness tasks were related to the job (*Harless v. Duck*).[43] These legal challenges ultimately unlocked the door of patrol work to policewomen.

Specific to policing, the Crime Control Act of 1973 banned sexual discrimination by police agencies that received federal funding from the Law Enforcement Assistance Administration (LEAA).[44] Departments that discriminated against women faced the possibility of losing federal grants needed for equipment and education of officers. Given that the LEAA gave $1 billion to improve forty thousand departments, courts, and correctional facilities, it had immense political clout. However, there is considerable debate about how influential the LEAA was in reducing discrimination in police agencies. This is mainly because the 1974 US Commission on Civil Rights found that the LEAA was not enforcing equal employment opportunities for women. It did withhold funds from the Chicago Police Department in 1974 because the department was found to have treated women, blacks, and Hispanics disparately in hiring, promotion, and disciplinary practices, but not until Chicago had already received nearly $5 million in crime-fighting funds. Despite this debate, it is safe to say that the public stance of the LEAA, even if it was only symbolic, made it clear to departments that practices and policies that involved blatant sex or race discrimination needed to stop.

Second, police departments nationwide faced a variety of social pressures to change in the late 1960s. Despite technological advances and growing police resources, this period of time in policing is marked by rising crime rates, challenges to traditional police effectiveness, and riots and unrest in many urban areas.[45] Opportunities for minority officers increased due to police reforms, urging police departments to hire more diverse officers in an attempt to smooth tensions between police and minority community members.[46] With regard to female officers, the 1967 President's Commission on Law Enforcement and Administration of Justice suggested, "Policewomen can be an invaluable asset to modern law enforcement and their present role should be broadened. . . . Their value should not be considered as limited to staff functions or police work with juveniles; women should serve regularly in patrol, vice, and investigative divisions."[47]

Of course, not everyone agreed with the commission's recommendation to expand the use of women in patrol, vice, and investigative units. In fact, opposition to women police was widespread and blatant as women tried to break into patrol work. Former police chief Penny Harrington discussed the opposition she faced:

> The biggest obstacle I had to overcome in my career was the attitude of the male officers. . . . When I began my career in 1964, women were not allowed to be on patrol. We did all of the cases involving women and children. So we were not a threat to the men, and they liked to have us there because they hated the "social work" of dealing with these issues. But then, as we broke into patrol and other units, they immediately took the attitude that women could not do the job. This attitude was not based on facts or events, but just on their bullheaded beliefs.[48]

Comments from male officers at the time confirm the opposition that Harrington mentioned and centered on female officers' strength and ability to protect themselves and their partners. One said, "Policing is men's work. The only woman I'd feel comfortable with is built like an Amazon." Another said, "Women can't hold up their end in fights. I'm no babysitter."[49]

Due to the perceived danger of the occupation, administrators, fellow officers, and the public in general were all concerned with the physical and emotional abilities of policewomen. This debate was eventually settled through several evaluations, which confirmed that female patrol officers performed police duties just as effectively as men.[50] In 1972, the Police Foundation, along with the Urban Institute, designed a yearlong study to measure the effectiveness of female officers and the public perception of their role. The results suggested that not only did women perform quite well, but residents of Washington, DC, also generally approved of having policewomen patrol the streets and respond to police calls. However, it was clear that sex stereotypes were hard to combat. One supervisor recalls observing a male and female team responding to a call. Much to his frustration when they arrived at the scene, the male partner went around the car to open the door for his female partner. These habits would be hard to break.

The first major metropolitan department to have women on street patrol was Indianapolis, Indiana. In 1968, Betty Blankenship and Elizabeth Coffal Robinson made history as the first women assigned to patrol. Robinson described her experience to Robert Snow, in his text *Policewomen Who Made History*: "The night before Betty and I went out in Car 47, it was so exciting. At last, we had our chance to show that women could do the job of street patrol."[51] Of Blankenship and Robinson's historic entry into street patrol, the *Indianapolis News* commented, "It seems improbable that we will soon see a policewoman apprehend stick-up men or shoot it out with criminals. But then again it seemed unlikely, not too long ago, that we would see them driving patrol cars."[52] By the end of the 1970s, women were on patrol in most of the major metropolitan cities.[53]

In the coming chapters we will discuss the legacy of Matron McCarthy (New York); Policewomen Marie Owens (Chicago), Lola Baldwin (Portland), and Alice Stebbins Wells (Los Angeles); and Patrol Officers Betty Blankenship and Liz Robinson (Indianapolis) and the many changes they brought about. Their bravery, along with the many women who served as matrons and policewomen from the 1850s up into the 1970s, created opportunities for those who entered policing in the 1980s after the door to patrol had been opened. Chronologically, the first section of chapters picks up where this introduction leaves off, in the 1980s and the so-called modern era of policewomen. Women who entered policing in the 1980s did so in many cases as the first couple of female police officers in the history of their department, as 96 percent of all sworn police personnel in the United States were men in 1980. Women not only fought to get into policing but also, once in their departments, fought to overcome gender-specific stereotypes and the notion that policing was simply a "boys club" and women need not apply.

Section I

FEMALE POLICE OFFICERS
OF THE 1980s

Title Niners

L ISA WRIGHT CAREFULLY TIMED HER ANNOUNCEMENT to her father: "You will never guess what I applied for . . . a patrol position." Her father, a veteran police officer, told her, "You are not doing that!" Lisa was already a corrections officer at the county jail managed by the sheriff's office. Sheriff's offices are unique compared to other police agencies in that, in addition to patrolling the county (i.e., on the road), they are responsible for running the jail, serving warrants, and maintaining security at the courthouse. In fact, there are many different types of police agencies, and they each have a unique mandate and jurisdiction. Local police agencies, including city or municipal police departments, sheriff's departments, and campus police agencies, are the most common and visible type of law enforcement departments. There are about 12,700 municipal police departments, 3,100 sheriff departments, and 861 campus police agencies in the United States.[1] Municipal police departments range in size. For example, New York City Police Department has 35,000 full-time police officers, one of the largest departments in the nation. However, agencies of this size are not common. In fact, the average American department employs fewer than ten full-time officers. With almost five hundred thousand officers nationwide, municipal police officers are the face of policing. These local officers are tasked with solving and preventing local crimes, responding to requests for services, and patrolling city streets to maintain safety.

The jurisdiction of local law enforcement officers is limited to geographic boundaries of the communities they police. For example, sheriff's departments are primarily responsible for law enforcement throughout the county in which they are located, and campus police agencies are responsible for the crime on their campus. However, modern police agencies agree to help each other out, expanding their jurisdictions through a sharing agreement usually called a memorandum of understanding (MOU) or mutual aid agreement (MAA). Through this agreement, agencies formally acknowledge their agreement to work together to bring about safety and crime control in the communities they police. In addition to local police agencies, there are forty-nine state and seventy-five federal agencies that enforce state and federal laws. While we have federal police agencies, the United States is unique in that we do not have a national police force, resulting in a highly decentralized system. Instead, the police structure in America is primarily built around local law enforcement, with each city and county having its own unique police agency. These agencies are accountable not to a centralized police agency but to the communities they police.

According to Lisa's father, corrections work at the local county jail was "a safer, easier gig" compared to patrolling. Jobs at jails and prisons were readily available due to the steady increase in imprisonment during the 1980s. This was the start of the "get tough on crime" movement in the United States. From January 1975 to 1983, the prison population rose 42 percent, or almost one hundred thousand prisoners. With the increase in imprisonment, overcrowding in jails and prisons became the norm. The conditions in many jails and prisons became "shocking," with prisoners forced to sleep on the floor without decent sanitary or recreational facilities.[2] Much of the increase was due to the war on drugs, which President Reagan launched in 1982, increasing the penalties for drug use and possession.

Despite her father's protest, Lisa Wright asked for an application to be a sheriff's deputy. The desk sergeant warned her at the time of her request that women were not cut out for patrol because they struggle with the physical requirements of the dangerous task. Patrolling the streets was a safety concern during the 1980s, especially in inner cities, where stories of lawlessness prompted a new get-tough police strategy in fighting the war on drugs—the police crackdown. A crackdown in New York's Lower East Side is illustrative of the typical process: the streets were flooded with police officers, "dispersing crowds, stopping and arresting suspected drug buyers and sellers, writing traffic tickets and making high volume arrests (more than 1,000 in the first month alone)."[3] The effectiveness of these strategies was called into question and the relationships between residents in these neighborhoods and police were rife with allegations of discrimination and abuse.

At the same time, a revolution was taking place in policing, prompted by a new theory that suggested the policing of disorder or "nuisance" crimes could prevent larger, more serious crimes. The broken windows theory, introduced in 1982, suggested that because a broken window symbolized an invitation for crime in high-crime neighborhoods, policing disorder offenses (i.e., public drunkenness, drug use, vagrancy, graffiti) would reduce serious crime. One of the first tests of the broken windows theory, by Philip Zimbardo, was used illustrate how the theory worked. Zimbardo arranged to have cars without license plates parked in a street in the Bronx and on a street in Palo Alto, California. What happened next was important:

> The car in the Bronx was attacked by "vandals" within ten minutes of its "abandonment." The first to arrive were a family, a father, mother, and young son who removed the radiator and battery. Within twenty-four hours, virtually everything of value had been removed. Then random destruction began—windows were smashed, parts were torn off, upholstery ripped. Children began to use the car as a playground.[4]

However, what happened to the car in Palo Alto, an affluent community, was even more illustrative of the theory's name. The car sat untouched for more than a week, so, to move things along, Zimbardo smashed part of it with a sledgehammer. It was not long before others passing by joined in, destroying the car in a few hours. The lesson was simple: the best way to address crime was to police disorder to prevent it from turning into serious crime. Broken windows theory was the launching pad for future police innovations, such as hot-spot policing, problem-oriented policing, and zero-tolerance policing, all of which have unique strategies to reduce disorder that are being used in neighborhoods today.

Lisa Wright passed her tests with flying colors and added to the law enforcement legacy in her family. However, it was not long before the desk sergeant's concerns became public following a tussle Lisa had with a suspect. Despite the fact that she held her own, her supervisor told her and her fellow officers, "This is why women should not be in law enforcement." It was a bitter lesson for her, one she described as a "disappointment," but she was not deterred. Today, thirty years later, she is a police chief in a large municipal police department, part of the 1 percent of police chiefs who are women nationwide. Lisa acknowledged that her work ethic was the secret to her successful tenure.

Women like Lisa Wright, hired as police officers in the 1980s, were the first generation to be impacted by Title IX and the Civil Rights Act of 1972, both of which increased opportunities for women. These policy changes brought about an increase in the number of women in policing. In 1980, there were 518,386 sworn law enforcement officers working in local, state, and federal agencies, of which 13,996, or 3 percent, were women. By the end of the decade, these numbers would triple. The average female police officer in the 1980s was employed in a large, municipal agency, like Los Angeles, where women made up 13 percent of the police force and were supervised by male officers, as women held less than 1 percent of all supervisory positions in 1980.[5] In many jurisdictions, these women were the first to be employed by their agencies. Being the first had its drawbacks. One was that sexism and harassment were common experiences, starting at the police training academy and continuing throughout their field training experiences and beyond. Another was that they faced skepticism regarding their ability to patrol alongside male officers. Remember that in the 1970s women were still primarily in specialist positions doing police work limited to women and children. Women police in the 1980s had to prove they were up to the task, as officers, administrators, and even police wives raised concerns about their ability to handle the job.[6] This section includes chapters on the most pressing issues of this era: chapter 1, "Girls, Why Do You Want to Be Police Officers When You Grow Up?"; chapter 2, "Becoming a Police Officer"; chapter 3, "Changing the Gender of Policing"; chapter 4, "Facing the Intimidations of Harassment and Discrimination"; and chapter 5, "The Dangers on the Beat."

1

Girls, Why Do You Want to Be Police Officers When You Grow Up?

IN 1974, THE NATIONAL BROADCASTING COMPANY (NBC) debuted the crime drama *Policewoman*, featuring Sergeant Pepper Anderson, played by Angie Dickinson, who was cast as an undercover agent for the Criminal Conspiracy Unit of the Los Angeles Police Department. *Policewoman* was the first successful show to feature a female police officer. Wildly popular, it became number one in the television ratings almost overnight. The show was advertised with a series of posters. One of my favorites features Angie Dickinson holding a very large handgun with the caption "Cold steel on the outside . . . all woman on the inside." The sexed characterization of Sergeant Pepper likely had something to do with the show's popularity. Her undercover work often had her posing as a prostitute or Vegas showgirl. At the 2012 WE TV event celebrating forty years of the crime drama heroine, Angie Dickinson acknowledged, "It's one thing to be tough and sexy but how many male leads in police series were required to do shower scenes?"[1] The women featured in this chapter, who became police officers in the 1980s, grew up watching *Policewoman*. In fact, it was widely reported that there was a huge jump in female police applications soon after *Policewoman* began airing. Given its popularity, even if they didn't watch it, they were likely aware of the show or the many other crime dramas that followed.

However, TV shows and movies were not the only reason women joined the ranks during the 1980s. Several federal laws made the education and working worlds more female friendly. First, in 1964 Congress passed Public Law 88-352, which forbade discrimination because of sex and race in hiring, promoting, and firing. While the Civil Rights Act of 1964 did not mention the words "affirmative action," it did authorize the establishment of a body to make rules to help end discrimination—the Equal Employment Opportunity Commission (EEOC). The EEOC was given the authority to help individuals fight sexual harassment and discrimination. In the next decade, Congress would gradually extend EEOC powers to include conducting investigations, creating conciliation programs, filing lawsuits, and managing voluntary assistance programs. With these changes, the federal government took a stand against blatant sex discrimination and allowed women access to equity in the workplace. Later, in April 1972, the act was made applicable to municipalities, knocking down the last major legal obstacle facing women interested in police work.

The second reason women joined the police ranks in the 1980s is Title IX. When people hear about Title IX, they often think about its influence on sports programs, as it resulted in greater gender equity in the participation of men and women in both high school and collegiate sports. However, Title IX of the Education Amendments also expanded the opportunities for women at institutions of higher education (i.e., colleges and universities) when it was passed in 1972, and women have enrolled in college in greater numbers ever since. Former president Barack Obama recently wrote a pro–Title IX op-ed piece published in *Newsweek* magazine arguing that "the law had achieved far-reaching gains in improving equality between the sexes."[2] The reason that this section on women who joined the police ranks during the 1980s names them "Title Niners" is that Title IX introduced the term "equity" into the public forum and gave girls opportunities in athletics and education previously reserved for men. Unlike women who entered in the 1970s, women who entered policing in the 1980s believed they should have equity in their police role, largely because of their educational experiences with Title IX.

Finally, women entered policing in the 1980s because many departments implemented court-ordered and voluntary affirmative action plans designed to increase the number of women and people of color in policing. In the 1980s, more than half of the police agencies serving populations of fifty thousand or more were under affirmative action hiring plans.[3] Many agencies set quotas for their hiring classes to ensure that women and other underrepresented groups, like people of color, were recruited. Agencies that were court ordered (Miami, Denver, Detroit, Buffalo, and forty-three others in 1986) were required by the Justice Department to increase the ratio of women and minorities.[4] Often, the court-ordered mandates came as a result of women who sued departments that had tried to keep them out. In response, the courts began to impose sanctions against departments in the form of consent decrees (i.e., a percent of every recruit class that must be female until the department reached a target percent or number in the department). Advocates of affirmative action plans saw it as a correction of the past inequalities that kept women out of policing. Opponents disagreed, classifying these programs instead as a form of reverse discrimination. Eventually, the numerical quotas utilized in affirmative action plans were discouraged by President Reagan's administration (1981–1989), but not before they had a revolutionary impact on diversifying urban police departments. For example, Cara Smith, a master colonel with a state police agency, was hired under an affirmative action plan following a lawsuit against her hiring department: "I was the tenth woman hired into the uniform ranks and the very first class of women . . . as a result of a lawsuit, so I was in the next handful that followed. And so when I got assigned to my district, there were no female officers up there . . . which was pretty typical." Her successful thirty-year career started because of the opportunity created through affirmative action. The popularity of police dramas, combined with the increased opportunities for women in education and employment and affirmative action programs, led to a rapid increase in the number of women in policing and by 1986 the percentage increased to 9 percent of municipal officers, up from 3 percent in 1980.

The reasons women gave for wanting to be police officers in the 1980s were very similar to the reasons men gave: job security, excitement, the camaraderie of the profession, and the opportunity to help people and to make a difference in the fight against the social problems of our society. Teri Hamm, who joined a state police agency in 1981, reported that she knew she wanted to be a police officer to help people and because the values of police work matched her own:

> I have this sense of right and wrong and I wanted to not only have that but be able to manifest that and help people. That's really in my opinion what policing is all about is being able to help people. It's normally in the sense of you know you're helping an old lady across the street but it's helping somebody change a tire or you're helping them at a crash scene because now they have to think about what do I do with this report and insurance and helping them navigate through that. And when arresting a drunk driver you are probably saving his silly neck or her silly neck. So it's helping people in so many different levels.

Helping people and solving the social problems that lead people to crime are the most common reasons that recruits report for wanting to become police officers, even today. Tammy Victor joined policing in 1985 to be a part of the solution fighting the inequalities of the system:

> It is funny that people will tell me that when I grew up that it could have gone either way which side of the law I could have been on. It's like, "Okay. I really just wanted to just be fair." I had a brother. . . . He would get in trouble with

the police a lot. . . . In a small town, it just didn't seem like he could walk across the street unless he was getting the blame for something. . . . Even if he wasn't in town they were like, "It had to be him." I remember being in the car with my sister one time and she turned the corner and the tires squealed a little bit and a police officer stopped her and said, "You know you guys are going to turn out just like your brother." And I hated that. I just hated the stigmatization of thinking that just because your brother got in trouble that it kind of stuck with you just a little bit. He wasn't really a bad person. In this day and age, the things that he would do weren't really bad. So I just wanted to be a fair person.

Others were drawn to the camaraderie and sense of "joining a brother-hood" that went along with joining the police family. Lisa Bailey, who joined a municipal police department in 1982 after an internship with the state's attorney's office, got into policing because she was impressed by the uniform and the respect it was given: "I joined policing because I saw the camaraderie and fellowship among the officers and I wanted to be a part of the organization. But, I was isolated once I became an officer. It had all changed, but I was too young to understand the difference."

Sam Johnson joined policing in 1985 because of the excitement and job security of police work:

Originally I was an education major in college and that was a very typical career path that colleges kind of funneled females into. Part way through the educational system, I just decided, having been brought up with my parents expecting whatever career path you went into that you should anticipate doing it, being able to do it for thirty years. That was just the guidelines that my dad and I always talked about. I grew up working in the family business originally, and I looked at education and said it was too repetitive. I couldn't do it for thirty years. I took several different internships, among them some criminal justice ones where I worked in police, corrections, and courts, and the police work appealed the most to me because of the variety. I am typically not a desk jockey type of person. I like to be physically active and engaged.

Others joined policing because of the pay and benefits. Historically, policing is a blue-collar job, meaning that most police applicants come from lower-middle-class or working-class backgrounds. In the 1980s, as today, policing was an attractive option for employment, given that most police agencies only require a high school education for application but offer long-term job security. Formerly, police departments maintained separate wage scales and eligibility lists, obliging women to have more education and higher test scores—often for less pay—than male applicants. However, by 1975, "a female rookie with a high school diploma could start, like her male counterparts, at an annual salary of $12,024 in Chicago, $12,441 in Philadelphia, $11,944 in New York City."[5] Lana Sykes, who joined policing in 1988, confirmed that salary was an important part of the decision to join policing: "The police department more than doubled my salary, so I took it. I figured I would go back to school while I am there and in the meantime, I could move out of my parent's house and buy my own clothes. So that is what I did." This made policing an attractive employment option, especially in comparison to the "pink collar" options open to women such as secretarial work, which did not have the same pay, benefits, or job security.

In sum, women entered the nation's police forces following the passage of the Civil Rights Acts and Title IX of the Educational Amendments, which opened doors to women for education and employment previously closed. Their motivations for police work were very similar to those of men. However, as they entered police work, the primary question became how the nation's men in blue would handle a "female invasion." In all fairness, while the distorted image of the role policewomen portrayed by televisions shows like *Policewoman* may have popularized women in policing, it did little to suggest that women were equal to their male counterparts in the dangerous world of policing. Much to the contrary, the highly sexualized Sergeant Anderson only fulfilled non-uniformed, specialized, protected, and sexy assignments, with plenty of male backup ready to step in. This was far from female officers' experiences in the 1980s.

How do you become a police officer? What was the hiring process like for women in the 1980s? The hiring process and experiences from the police training academy are in the next chapter.

2

Becoming a Police Officer

So let's say you want to be a police officer. What are the steps to becoming one of the men or women in blue? The first step is the application stage. To apply, police departments have minimum requirements that all applicants must meet. These vary but usually include a high school diploma, being age twenty-one or older, and being free of a felonious criminal record. While a criminal record for misdemeanor crimes like driving while under the influence (DUI), shoplifting, or minor drug use may not automatically disqualify a person from police service, felony crimes such as robbery and murder would. Police applicants, who meet the minimum requirements for police employment, are eligible to apply.

Police agencies invite applications when interested in hiring new recruits. Most departments keep a list of eligible applicants and then hire from the list when they are given the authorization to hire. To make it onto the list, recruits must pass a series of tests to progress to the police training academy stage. Each department utilizes its own process, but there are considerable similarities. For example, almost all police agencies require criminal record checks and background investigations to screen applicants for past criminal and ethical violations. Variability comes into play with departments' use of personal interviews, psychological evaluations, written aptitude tests, physical agility tests, personality inventories, and polygraph examinations.

Pre-Employment Testing

The Written Test

Most police scholars agree that the best predictor of a successful police career is the ability to communicate, orally and in writing. For this reason, many agencies have created written assessments to measure applicants' ability to read and write. In the 1980s, the educational pre-employment testing requirement for police work benefited women, who generally entered policing with a higher education level. This may be because in many departments in the 1970s the requirement for policewomen was a bachelor's degree, while only a high school degree was required for policemen. A national survey of policewomen conducted in 1988 showed that 56 percent had some college education, 24 percent had bachelor's degrees, and 11 percent were pursuing graduate work, leaving 9 percent with high school diplomas. This was higher than the 41 percent national average of men who had some college.[1] While women excelled at the academic requirements of the application process, the physical requirements kept women out of policing.

Physical Agility Testing

Pre-employment testing requirements related to physical agility have historically kept women out of policing. First, there were height and weight requirements. The thought was that police work required officers to be tall and muscular, what one female officer referred to as a "doorframe with a head." After the 1972 Civil Rights Act opened the door of patrol to female applicants, height and weight requirements were the most consistent barrier. In the 1973 court case *Smith vs. the City of East Cleveland* the courts decided that these requirements unreasonably discriminated against female officers. For example, Ohio's 150-pound weight requirement disqualified 80 percent of female applications and only 20 percent of the males, and had very little to do with the performance of police duties. The court determined that the larger size did not improve police performance and was, therefore, discriminatory under the 1964 Civil Rights Act.[2] Later, in the 1977 Alabama case *Dothard v. Rawlinson*, the Supreme Court confirmed that height and weight requirements discriminated against women. However, long after the height and weight requirements were struck down, barriers to police employment remained in a new form: physical agility tests.

This is because physical agility tests overemphasize upper-body strength. Physiologically, women on average have only about 60 percent of the upper-body strength of men. Because departments force women to take the same test as men, knowing they are much less likely to pass, many have argued that the continued emphasis on upper-body strength is really about keeping women out of policing. Physical agility tests vary widely from agency to agency, but these tests can generally be divided into two types: a calisthenics test or an obstacle course test. Some agencies' agility tests require applicants to do calisthenics tests: a certain number of push-ups and sit-ups and a specific distance to run in a prescribed amount of time. For example, the Illinois State POWER test requires police officer candidates to engage in the following activities: a sit and reach test, a one-minute sit-up test, a one repetition maximum bench, and a one-and-a-half-mile run. To deal with the physiological differences between men and women, the POWER test has prorated activities. For example, women aged twenty to twenty-nine must bench press 58 percent of their body mass and sit and reach almost nineteen inches, while men aged twenty to twenty-nine must bench press 98 percent but only sit and reach sixteen inches.[3] These activities are prorated based on age as well as gender.

Others departments utilize an obstacle course–style of test, made up of tasks such as being able to carry an incapacitated person a certain distance or jump over a fence. For example, in Belton, Texas, the following obstacle course must be completed in seventy seconds or less:

1. Exiting a patrol car and running 62 ft. 6 inches to the first of four serpentine cones.
2. After weaving through the four cones and upon exiting the last cone, the applicant/officer will proceed 26 ft. 3 inches to a 4 ft. simulated chain link fence. The applicant/officer must successfully navigate themselves over the fence.
3. After navigating the fence, the applicant/officer must run 33 ft. to the balance beam. The applicant/officer must cross a 10 ft. long beam without falling off.
4. After completing the balance beam, the applicant/officer will advance around the next barrier cone, a distance of 23 ft. 2 inches, and continue to the 6 ft. wall. The applicant/officer must climb over the 6 ft. wall.
5. The applicant/officer will then proceed to the open window, a distance of 41 ft. The applicant/officer must go through the window and advance to the simulated victim.
6. The applicant/officer will retrieve the simulated victim (a manikin weighing 150 pounds is used to simulate a victim) and drag the simulated victim 30 ft. to safety.[4]

Note that this test does not prorate based on age or gender. According to an assessment completed by criminologist Patrick Maher in 1984, physical agility tests that were timed and required applicants to scale a wall, swim, run, broad jump, complete an obstacle course, and walk across a balance beam had the largest adverse effect on women, meaning women were much more likely to fail these tasks than men.

Adding to this debate, when challenged, these tests have routinely been struck down by the courts. For example, in the 1985 case of *Thomas v. City of Evanston*, several women argued that the physical agility test used in 1976 and 1979 were discriminatory because they excluded women disparately. The test required applicants to sprint, run, throw a tear gas canister, fit comfortably and safely in a standardized police car, and pass a test of strength to determine the physical ability to subdue or handcuff a 175-pound man. The courts agreed, throwing out the test as discriminatory, as the "test eliminated about 85 percent of the women applicants and only 10 percent of the men," establishing a "significantly discriminatory pattern" of selection.[5] The courts found the job analysis performed by the city was clearly insufficient, arguing that it was full of "ingrained stereotypes and speculative assumptions."[6]

The debate over whether upper-body strength is necessary to police work, or a job-related standard, is not clear-cut. In employment law, such a standard, also known as a bona fide occupational qualification (BFOQ), is permissible under Title VII of the Civil Rights Act even if it may exclude members of a protected class. It just must be reasonably necessary to the work. For example, if a physical agility test excluded 80 percent of female applicants and only 10 percent male, but it measured a reasonably necessary skill to police work, or a BFOQ, it would be upheld by the courts.

In policing, deciding what is reasonably necessary to do the work seems to be the issue. No research has ever found that strength is related to police functioning or that physical strength is in any way related to a person's ability to manage conflict or danger. Plus, much of what police do is respond to citizen calls for service, which involves driving a police car and communication skills. However, physical exertion can be a real part of an officer's day, including chasing and wrestling suspects; it's just the exception, rather than the rule. The fact that most municipal police agencies do not require officers to repeat the upper-body strength requirements throughout their career only fuels this debate. Think of all the jokes about police and doughnuts. If scaling a six-foot wall were necessary to do police work, shouldn't the test be repeated every year? What about police officers, male and female, who successfully police the city streets every day who are overweight and out of shape, like most Americans? Doesn't their ability to do the job prove that there is more to policing than physical fitness? One police administrator argued against the emphasis on upper-body strength and instead suggested a focus on physical fitness and communication for recruits:

You have to convince yourself that it isn't about brawn and it isn't about muscle strength. It helps, but women depend on communication skills. . . . You have to be physically fit, you have to be sound, you have to be able to drive, you have to take care of yourself, and you have to qualify with weapons and do all those things. But, you are not likely to be in a physical confrontation because you are going to be using your head and your mouth.

Despite the overemphasis on upper-body strength in the testing of applicants, the number of women in policing soared during the 1980s. How did these women make it if the requirements were so tough? Many departments sought to reduce the adverse impact the tests had on female applicants. For example, the Los Angeles Police Department created a pre-academy and pre-application program designed to improve women's fitness as well as strategies to pass the tests. Others created a remedial program for applicants who failed the physical testing. For example, the Miami Police Department placed applicants who failed the test on a six-week hold, during which they could retake the test. This worked well, as 95 percent who failed the first time passed at a later time. These and other innovative programs contributed to the increase in female recruits during the 1980s.

In most agencies, the written exams and physical agility tests screen out the majority of applicants, leaving a small viable pool of applicants who may be required to complete an oral interview, a polygraph, and/or a drug and medical screening. Policing is reliant on the civil service or merit system for selecting applicants. This system involves selecting in rank order those individuals who scored the highest combined score in the testing process. Applicants who rank the highest in the testing process move on to the next step, the police training academy.

The Police Training Academy

All officer recruits undergo two training experiences. The first is the academy experience. Usually about 760 hours, recruits learn about physical training, law, tactics, firearms training, driving, and human relations at the police training academy. Each state and jurisdiction has different training requirements based on the state's Commission on Peace Officers Standards and Training (POST) requirements for certifying or licensing police officers. In addition to the different state standards, some departments provide substantially more training than is minimally required. Large police departments may maintain their own police academies while smaller agencies typically send their recruits to a regional or county academy. Departmental preference for where recruits train depends greatly on the academy's program orientation (e.g., boot camp,

classroom based, problem based), philosophy (e.g., training versus education), and instructional content (e.g., some of the more unique programs
include conflict management, computer information systems, and foreign
language). Departments often choose the academy based on academy reputation and availability of space.

Academies vary significantly in the design and delivery of recruit training,
but for all the focus on firearms and basic self-defense, training takes priority.
According to Lisa Bailey, it is both hands-on and classroom-based training:

> You know, because you have so much to learn, and in a split second you have
> the authority, the ability, the capability of taking someone's life or not. There are
> some things that in some situations you can't learn in a book. You can't learn
> by watching; you have to get out there and do. But you have to have that firm
> foundation to know what to do when to do it, and how to do it.

There were varying opinions on whether previous educational experiences
were helpful in the training academy, likely based on differences in the academy attended. Kim Black found her previous educational experiences helpful:

> The academy experience was good. I had a huge advantage due to education.
> There is a change in attitude. In policing, originally all you needed was two big
> fists and a hell of an attitude, and the ability to talk and write reports did not
> matter. Now, they understand the importance of both. You need to have a brain
> too.

By comparison, Heather Noell felt her previous educational experiences were
not helpful because the academy did not prize "book smarts":

> I got my undergraduate degree from the [state university] and I'm not saying
> that undergraduate education is the best ever but I was shocked at how terrible
> the academy was. Seventy-year-old men telling fifty-year-old stories, people
> with very little adult education experience.

In the 1980s, the police training academy most resembled a military-style boot
camp with the aim of producing well-groomed and disciplined officers. One
purpose of this style of training was to teach recruits to adopt the police identity,
professional demeanor, and respect for authority. It's intended to tear a person
down and rebuild them in the image of a police officer. Boot camp was a shock
to most recruits, who were unaware of how militaristic the training academy
would be. For example, Teresa Bosch said that the police training academy

> was the most militaristic place I have ever been in my life. They get you out of
> bed in the middle of the night and put you in the push-up position and those

parking lots were gravel and it was cold in the middle of January. You hold push up position with that big riot baton on that gravel and there are bloody knuckles. It's a lot more relaxed now. I mean now, compared to what we went through it is nothing.

Many police training academies today have a more collegiate feel to them as compared those in the 1980s. In keeping with the military influence, Teri Hamm believed that grooming and uniforms also became an important avenue for maintaining discipline:

In the academy, the officers would get in our faces. One of my shoelaces was touching the floor and he was screaming at me, but I couldn't look down to see: "Don't you look down when I am telling you to dress!" I had to write a memo on it. Whoa! My shoelace is untied and apparently, this is the end of the world. The method was to see if I was going to cry or lose it. Some people lose it. They'll lose their temper. The officers will try to hit you on your hands because your hands are on a stick and there is no give and see how you react. Are you going to break rank? I had a guy in my class that did that. Threw down his stick and ran after one of the instructors. He was done! Bye-bye.

Recruits often wear uniforms for the first time in the academy. This can be an awe-inspiring and exciting opportunity. Now recruits had to look the part of police officers. Uniforms and haircuts are symbolic to the quasi-military roots of the police. In the 1970s women were assigned uniforms that consisted of skirts, heels, and handbags in which they were instructed to carry their weapons. These uniforms were not practical for climbing, running, or scuffling with suspects. Chief Wilson of the Washington police department humorously commented that the early policewomen uniforms "looked like air hostess uniforms, done up in yellow, pink, and blue."[7]

By the 1980s, it was clear that skirts and heels were not the answer; however, the solution to give everyone the exact same male-fitting uniform was met with shock, humor, and anger by many female officers: "When I got my first shirt and pants they were men's. They told me they did not make women's uniforms. They told me to take it to the tailors. I demanded a female uniform. Eventually, they gave in and found female uniforms." It seemed to be a rite of passage for many women who faced administrators who ordered men's sizes under the belief that "if you have a man's job, you will wear man's clothes."

What was the big deal? "Uniforms are built for men and if you're a woman who has curves, then you will have somewhat of a problem." This created all sorts of physical discomforts: "So I got my vest and the joke was that you could see my blood type through my shirt because it was so tight." Of course, besides comfort and fashion, there were practical considerations as well: "Women's shirts are smaller than men's. They button different. . . . We are required to carry a pen in our pocket but we can't get a pen that fits. So, as unimportant as it may seem, they got us pens." The issue of women wearing ill-fitting men's uniforms is still common today.

The policing of hair was also a big deal in police agencies in the 1970–1980s, as men's hairstyles were longer. Think Bon Jovi, John Travolta, and Michael Jackson. However, the rules for hair also applied to women. Many agencies required officers who had long hair to keep it "tucked up, away from the face." This was for tactical and professional reasons. Other agencies required that recruits and officers cut their hair. Hesitancy in cutting their hair has been identified as a reason that women do not apply for police work. Lisa Wright faced consternation over her long hair in the academy: "A supervisor asked me to cut my hair. She said: 'How could anyone take you seriously when you have bright green eyes and flowing blond hair?' I have been treated like a blond bimbo on many occasions since."

By the 1980s, men and women were attending the same police academy training. Academies had to find separate accommodations and figure out how to deal with the "gender" issue. Keep in mind that a decade prior women were often given different training from men. If you consider that women were going to be doing juvenile or secretarial work, it makes sense that they would have different training than the male officers. In 1985, many facilities didn't even have women's locker rooms or restrooms. One woman commented that "when we first went on the street we didn't have locker room facilities; women had to use the public restroom to change."[8]

The entrance of women into the academy raised some interesting questions about how police were trained and housed at the academy. Could they still call recruits "guys" when training? Should men and women face off in hand-to-hand combat? How carefully did they need to monitor their usual canteen humor? Many of these decisions were made in the moment rather than any preordained sweeping changes in policy or practice. Cara Smith illustrates an example in the academy when considering the procedures for same-sex versus opposite-sex police searches:

> When I was a cadet in the academy, we had a policy when they were teaching us arrest—how to conduct a search—we got to the topic of if its someone of the opposite gender. And so the policy in place was if it was in transporting someone of the opposite gender. So typically the policy was written with male officers in mind transporting a female. And you would call in your mileage and let them know you were transporting a female, and part of it was to protect an officer against any allegations that he sexually assaulted her because it was a very specific procedure. And I remember raising my hand and asking, "What should I do?" I'm thinking the whole point is for male officers with females, and I asked:

"Do I do the same thing with a female?" And they said, "Yeah." And I thought that was stupid. I guess they hadn't thought about it. So there was little things like that that they were not prepared to deal with.

In their article "There Oughtta Be a Law against These Bitches," scholars Anastasia Prokos and Irene Padavic argue that the police training academy was the first line of defense to stop the "female invasion" in policing.[9] There is no doubt that some female recruits felt isolated and persecuted during their training academy experiences. Teresa Bosch felt that a physical injury at the academy was used to force her out of her training class, despite her success as the "first female class president." Thirteen weeks into her sixteen-week training academy experience, Teresa discovered a tumor on the back of her knee. The doctor examined it and recommended immediate surgery. When she told the administration at the academy, they told her:

"Sign the papers. You either resign or get fired." I was like, "What the heck?" I had to leave. I needed surgery. So I came back to the very next recruit class (number) and the first thirteen weeks were totally the same. So I only had three weeks that were different so that was an awful experience. We wouldn't do that to anybody now. In fact, in that second class, they had a guy whose dad was a sergeant who broke his leg in the second week and he stayed, he never did physical activity again. I mean that's the kind of stuff they did then. Now they still do it; they are just more covert. We, still to this day, we have not had another female cadet class president.

After successfully meeting current paramilitary standards for being a police recruit, many female officers recounted being singled out by their trainers and field training officers for both physical and verbal abuse in front of their classmates. Sara Decker recounted the physical abuse she experienced during her training experience:

I just had the most horrendous time at the academy. The control tactics instructor was this massive six-foot-six, three-hundred-pound meathead, muscle man. Whenever he would demonstrate something, he just loved ripping me out of my shoes. I'm like, "Oh good, you can pick on the five-foot-two girl. Why don't you pick on someone your own size? Anybody in the room can throw me."

Jessie Langston, who went to the academy in 1985, found the language and degradation especially difficult: "They yelled and screamed at you and tried to make you quit. They called women the 'C' word, fat, and ugly. That behavior was accepted."

Another way that women were made to feel as outsiders was by objectifying or denigrating them as sex objects. Policing is known for canteen humor associated with building rapport and solidarity in police work. While sexual innuendo was expected in the male-dominated culture of policing, reports of overt sexual harassment in the academy were not uncommon. Lana Sykes attended the police academy in 1988.

> My first day at the academy is a great story. So this instructor goes up and starts writing down clearly they are bar names on the board right and I am going: "Huh. They are going tell us to make sure you stay out of these places." He starts talking to the guys. He starts pointing to these places. He starts pointing to out all of these places and telling the guys "this is a good place to get laid. This is not a good place to get laid." I swear to God, I swear to God. And then to top matters off . . . I must have had dropped jaw, a completely dropped jaw expression on my face. He looks at me and he goes "and honey if you have any problems getting laid give me a call" in front of the whole class, the whole class. And I said to my-self "what in the fuck have I gotten myself into? You have got to be kidding me. This is really going on, you Neanderthal." They all started laughing, of course.[10]

Field Training

As graduation day approaches and recruits leave the academy, having lived through the academy rite of passage, another important training session is just beginning: the field training experience. At this time, official probation-ary police officers shadow a more experienced police officer, usually called a field training officer (FTO), to learn more about how officers in their home department do the job. While the police academy teaches recruits the laws for the state and established safety procedures, the FTO will train the proba-tionary officers in how their agency does police work. This is that part in cop movies when a veteran officer tells a new rookie recruit to "forget everything they taught you in the academy; now I will teach you how to really do the job." During this time, recruits are on a probationary status, usually lasting from six months to one year, and at any point during this time, if their performance is unsatisfactory, they can be immediately terminated.

The FTO process usually is composed of three phases. In the first phase, recruits learn the agency's policies and local laws that they may not have learned in the academy. During the second phase, the officer observes how his or her department carries out police work. In some agencies, this means spending a couple of weeks in each of the department's bureaus (i.e., traffic, juvenile, major crimes, etc.). In other agencies, this means responding to calls for service and patrolling in a variety of different neighborhoods. In the final stage of the field training program, the FTO observes the recruit and evalu-ates the recruit's readiness for solo police work. Many police agencies utilize single-officer patrol cars, so once officers are released from their probationary status they need to be ready to patrol alone. Probationary officers must receive positive ratings to be released from probationary status.

Women reported a variety of field training experiences, ranging from supportive, career-long friendships to discriminating and harassing rites of passage. Each emerged from these experiences to become successful police officers. Teri Hamm recalled the support she felt from her FTO:

> I had a field training officer that took me under his wing like a little sister. He had twelve years on the job. He told me, "you know if they want to give you a bag of crap, you take it and you decide later what you're going to do with it." . . . I really didn't have a mentor except for my field training officer, and he was still at [location] so I would call him at home and say, "This just happened; what should I do? Or this guy said this to me, what should I do?" He would walk me through and that helped me a lot.

Female FTOs were almost unheard of during this time, as most women had yet to become tenured officers, due to their entrance in most agencies only a few years prior. Almost all role models and FTOs for women in the 1980s were men. Cara Smith discussed how she altered what her FTOs taught her to make it work for her:

> All my FTOs were men, and they were wonderful men, but what I found is their techniques sometimes didn't work for me. You know, a guy could come across in a bullying kind of way, or very assertive, and I found that with my smaller stature, people would kind of just laugh at you. Like I said, they wouldn't take you seriously. So I found that didn't work. So I had to take what they showed me and then adapt it to the way that would work for me, and I found that most women, you know, you communicate and talk your way into, out of, and around situations, and I had to learn to do that a little more on my own. And there weren't a lot of female officers you could talk to. So a lot of it was just trial by error.

FTOs often introduce recruits to the culture of the department. The paramilitary model of policing values loyalty to coworkers and respect to senior officers. Lisa Bailey recounted how some in her department did not appreciate "rookies" speaking to the rank and file:

> When I first came on, my first obstacle that I hit was, you know, I'm from [location]. You say hi to everybody, wave. Yeah, you don't know a stranger. And when I walked past somebody, I said, "Hey, how ya doing?" and kept walking. Next thing I know, after roll call, I got pulled to the side and . . . my FTO came up and said, "What's your fucking rookie doing talking to me?" And I and one

of the other guys that were working the same shift that got hired together, we were both told, "Keep your mouths shut."

Field training officers also targeted female officers, making them feel unwelcome in their departments, as Teresa Bosch recounted:

> I got into the car with an FTO who told me "Because you are a woman you don't belong on the fucking job. You won't make it through my fucking FTO program. Go to work. I am not even here." That was my FTO Program. And in fact my first training officer, the first day I came on the job, I said "I don't need any job this bad." It was just miserable.[11]

This level of harassment was common in the 1980s and is discussed in more detail in chapter 4. This behavior led many to believe that the academy was intended to stop what was perceived as a female police invasion as women entered policing.

Despite the obstacles presented to women entering policing, the number of women who joined police work in the 1980s is the biggest increase ever recorded, from 3 to 9 percent of municipal officers. As women graduated from the academy and entered the field, they blazed a path in their agencies, achieving new "firsts" every day. However, being one of the firsts was tough, as the visibility of being the "token female" coupled with the expectations of being both a "woman" and a "police officer" at the same time created conflict. How women managed this conflict and overcame it to find acceptance in the police role is heartening, as women proved their worth in the boys club of policing. The next chapter explores what it's like to be first.

3

Changing the Gender of Policing

As women joined police agencies in the 1980s, we saw many firsts
in policing. Keep in mind that just a decade earlier women were only
allowed to do police work behind the scenes—helping children and women
and typing reports. This expanded role for women brought lots of firsts to
the forefront in new and previously unexplored police positions. Women
worked undercover in vice units, patrolled city streets in cars and motor-
cycles, and even served as supervisors in some municipalities. For example,
Teresa Bosch, one of the first women hired in her agency, discussed the difficulties of being the first women in the agency: "I was the first female. They
never had a female until this captain retired. He said as long as he was there,
there would not be a female. So when I went there I was not well-received."
Interestingly, women police who had previously served in the military and
believed they had "seen it all" reported surprise at the masculine culture
of policing. Sara Hitte, an officer hired in 1979 at a municipal department,
mentioned:

> I was the first female officer here. It was a little dicey, which was a reality shock.
> In the military, this was not a problem. It did not dawn on me this would be a
> problem. . . . I would say there's no other job I've ever worked, even being in
> the military, that I ever felt my gender showed more than my police work, and
> it completely surprised me.

Tokenism

Being first had its benefits and drawbacks. Because women were the minority in the police station, their differences were highlighted and their mistakes were much more visible. According to Rosabeth Moss Kanter, that is what it means to be a token. In her 1977 book *Men and Women of the Corporation*,[1] Kanter coined the term *tokenism* to describe what was happening to women as they joined the business world. She argued that when women (or really any group that made up less than 15 percent of the occupational workforce) joined a male-dominated occupation like policing, they experienced greater visibility compared to the rest of the group, which heightened the consequences of their actions. They felt like everyone was watching them even when they were not. Nancy Gyra, a municipal police chief, described being a token: "I was the first female sergeant in the county. Then the first female lieutenant. Now I am the first female chief. It gets old being the first. Everyone looks at you. It's like being in a fishbowl." This heightened visibility leads to greater stress and can also cause a decrease in job satisfaction. The pressure to succeed was a great source of anxiety among female police officers. Kim Centra, a captain with a state police agency, mentioned how little mistakes become big mistakes when made by a woman because of her visibility: "If she goes out and makes a mistake it becomes *this big* because there are so few of us." Sam Johnson, a captain with a state police agency, agreed: "I think women stand a higher risk of being described in the negative by their mess-ups and by their errors, which we all make. If a woman screws up I think it has a tendency, reputation-wise, to stay with her longer than a male." The visibility becomes part of a female police officer's working personality: "Well, I am a female in a male-dominated organization. I'm not particularly tall. I'm not particularly short. I'm not particularly fat. I'm not particularly thin. So what sets me apart? My gender does."[2]

This is because the organization expects you to act "like a token," fulfilling stereotypical roles. For women in policing, this means doing "women's work." Kim Black, a detective in a municipal police department, believed she was brought along on raids for her mothering skills, even though she was the only one on her team who did not have children: "I would get called along to go on raids if they knew there would be children there. Once, we were getting ready for a raid and I looked around and I was the only person there who did not have kids. What was I doing there?"[3] Often this occurred because male officers or supervisors assigned a female officer to cases dealing with women and children, a throwback to the earlier days when women in policing really were "sex specialists."

This created a problem for many women in policing because it forced them to choose between femininity, which is expected of women, and an image of professionalism and masculinity, which is the expectation for a police officer. They have to choose—their gender identity versus their career—to manage the conflict between what's expected of women and what's expected of police officers: "You are either a slut or a lesbian; there is no happy medium for the family woman."[4]

This role conflict was first identified by Susan Martin in her groundbreaking analysis of female police officers' experiences in the 1980s. She concluded that the conflict between sex roles and occupational role norms resulted in women adopting either the *police*woman identity, which stresses overachievement and conformity to the police subculture, or the police*woman* identity, which emphasizes conformity to stereotypical feminine roles. Either choice has consequences. Policewomen who attempt to meet the crime-fighting image of ruggedness and masculinity may be negatively labeled as "butch or dyke," but female officers who do not attempt to meet this perceived ideal may risk being defined as weak or "pansy police."[5] As it turned out, being weak was preferred. Female officers in Martin's study reported that male officers were more supportive of women who were incompetent as police because it kept them in their place. By comparison, women who pulled their weight in the workplace and expected respect in return were ostracized, being stereotyped as "castrating," "bitchy," or "lesbian."

Proving Yourself

Most women acknowledged the difficulty of being tokens and discussed solutions to overcome the stereotypes. Cathy Thomas, a detective in a rural county sheriff's office, argued that the only solution to tokenism was "to prove yourself." Cara Smith, a master sergeant with a state police agency, agreed: "Women have to work twice as hard to be half as good. Don't spend your energy complaining about it; just spend your energy being twice as good."[6] Proving yourself and gaining a sense of acceptance in policing usually occurred through achieving a rank or position that demanded respect, through a show of force, or by being unique or different from the male officers.

In policing, rank demands respect. The rank system is a throwback to Sir Robert Peel, who is credited with the creation of the first organized police force. He recommended that police follow a military model. While few police agencies follow all the rules of the military model, the rank system by which police are organized lives on. In most large municipal agencies, the chain of command follows chief, assistant chief, deputy chief, commander, captain, lieutenant, sergeant, and patrol. Moving up the supervisory chain of command is associated with prestige and greater decision making. Sam Johnson, a captain of a state police agency, argued, "There is a certain amount of courtesy that is perfunctory because I wear this particular rank."[7] Jessie Langston was always aware that she was a role model for others: "I've always been really cognizant that what you do helps other people see. 'See, she did it. I could do it too.' They can see there's someone like them, especially when I was the [high-ranking training officer] for a while. I thought that was particularly important for recruits to see."

Another way of proving yourself and gaining a sense of acceptance in policing is a show of force. Amanda Kaminski, a municipal police officer, found that out after a near-death experience in a hotel room: "Probably the most acceptance was when I was almost killed in a hotel room. I had to use my gun on a seventeen-year-old. I think you hate to say it that way, but I think officers felt, 'she can do the job. She did prove that she made it out of this hotel room alive and protected herself.' So, I think you can get accepted in a way like that."[8] Lana Sykes had a similar experience early in her career:

> They became friendly after I got to my first fight. Before that, no one would really speak to me. I was in the FTO program. My FTO and I got into a big fight in a bar that was in the south end and I drug the guy that was jumping on him and I flipped him over and handcuffed him and cussed at him and drug him out of the building and after that, they all spoke to me. But it was really kind of like a waiting game that I didn't know existed, that they were just waiting to see what I would do if there was actually a fight. Once they saw that I was going to jump in and help somebody and actually win the fight, then it was, you know, "Oh we will slap you on the back. We are going to keep a watchful eye on you, but you are okay as far as we are concerned." It's a very simple mentality that works here.[9]

Female police officers, who are successful at managing the delicate balance of expectations associated with their femininity and police professionalism, may find ways of making their visibility an advantage. Cara Smith believed her uniqueness and her physical attractiveness paid off: "I had a lot of opportunities being in the state police organization back then because I was very unique. So I think I had the opportunity to do a lot of things that maybe others might not have had, in part because I think the department was showcasing me. You know, I looked good in a uniform."[10] Lisa Bailey discussed how being a woman influenced the way she did her job in ways that men could not:

> Well, I think one thing is, in the past, I've been criticized because I've not been in a knock-down, drag-out fight. And my response was, "Why do I need to be if I can walk up to John Doe and say, 'Excuse me, sir, you're under arrest. Would

you please put these handcuffs on?'" And I go home with no scratches, bumps, or bruises.

Tokens do not have the same informal bonds, leading to less support on and off the job. One consequence is that female officers feel isolated and subordinated. Margaret Stack, a sheriff's deputy in a small, rural county, argued, "I have never had a problem. I think because of my attitude. I don't try to compete with the men. I try to do the best I can do and I try to work with them. By 'compete' I mean I don't butt heads with them."[11] Another consequence is that women may have higher expectations for their female coworkers than men do. If they screw up, it's seen as a reflection on all women, and it makes it harder for them all. One of the many women who found themselves pushing other female officers harder was Jackie Heath:

> When I first came on the department I was in the police academy, and our eighth week we had a shooting at our academy, and it was a female officer who shot another classmate. And that really shaped my values about what I thought about women in police work. And even though I didn't really want to, I was so hard on the other females because I have such a high expectation of myself, and I want that to be in other people also. So, you know, when she shot him, all the guys were now looking at every other woman in that academy class going, "Is she going to shoot me next?"[12]

In her book *Breaking and Entering: Policewomen on Patrol*, Susan Martin predicted, "It is likely that the dynamics of tokenism will continue to operate, leaving policewomen with a number of difficult choices in the face of expectations that they will think like men, work like dogs, and act like ladies."[13] The consequences of tokenism, including the isolation of women, exaggeration of the differences between females and males, and the definition of appropriate work for women compared to men, are based on the idea that women are tokens and novel. The flipside is that as the number of women in policing increases, their novelty and token status will go away. Sadly, few departments today have moved beyond Kanter's 15 percent marker to test whether the numeric increase of women would decrease their visibility and perceived difference in policing. Only time will tell whether their token status will become a thing of the past.

The next chapter describes the experiences of women navigating the male culture of policing in the 1980s and their strategies for overcoming sexual harassment and discrimination. Sexism and harassment were significant consequences of tokenism and another tool to drive women from police work. The continued resistance to the idea of gender equity in police departments manifested in sexism, sexual jokes, harassment, and discrimination, which by all accounts were daily occurrences for female police officers in the 1980s.

4

Facing the Intimidations of
Harassment and Discrimination

IN HER ARTICLE "MALE PEER SUPPORT AND THE POLICE CULTURE: Understanding the Resistance and Opposition of Women in Policing," Courtney Franklin reported that sexual teasing, sexual harassment, and discrimination are all tools in the arsenal intent on keeping women from being accepted as equals in policing.[1] Why? To answer this question, we have to understand the root of sexism and its manifestations as harassment and discrimination.

We all have biases, and those biases often influence how we see others and attribute worth to them. Sometimes our biases affect how we behave. We generally divide biases into implicit and explicit biases. Implicit bias refers to the attitudes or stereotypes that affect our understanding, actions, and decisions in an unconscious manner. These biases reside deep within our subconscious, but we are not aware of them, and for this reason, we cannot conceal them. Everyone has implicit biases, and they change over time based on our experiences. Explicit bias, by comparison, refers to the attitudes and beliefs we have about a person or group on a conscious level. Explicit bias occurs as the result of deliberate thought and for, that reason, can be consciously regulated. Interestingly, actions based on explicit bias, such as harassment, are most likely to occur when a person perceives an individual or group as a threat to his or her well-being.

In policing, sexism may be based on concerns about what the female invasion may bring to the profession of policing. These biases manifest as discrimination and harassment. Discrimination refers to when someone is treated less favorably than another solely because of the color of his or her skin or his or her ethnicity, sex, age, disability, marital status, faith, or even sexual preference. This is illustrated in the obstacles to advancement in promotion or the lack of female-friendly uniforms and locker room facilities. Behaviors that are considered unwelcome sexual advances, as well as those that create hostile working environments, constitute sexual harassment. Sexual harassment also involves unwelcome behaviors that happen to workers because of their sex.

Sexism is not unique to policing. In fact, between one-fourth and one-half of women in the workplace in the 1980s reported experiencing sexual harassment. In one-fifth of the cases, the harassment was devastating enough that it resulted in the woman quitting her job, being transferred, or being fired. Sexual harassment is generally higher in workplaces that are male dominated and have a history of excluding women, so the argument could be made that female officers experienced a significant amount of sexism on the job. The core values of the police culture illustrate how the entrance of women disrupted the solidarity of this previously all-male profession. These values are critical in understanding how sexual harassment and discrimination became common issues in policing during the 1980s.

Police Culture

Culture refers to a shared set of values, norms, and behaviors that form a particular way of life. Police culture (sometimes defined as a police subculture) refers to values that guide police behavior. Criminologists Malcolm Sparrow, Mark Moore, and David Kennedy have defined five core values of police culture that guide police behavior.[2] First, police believe that they are the primary crime-fighting organization in the United States. As discussed previously, little of what police do, about 15 percent of their activities, have anything to do with crime fighting. However, crime fighting is seen as real police work and is prized over other types of police duties. Keep in mind that this is because the authority to use coercion or force is what defines police work. Second, police officers believe that no one other than the police understands the true nature of police work and what is necessary to get the job done. Often, this is discussed as "us versus them," as police see themselves as "belonging to an exclusive group of men who are braver, smarter, and more self-reliant than the civilian population they serve."[3] Third, police believe they have to stick together because everyone else is unfair in their critiques of the police. Concerns that the public, politicians, and administrators are unduly critical of police and even "Monday-morning-quarterback" police decisions are common. Fourth, police believe they may have to violate ethical, organizational, and legal standards to get the job done. Criminals fight outside the rules, and sometimes police also have to exceed the boundaries set forth by their jurisdiction. Police studies professor Victor Kappeler argues that police are taught by the subculture that "if you get caught off base, don't implicate anybody else." This means that if you get caught violating an organizational ethical or legal rule, you should accept your punishment and not implicate others.[4] Finally, the last core value of police culture is that the public does not understand, support, or appreciate the police. This belief, coupled with shift-work constraints, secrecy, and cynicism, limits relationships that police have with non-police. The culture in policing is an outgrowth of the work that police do. It gives them protection and support to do an increasingly tough job. Unfortunately, these same core values "form the social systems that serve to keep women from fully participating in policing."[5] They do this through the influence they have on the organizational climate of police agencies, defining police practices and what behaviors are rewarded, how communication flows in the agency, and who has access to power and decision making. Often the police culture impacts the organizational climate by normalizing police practices; for example, the focus on danger and crime fighting not only legitimizes the increasing militarization of police but also leads agencies to overemphasize physical fitness standards in the hiring process, and it discourages women from seeing policing as a rewarding profession.

Sometimes the culture influences the organizational climate in nuanced ways. Cara Smith discussed how the language used in the organization sent a subtle message to women that they did not belong in policing: "If people use the word 'manpower' or some sexist language like that, I'm the first one to jump all over them. And a lot of people will react like, 'Oh you're making a big deal out of nothing,' and I always say, 'No—you're sending a strong message that only men can do it.'"

Sometimes the messages are not subtle. Police solidarity or the blue curtain makes it very difficult to investigate and punish officers who engage in harassing and discriminatory behavior against their colleagues, as well as silencing officers who have been victimized out of fear that they will be labeled a snitch and further ostracized. The male solidarity in the agency Teresa Bosch joined resulted in her primary training officer admitting that "he was promised a promotion if he could get me to quit because they just didn't want women." In the district Kim Centra joined, she was physically attacked by one of the other male trainers at the police training academy she attended, describing it as her district's "first sexual harassment." She was hesitant to report the attack because she knew better than to report "one of your own." She also knew that her superior officers "thought it was funny." In this way, the police culture fostered an organizational climate accepting and protective of sexually harassing and discriminatory behavior.

Sexism and Discrimination

Male police officers' opposition to female officers has been amply documented.[6] In his 1980 book *Women in Law Enforcement*, researcher Peter
Horne illustrated that male resistance "has been the most significant factor
in hindering the advancement of policewomen."[7] In studies of women's
entrance into patrol in both St. Louis and Washington, DC, male officers
reported overwhelmingly negative attitudes toward policewomen.[8] Their
concerns regarding the female invasion into policing revolved around sex
roles or the proper role of women and men in work access to promotion and
other specialized positions and doubts that women could handle the dangers
of police work. Sex roles, or what is considered natural or normal behavior
for men and women, suggest that women do not belong in the very dangerous
and masculine occupation of policing. As one officer put it, "Women don't
carry guns, women don't fight, women don't arrest people, and women don't
earn $20,000 a year."[9] For some female officers, policemen responded to their
presence with paternalism and chivalry. A Washington, DC, officer reported
that her male partner kept "holding the door for me." These paternal actions
kept women in subordinate positions because, as the term *paternal* indicates,
it's hard to be an equal to your father.

By the 1980s, officers were skeptical that women were expected to be
equals. For many, "the very notion of a woman officer violates the self-image
of these individuals and the organizational and social myth that law enforcement is a man's job."[10] These were very powerful beliefs, which officers went
to great ends to protect. Kim Centra, a captain with a state police agency,
recalled the resistance she faced because she was a woman entering a very
male world in policing: "I had sergeants sit there and tell me walking into
headquarters when I was a trooper, 'You don't belong here. It's a job for the
White man.'"[11] In his 1987 analysis of the beliefs of 191 men and 42 women
officers in the Illinois State Police, Ralph Weisheit confirmed that the policemen in his study generally shared the unspoken belief that "if a woman
can do it [the police job], then the job isn't worth much."[12] Joanna Bunker
Rohrbaugh argued that this kind of behavior occurred when women entered
other male-dominated occupations as well, such as business, academics, and
law, with the express purpose of reminding women that they are not bona fide
members of the group.[13]

The competition for scarce administrative positions added another reason
why men fought against adding competitors for promotions and access to
specialized positions, such as SWAT (Special Weapons and Tactics) team or
school resource officer. In a 1987 study of male state police officers,[14] they
reported that they felt that female officers used their gender to get jobs and

move up the ranks. For this reason, women who sought promotion faced considerable resistance. While promotion is covered in detail in the 1990s section, this was and still is a serious obstacle to women's advancement in policing, and the resistance turned many women away from the promotional process. Lana Sykes, a captain in a municipal police agency, discussed the sex discrimination she faced in the promotional process:

> I wanted to try and do some other things, and I started to put in for some other positions. And I wasn't getting those positions even though I had a really good work record and I had really good relationships with my coworkers and my peers. One of the guys that got a position that I didn't get was a complete idiot. So I started to say, you know what, the writing is on the wall. They are not going to let me go into what I want to do. There is still some stigma going on here. There were still some issues with where they wanted females to go. Both of those positions had never been held by anyone but a guy. The writing is on the wall. They are not going to let me go anywhere. So they created their own worst nightmare. Now I am going to try to get promoted and I am sharp enough that I probably will be. So they should have let me go where I wanted to go. Now I am going to be your competition for promotion exams. So that's why I did it.[15]

Much of the discrimination centered on women's abilities, as male police officers refused to see female officers as equals. Tammy Victor recalled how her administrator refused to treat her in the same way as male sergeants following her promotion:

> Well when I got promoted, I remember there was a gruff old master sergeant down there and he felt one of the other guys should have got promoted. . . . I can just remember that he questioned every decision that I wanted to make, and you could just tell he just did not like that I was in the position. I remember finally just going to him after a few months. I just walked in there and was like "I don't know what I have done to you or what is wrong with you. I don't know what we have to do to resolve this but I am not going to continue to go on like this here." So I spoke to the captain and said: "Hey, this guy needs to treat me the same he treats everybody else or I am going to have to do something different." . . . And after I kind of called this master sergeant on the carpet, I guess he just left me alone; it was like, "Well okay, here she is going to stand up for herself," and he was apologetic. . . . He left me alone. It worked out pretty good after that.[16]

Even other women were involved in resisting women's expanding role in policing. In the 1970s, female officers also felt that men were more competent. When asked whom they wanted to partner with, many female officers chose men, expressing a greater trust in the policing capabilities of males.[17] The alienation of women toward other women in the occupation is common in tokenism. The price of being "one of the boys" means occasionally turning against other women who are not.[18] Kim Centra recalled the bittersweet moment when she met the other female officer stationed in her police district:

> I will never forget this experience when I remember I met my female counterpart up there who was on the road; there were only two of us there at the time. And . . . I went to introduce myself and I stuck my hand out and she turned her back and walked away.[19]

This creates an isolating effect by which women are socially cut off from both formal and informal power structures at work in their agencies. Women may avoid informal interaction with their male colleagues in order to prevent the implication of sexual impropriety. If female role models are unavailable or unwilling to build interpersonal relationships with them, their access to mentors and career advice is blocked. Without access to the informal political network in their agency, women are more likely to be overlooked for promotions and other specialized police positions and to feel isolated at work.

Sexual Harassment

In the 1970s, administrators, policemen, and even police wives warned that mixed-sex socializing inherent in adding women to the masculine culture of policing would result in a variety of dramatic problems for agencies.[20] Police solidarity is an important part of the police culture, as police rely on one another for backup, camaraderie, and support. This is especially true for police partners, as they not only depend on each other but also develop strong attachments as they work together. It is often said that police partners spend more time with one another than they do with their spouses.

The entry of women into policing threatened this camaraderie and solidarity. Police wives felt threatened by the presence of women on the job. Husbands, in turn, felt some resentment at being placed in an uncomfortable position at home because of the departments' hiring of women. Of course, this situation worked against female officers at home too. In her 1983 study of policewomen, Patricia Remmington found a number of female officers in her survey got divorced after becoming police officers.[21] Their husbands were concerned that they were participating in extramarital affairs with fellow officers in the privacy of the police car. In response, some agencies even passed fraternizing rules prohibiting officers from dating other officers.

By comparison, as women entered policing in greater numbers, agencies, by and large, failed to take measures to prevent incidents of sexual harassment. One expert suggested that in 1988, most police did not even understand what behavior constituted sexual harassment. While that may be hard to imagine today, keep in mind that when University of Oklahoma law professor Anita Hill testified at Clarence Thomas's Supreme Court confirmation hearing in 1991 describing his sexually harassing behavior, it shined a light on a problem facing many professional women in the workplace that had been ignored or hidden up to that point in time.

Sexual harassment is a very specific term that describes unwelcome behavior that happens to workers because of their sex, and, by all accounts, it was a daily occurrence for female officers in the 1980s.[22] Kathy Frank, a police chief, argued that the obstacles she faced, including "discriminatory and disrespectful behavior" and being made the "butt of jokes" aimed at her sexuality, when she became a municipal police officer in the 1980s were clearly due to her gender: "The things that impeded me were done because I was a woman. It was very clearly directed at me because of my gender." Susan Martin found that 63 percent of seventy-two women officers interviewed in five large urban departments recounted instances of sexual harassment on the job: "Most women officers have experienced both sex discrimination and sexual harassment," and frequently these behaviors were "blatant, malicious, widespread, organized, and involved supervisors; occasionally it was life-threatening."[23]

Sexual harassment can be perpetrated by anyone in the workplace, including supervisors, and includes unwelcome sexual advances, requests for sexual favors, and verbal or physical conduct of a sexual nature. When submission to the conduct is used as a basis for employment decisions or is made a condition of employment, that harassment is called *quid pro quo*. When the conduct is so severe or pervasive that it creates an intimidating or offensive work environment, it is called a *hostile work environment*. According to the courts, a few common mannerisms that may create a hostile work environment include the frequent use of terms like "honey," "sweetie," "babe," and so on; sexual gestures; sexually explicit jokes; distasteful physical contact; displaying sexually suggestive pictures or posters; asking questions of a personal and sexual nature; and repeated requests for dates.[24] This was very common in the culture of policing during the 1980s. Teresa Bosch described the sexual comments that littered her field training experiences:

> I was with a training officer one night, afternoon, it was Easter and it was not like you have all the places now with things open, and it was like, "What are we going to find to eat today?" He was like, "Let's go to the Y," and I am thinking, "The Y? Are they having some kind of like family dinner?" He was like, "No. The Y. Get it?" I was like, "No. No." He's like, "The Y between your legs." Because that's the kind of treatment you got, every day.

One perpetrator of sexual harassment in an agency could alter the work experience of all the women working in that agency: "We had one supervisor here who . . . single-handedly alienated every single woman in the organization at some point. . . . He was like a lawsuit waiting to happen."[25]

Cara Smith described a very creative way that she dealt with a colleague's attempt to create what she perceived as a hostile environment for police recruits as an administrator at the academy:

> Early on in my career, I had gone into a colleague's office. He worked in a different work unit, but we were both assigned to the training academy. I went to him on an issue. As I am sitting there talking to him across his desk, I can't help but notice he's got a calendar hanging right behind him of all these scantily clad women in lingerie. So I said to him, "You know, you need to take that calendar down, that's not appropriate." He said "Why? I like it." I said "Well, you know, you're going to have cadets in here and talking to you and that's just inappropriate. You shouldn't do that." He said: "Oh . . . do not make such a big deal out of it." Well, it bothered me, and it was not the environment where I could go to EEO or I could go to his boss or even my boss, for that matter, and complain about it. At least I did not feel . . . and I felt that I would be ostracized, so I talked to another female coworker of mine and said, "You know, we got to get that calendar down. That's just wrong." So we got an idea. So that night after work, I went to Toys-R-Us, and I got paper dolls with clothes and I went back to the office, got the key for his office, and I went in, and I took the calendar, went back to my office, cut out [the clothes] and I dressed them all. I put hats on and shoes and purses. I just had a great time getting them all fully clothed, then snuck back into his office, hung it back up, and left it at that. Well, the next day, I'm having coffee; he comes in and says "OK. You win." And I said, "What are you talking about?" And he tosses the calendar at me and said, "You win. Nobody ever says anything about it, and you complain about it and look what's happened to this calendar." I said "What a clever idea! I wish I could take credit for this. What a great idea."

Cara's experience makes clear that there were organizational remedies to the behavior but that she did not feel she had enough support to report the behavior. Instead, she got creative.

Responses

Because sexual harassment is a form of sex discrimination, which violates the law against sex discrimination in the workplace outlined in Title VII of the Civil Rights Act of 1964, employers can be held legally responsible for the harassment and liable for damages that result, regardless of whether the acts were authorized or forbidden and regardless of whether the employer knew or should have known of the occurrence. Some women filed lawsuits against their departments to fight back. Teresa Bosch filed a lawsuit against her department for disparate treatment regarding her promotion process. She had no idea the lengths the department would go to protect those who had engaged in the discriminatory practices. Her ten-year battle started when her ratings in her written exam were altered to promote men ahead of her: "Two guys were eleven points higher than me. You have got an eleven-point gap, then me, then everybody else. It was like, 'This is a joke. . . . Those ratings are just a damn sham; they might as well get rid of them.' They knew I had a well-written test." Next, her direct supervisor promoted his best friend over her. She complained, making it clear that she knew that he had altered the written test ratings: "'You played with the ratings. I have got more time on and more time in investigations. He is your best friend. You guys hunt and everything together and that is horseshit. You are wrong.'" The very next day, she was visited by "an internal investigation for some kind of horseshit crap and I am like, 'Amazing!' My whole career I have never had a letter, never had an investigation." They fabricated a sexual harassment claim against her. She was called into the investigation to give her testimony, and in the testimony, they asked her about her sex life at home with her partner. Bosch was in a committed relationship with a woman who was a police officer in a neighboring police department.

> They kind of go skipping and dancing around and their first question was, and this is how I knew the whole thing was full of crap, was if I had sex with my partner that I am living with. . . . Because when you are in one of those internal investigations you have to answer. It isn't like a criminal with "I will plead the fifth" or whatever. They knew I wasn't going to answer the question and they were going to suspend me immediately. I was going to get fired because you can't do that.

Instead, Bosch answered their questions honestly at the encouragement of her counsel. Bosch waited for the result of the investigation and her punishment. She was not even aware of the person who made the claim. In the end, it became apparent that a colleague saw Bosch interacting with a witness and believed that it was "inappropriate" and, based on that belief, brought the case forward. Eventually, "the whole thing comes out and the [alleged victim] says that I have never done anything inappropriate and in fact, the only thing she has heard about the dating thing is from [the witness colleague]." Her colleague had suggested to the victim that Bosch wanted to date her. After fighting this battle for ten years, Teresa Bosch got her promotion. It came at a cost. Her relationship crumbled under the pressure of litigation and stress and the disbelief that this was happening to them: "Our relationship has like gone to shit over all these years of everything and this pressure because she can't believe the department has done this. . . . You know, I think her eyes are little more open now, but at the time she just couldn't believe people are doing this but there must be something I am not saying."

Sexual harassment and discrimination complaints are costly to agencies in terms of not only lawsuits but also lower job satisfaction and, in some cases, loss of quality employees through turnover. Some women, when faced with sexism, harassment, and/or discrimination, left the profession. Several studies have confirmed the higher rates of turnover of women police than men during the 1980s. For example, in a study of policewomen of the California Highway Patrol, female officers had a higher attrition rate than male officers—three times the male rate.[26] In Lincoln Fry's examination of the factors related to turnover of women in law enforcement, he found that women were more likely to leave both the police training academy and police employment than male officers.[27] Interestingly, he reported that they often left to accept employment with other agencies, likely for improved opportunities for promotion. Can we blame them? Experiences of harassment and discrimination can have a serious impact on women's physical and emotional well-being, and often involve anxiety, depression, sleep disruption, weight loss and gain, and headaches. Detroit policewoman Cheryl Preston filed a lawsuit against her department in 1984 alleging sexual harassment that was so egregious that it caused her to have a nervous breakdown. The courts agreed to award her $900,000 plus interest based on her experience.[28]

Others have responded to sexual harassment and discrimination by simply persevering: "I have never filed any lawsuits against the department. I have had women say, 'Hey, you want to get on this little class action thing or say something about not getting promoted?' Nope. . . . I just ride on my own, do my own little thing out here." Kim Black survived by "refusing to let the bastards get me down. In the beginning, they tried. I was cut down by my commander. They made destructive comments. They are gone now. I outlived them."

At the end of the 1980s era there is some evidence that sex discrimination improved. As Lieutenant Heather Noell said, "The blatant sexism and racism has been gone for a while." Women surveyed in 1990 reported that discriminatory behavior had improved for women hired later in the 1980s, but that the sexually harassing behavior stayed the same. Maybe the discriminatory behavior improved because it became obvious that women were in policing to stay. Perhaps departments became increasingly aware that they would be held responsible for the behaviors they were using to keep women out of policing. Some women argued that sexual harassment and discrimination were a thing of the past by the 2000s; others believed that perpetrators simply became more covert.

The lingering question of the 1980s was: Can women handle the physical dangers associated with policing? Only the brave acts of women put into the line of fire could settle this debate. Important to this debate is an understanding of how dangerous policing really is. While police work has the potential to be dangerous, most police work is actually pretty mundane. The next section explores the dangers of police work and the ability of women to survive those dangers.

5

The Dangers on the Beat

I N 1991, THE PUBLIC MET OFFICER PAT LOGAN of the Pittsburg Police Department in the new television reality series *Cops*. According to its founder,
Cops was one of the first true and unscripted reality shows that followed the
activities of police officers by embedding camera crews with police units.
While shooting in Pittsburg, Logan described police work:

> Officer Pat Logan says on the job they've broken his arm, fractured his skull,
> stabbed him four times, run him over with a stolen car, smashed into him with
> a stolen car and put him out of commission a couple of time. He's been in four
> gun battles and one where he saved an officer's life. He still has nightmares
> about gun battles and getting shot at, every once in a while wakes up in a cold
> sweat. . . . He says it's not his fault the way the world is. It's good. Or guys who
> don't believe that wind up chewing on a gun barrel leaving a family behind who
> doesn't understand.[1]

Is his experience common? Do all police have a list of broken bones and
psychological troubles at the end of their police career? Unlike what is popularized on television crime shows, most police retire without ever even un-
holstering their firearm, and violence between police and citizens is rare. To
give you a picture of how rare it is, in 2013 in New York City, only one police
officer out of 850 shot a suspect intentionally.[2] Citizen attacks of police are
also rare. Staying in New York City, from 2008 to 2012, only one police officer
was killed by a firearm in the line of duty. In fact, there are occupations where
fatalities are much higher. For example, jobs in mining and construction have
much higher fatality rates than policing.

In reality, most police work is routine and rarely matches the sexy types of crime fighting seen in television crime dramas. Police work includes preventing crime, protecting life and property, enforcing laws, maintaining peace, and providing service to the public twenty-four hours a day. In the 1980s, similar to today, the most common types of police calls involved requests for service to the public and had little to do with crime. However, according to well-known police researcher Egon Bittner, what makes police unique is their ability to use coercion or force to establish social control. Think about it: What other occupation is authorized to use force, even deadly force against citizens? So, while only 10–15 percent of police work really has anything to do with crime fighting, it is the most visible part of the job. The pursuit of criminals is perceived as real police work because it has embodied the danger and authority that are stereotypically inherent in the police role.

This is why danger is an ever-present possibility in policing. Who knows if a traffic stop will result in an ambush attack on police? Will the citizen who is being stopped and frisked for weapons be a career criminal who is more willing to fight or shoot police than serve his or her time on an outstanding warrant? The paradox of danger and policing is that while actual danger is rare, the potential for danger is constant. Seeing the police as legitimate users of force, coupled with the potential danger faced, helps explain why physical prowess and ability to maintain authority are thought of as important police skills. It is no surprise that one of the most frequent concerns about female police officers' entry into the most dangerous aspects of policing is that they are physically weaker and therefore less capable. Although the research from the 1970s and 1980s consistently reported that women were as capable as men in the police role, doubts remained, especially in the aftermath of officer-involved shootings and fatalities.

First Female Officer Down: Gail Cobb

In 1974 Gail Cobb, a Washington, DC, patrol officer, was the first police-woman killed in the line of duty. Cobb was only six months out of the police academy at the time of the shooting. She applied to be a DC Metropolitan Police officer in October 1973, following the department's historic decision to lower its height requirement to five feet. She graduated in April 1974, one of thirteen women hired.

Cobb was fatally shot while chasing a fugitive on Friday, September 20, 1974. That morning two men, twenty-nine-year-old John Curtis Dortch and twenty-four-year-old John William Bryant, set out to rob the Eastern Liberty Federal Savings and Loan at the intersection of Twenty-First and L streets.

The police were waiting for them, as they had been tipped off to the robbery. When detectives approached the get-away vehicle, a Pontiac Grand Prix parked in front of the bank, and asked them for identification, they ran off.[3] As fate would have it, Officer Gail Cobb, age twenty-four, was writing a traffic ticket a few blocks away when someone told her that a suspicious person had just run into a nearby parking garage. John William Bryant had ducked down into the underground garage after fleeing police outside the bank. Cobb discovered him at the bottom of the ramp. Bryant turned and fired his gun. The bullet passed through her forearm and penetrated her heart. Cobb was pronounced dead forty-five minutes later.[4]

The nation was shocked. Her funeral involved a five-hundred-police-squad motorcade followed by her burial at the Lincoln Memorial Cemetery. At the hour of the funeral, President Gerald R. Ford called for a moment of silence as he addressed an International Association of Police Chiefs conference being held across town.[5] Of her violent death, *Saturday Evening Post* contributor Virginia Armat said, "The ceremony, one of the most impressive of its kind ever seen, was both a solemn avowal of the dangers policewomen face and recognition of women's new share in police work."[6]

Keeping Track: Law Enforcement Officers Killed and Assaulted (LOEKA)

Gail Cobb's death occurred at the peak of officer deaths in America. Federal Bureau of Investigation (FBI) reports indicated a disturbing trend and give us some idea why police were very concerned with danger in the 1970s: The number of US law enforcement officers feloniously killed in the line of duty per year more than doubled between 1960 and 1966 (from 28 to 57) and doubled again between 1966 and 1971 (from 57 to 126).[7] The number peaked in 1973 at 134 officers killed. It was clear that more needed to be done to understand why and how police were being attacked and killed.

In June 1971, executives from the law enforcement conference "Prevention of Police Killings" called for an increase in the FBI's involvement in preventing and investigating officers' deaths. In response to this recommendation, the FBI expanded its collection of data to include more details about the incidents in which law enforcement officers were killed and assaulted. From this information, the FBI created the annual publication *Law Enforcement Officers Killed and Assaulted*, commonly referred to LEOKA.[8] The expanded analysis about the details of incidents in which police were killed and assaulted led to important procedural changes that have improved the safety of officers. For example, we know from the LEOKA: (1) most police fatalities occur in situations the police already know are dangerous (the top three are while making an arrest, situations involving robberies, and traffic stops); and (2) most of the incidents involving fatalities are initiated by the officer rather than by the citizen. These findings prompted the wider use of protective vests, improved training, and a heightened awareness of dangerous police calls. These safety mechanisms attributed to the declining number of officer fatalities in the 1980s, as the number steadily declined after 1973.[9]

Strained police-community relationships influenced both officer and citizen perceptions of danger. By 1980, America was becoming increasingly urbanized. Inner-city communities were experiencing a new wave of immigration represented largely by impoverished African Americans arriving from rural southern states. This era is marked by increasing social, cultural, and racial distance between police and communities, resulting in allegations of abuse and discrimination. The strained police-community relationships from the early 1980s in major cities did little to calm police concerns of danger. Detective Alicia Kaminski, an eight-year veteran of a municipal police department, argued that police perception of disrespect breeds discouragement and fear and that this shift represented the biggest one of her career:

> Since I first started policing, the biggest change is that the respect is not there. You notice . . . the liability factors, and I mean when something happened and, you know, as police officers, that if we have to pull out our gun on somebody, lengthy reports have to be written. Everything has to be documented. People want to find fault with police officers now, and back when I first started, police officers were looked upon as very respectful people, and now it has become where it is very disrespectful. The police are always wrong, and they're always right. Everybody is carrying a gun and there is no respect for police. I mean, to kill a police officer these days is not uncalled for. Back when I first came on, that was something you never heard of much.

We know that the stress that officers experience is influenced by their perceptions of danger. The chance of being hurt or killed on the job is defined by police researchers as the "potential danger," and it causes stress-related consequences, including alcohol and drug abuse, emotional distress, burnout, and even suicide. Police are at a greater risk of all of these stress-related consequences than the general population.

Aftermath of a Police-Involved Shooting

Living in the aftermath of a police-involved shooting is devastating, especially when there are fatalities. In the late 1980s, young Teresa Bosch was in a shootout with a man who was facing charges for putting out a hit on his wife. The man and his wife were having marital problems and she was fearful for her life. As it turned out, she had a good reason for concern. The man would prove capable and willing to use deadly force. The police had been encouraging the suspect to turn himself in the day before the shooting, but negotiations failed. Because the man was heavily armed and a weapons expert, the decision had been made that meeting him on his home turf would not end well. Instead, the agency hatched a plan to stage a motorist in need of help along the route the suspect took to work. Teresa and two other male officers wearing street clothes waited for the suspect in an unmarked car along the highway.

The plan was to have Teresa walk up to the suspect's car alone, but her partner walked up to the car with her, and then he shined his flashlight and announced himself: "That was a bad deal because I was the only one supposed to be at the car window. My partner . . . broke the plan, came up behind me and was actually leaning on my shoulder." The suspect opened fire on the officers. Left with no choice, the officers shot and killed the suspect. Sadly, Teresa's partner, a longtime police veteran, was also shot and died from his wounds. The third officer at the scene was also shot, though not seriously injured. Teresa remembers the moment that the shooting began:

> This guy had the gun under his coat the whole time and just opened fire. The one that killed my partner burned the arm of my coat. I don't know if he is hit or dead during all the shooting. . . . We were in real close physical proximity by the time this thing was open; in fact, I emptied all my weapons. Backup comes and shoots him, but I think he is grabbing another gun, so I go charging up and I fire his last round into him. . . . I have got two empty guns, and this is the first time I see my dead partner. . . . I pick up his gun. . . . I still think he has tripped. I have no idea. . . . By that time he had quit moving so I rolled over to get my partner and say, "Hey, are you okay?" I did CPR work on him and I just pumped the rest of his blood out. I mean there was nothing. It was pretty much instantly. . . . My other partner got wounded, grazed in the head and wounded in the hand. . . . I mean I already thought I was shot. I had no idea I wasn't till it was over.

Posttraumatic Stress Disorder

In the aftermath of the shooting, Teresa suffered from posttraumatic stress disorder (PTSD). This psychological condition involves: (1) reliving the event (also called reexperiencing symptoms) through nightmares, flashbacks, and triggers in which the officer may see, hear, or smell something that causes the officer to relive the event; (2) avoidance, as the officer may try to avoid situations and people that generate memories of the trauma;

(3) negative changes in beliefs and feelings, leading to apathy in relation-ships, distrust, and the inability to discuss the negative event; and (4) hy-perarousal, such as having a hard time sleeping, trouble concentrating, or being startled by a loud noise or surprise. PTSD is a treatable condition, and most sufferers gradually improve. The US Department of Labor, Oc-cupational Safety and Health Administration recommends steps that will significantly reduce stress following a police-involved shooting or another critical incident: (1) limit exposure to noise and odors; (2) dictate an im-mediate fifteen-minute rest break; (3) provide a non-caffeinated beverage to drink; (4) provide low-sugar and low-fat food; (5) get the person to talk about his or her feelings; and (6) do not rush the person back to work.[10] Because first responders, such as police, firefighters, and EMTs, may suf-fer from PTSD after incidents they witness during their employment, most police departments have mandated counseling for officers who experience a critical incident like the one Teresa and her partner did. Both she and her surviving partner were required to attend counseling sessions.

She described some of her more troubling experiences following the shoot-ing: "I am thinking, 'Man oh man, this is bad.' It is nightmarish. You would wake up and see this guy. In my dreams, I always had physical contact with him [the assailant] because I thought that is what we were going to do. The thing was we just kept shooting and fighting; when [your gun was] empty, you found another one and I was going to find another one and if the third one had been empty it was like I am just going to wrestle him."

Soon after the shooting, Teresa's concern shifted from herself to her part-ner: "I really thought my other partner was going to commit suicide at some point." Officers are at great risk of suicide following debilitating stressors such as being involved in a shooting with police fatalities.[11] Nationally, the rate of police suicide is three times the rate of everyone else, and three times as many police kill themselves as are killed by criminals in the line of duty, prompting Laurence Miller to argue that "this makes officer suicide the most lethal threat in police history."[12]

The police culture and officer reluctance in asking for help exacerbate the problem of police suicide. In the article "Police Suicide, What Can Be Done?" a widow of a police officer who committed suicide in 1989 encouraged of-ficers struggling to seek help: "I know the stress that is placed upon law en-forcement officers in this violent society. Many officers believe that seeking help from a mental health professional is a sign of weakness."[13] A critique of the police culture has been that it holds the mantra that "real cops don't need shrinks or other outsiders to make sense of police incidents."[14] Officers fear stigma, confidentiality breaches, job impact worries, mistrust of the psycho-logical field, and stigma associated with medications.

While Teresa and her partner went to counseling following the shooting, their agency's decision to send them to the same counselor increased fears of confidentiality and stigma: "Then they sent us to the same counselor and it's like, 'Okay, first of all, that's bad, and second of all this counselor is telling me is that if I get married and have kids I will be fine. This has nothing to do with the shooting.'" Teresa finally found relief by seeking support on her own: "So finally I find somebody on my own and it was like, hey, this is perfectly normal." She described her eventual recovery from PTSD: "It was like flipping a switch. Your life before then, certain things will never be the same afterward, and the thing is you can live with it, which is fine but you have to realize what the hell happened and what you got." Long after the event, it is clear that the guilt of being the one who lived remains.

> So then this is what you should teach people, because you never think it's going to happen to somebody with you. You might get called to a scene, but not with you when they get killed and you don't. We still don't do enough with that. He has a family and kids and you are thinking, "I feel bad enough. This wasn't my fault." You know when you come on, you think it could be you or the bad guy. You never think it is going to be somebody with you, and they don't train us how to react to that.

In Teresa's case, the situation was exacerbated by the lack of support she felt from her department following the death of her partner. Social support at work can mediate the stressful consequences of a critical incident, but in her case, peer and supervisory support were lacking: "That whole office went into emotional crisis. Oh yeah, we didn't handle it well at all. It was like everybody wanted to hide it." Two years later, when the reenactment of the shooting came out, "a lot of people apologized." However, she felt her career suffered due to people's biases about her being involved in a fatality, especially as a woman: "I always wondered about my career. I mean there are still people who come on and hear about that and they don't get the right story." Teresa felt that her gender had something to do with her treatment in the aftermath of the shooting. She was one of the first female officers to be involved in an officer fatality. Both of the other officers at the scene, including the one who lost his life, had been police officers much longer. "Then throw a female in it, and they will just throw you to the wolves. . . . There are some people who had their mind made up . . . that if I wouldn't have been there, he would still be alive."

Despite the investigation of the shooting, the reenactment of the critical incident, and the acknowledgment she received for bravery and valor, she always believed that the shooting influenced her career and reputation because she was a woman, and for that reason, people had their doubts.

Can Women Handle the Danger of Policing?

The attitude that women were unable to maintain the authority and strength of the police role had always been the elephant in the room. Some of this attitude was indicative of the ideas about the proper role of women in society of the time, which held a general bias toward women working in traditionally male fields. Policing was far from alone in this attitude, as illustrated by the 1980s movie *9 to 5*, which highlighted the sexist culture of the business world.

The concern that women could not protect themselves in policing led to the overprotection of women in the types of calls they were assigned. For example, in Peoria, Illinois, Officer Marian Sleeth, one of the nine women patrol officers on the force, heard a trouble call dispatched in her vicinity. When she attempted to respond, the dispatcher discouraged Sleeth from responding until the police chief, Allen Andrews, intervened and ordered the dispatcher to send her to the call.[15] The radio dispatchers had actually been shielding female patrol officers from what they perceived as potentially dangerous situations.

Dispatchers, police wives, chiefs, and officers from cities across the United States raised concerns that women were unfit for the physical duties of patrol. They worried that suspects would resist policewomen more than they would policemen or that a female officer might miss her target and hit an innocent bystander instead. Despite these concerns, the Police Foundation in Washington, DC, conducted a study in which they could not find a single case in which the presence of a female police officer endangered the lives of her partners.[16]

Instead, they found that when violence did occur there was some evidence that a policewoman's presence reduced it. Researchers explained it like this: While potentially violent citizens may feel empowered to attack a policeman, they feel cowardly attacking a woman.[17] Coupled with finding that policewomen showed more concern, patience, and understanding in family violence situations, the ability of women to have a calming effect on potentially violent encounters suggests that they play an important role in policing. These findings prompted Katherine Van Wormer to write a tongue-in-cheek article in 1981 titled "Are Males Suited to Police Patrol Work?" in response to the mounting concerns that women were ill prepared for danger.

When prompted, women appeared to have little hesitation to use force, even deadly force when necessary. One of these remarkable policewomen who did just that is Officer Marty Green. Green joined the Louisville Police Department in 1971 with six other female recruits, the first woman to be hired by the department in fifteen years. Unlike some departments at the time that kept women in specialized roles, the Louisville Police Department made it known that women would complete the same tasks as the policemen in the department with no exceptions. Green had only been in the department for two years but had an impressive background of working in a youth bureau, as well as narcotics and homicide divisions. Even with an impressive background, Green's day to prove herself came in January 1973. She was sent to the scene of an armed hijacking of an Ozark Air Lines plane housed at Standiford Field. The hijacker was Dennis Durkin, a seventeen-year-old soldier who went AWOL, shot up the Standiford Field terminal, and proceeded to hijack the plane along with taking a mechanic hostage. The hostage situation lasted from 9:10 p.m. on Friday night to 3 a.m. Saturday morning, when Green successfully brought the young gunman down and the hostages to safety. Green convinced Durkin to let her take the place of his hostage, and as the exchange was made, Durkin gave up his weapon, giving Green an opportunity to tackle the seventeen year old, sending them both toppling down the airliner stairs.[18] Officer Green was one of the many female officers who proved that women are fully capable of completing the duties of a police officer even when they are faced with a dangerous situation.

1980s Summary

In conclusion, as women entered policing in the 1980s as equals in police work, their ability to handle danger was the biggest lingering question. Some departments gave their policewomen the opportunity to prove themselves by assigning them beats alongside their male counterparts; other departments kept women in the specialist positions in which they thrived in the 1970s, limiting their exposure to danger. The answer to the question of whether women could handle danger was settled by the efforts of the brave women, like Officers Cobb, Kaminski, Bosch, Sleeth, and Green, who by their performance quieted some of the concerns that women were not up to the police role. In policing, proving yourself is one of the few ways of gaining acceptance in the "all-boys club."[19] Following their heroic acts, many police administrators took note and became more open to the idea of women working in all areas of police work. As Chief Andrews admitted, the "situation has improved considerably as the policewomen have proved that they can handle dangerous and potentially dangerous situations."[20] Another police chief agreed, stating, "As far as I am concerned we are no longer hiring policemen and policewomen but police officers."[21]

During the 1980s, female police officers faced many obstacles in their quest to survive in an "all-boys club," including sexual harassment, discrimination, and tokenism.[22] Yet, as we see in the next era, the women of the 1980s shaped the culture for future generations, proving that women could handle dangerous policing work and could be counted on as competent partners. Their acceptance in the "all-boys club" opened new doors for women of the 1990s. Their work was not finished, as the generation of the 1990s faced the daunting task of representing the changing face of policing. The high-profile brutality cases of Rodney King and Abner Louima during the 1990s prompted attempts to make police departments more representative of the communities they policed. Women who entered policing in the 1990s were not facing the same obstacles in hiring faced by previous generations; instead, they faced the new challenges of promotion and integration into the "all-boys club." In the 1990s, policing was undergoing a revolution, as community policing, which relied more on communication skills and problem solving, was becoming the police modality of choice. This seemed a perfect fit for women, who were thought of as more natural communicators and consensus seekers. The stories of the women who entered policing in the 1990s are covered in the next section, "Female Police Officers of the 1990s: Crime Fighters or Communication Experts."

Section II

FEMALE POLICE OFFICERS
OF THE 1990s

Crime Fighters or Communication Experts

I N THE 1990S, AMERICANS WERE AFRAID OF CRIME. The perception was that crime was at an all-time high and likely to get worse. In 1995, John Dilulio, a professor at Princeton, coined the term "superpredator" to describe the new violent breed of juvenile offenders preying on inner-city residents. He famously predicted that the number of juveniles engaged in crime would increase threefold in the coming years and that by 2010 there would be "an estimated 270,000 more young predators on the streets than in 1990."[1] He was not the only one concerned. Criminologist James Fox joined in the rhetoric, saying publicly, "Unless we act today, we're going to have a bloodbath when these kids grow up."[2]

Of course, by the time John Dilulio coined the term "superpredator," violent crime rates among juveniles had already begun to fall. Ironically, crime fell sharply in all categories of crime in the 1990s. Homicide rates fell from 1991 to 2001, ultimately reaching their lowest point in thirty-five years. Robbery, burglary, and larceny each also fell every year between 1991 and 2000. The crime drop was without warning and unexpected. In fact, just about the time that experts were calling for a massive explosion in crime, rates started to fall. Why?

The most frequent explanation for the falling crime rates during the 1990s was the innovative police strategies implemented during this time. The two most popular strategies, zero-tolerance policing and community policing, were drastically different in their crime reduction methods. While zero-tolerance policing was characterized by aggressive order maintenance initiatives and arrest-driven approaches that targeted disorder, community-policing initiatives were characterized by the engagement of community stakeholders in the identification, development, and implementation of crime-reduction tactics.

An enormous amount of media attention centered on zero-tolerance policing strategies, including the increased enforcement of nuisance activities like panhandling and prostitution in high-crime neighborhoods and "stop-and-frisk" pat-downs implemented in New York City. Following the introduction of the zero-tolerance policing strategies, crime dropped, adding to its headline-grabbing popularity. Of course, experts are still skeptical that police strategy had anything to do with the reduction in crime, instead crediting the decline in the popularity of crack/cocaine, improved economies, and the incapacitating effects of the rising prison population. The fact that "stop and frisk" has since been ruled unconstitutional and considered a euphemism for racially biased policing has only added to this debate.

At the same time, the popularity of community policing as a national reform movement grew, encouraged by the federal grants available through the Office of Community Oriented Policing Services (COPS). Community policing promised to improve police-community relationships through working with racial and ethnic minorities to solve crime problems plaguing their neighborhoods. Its popularity cannot be overstated. There were annual conferences on community-policing strategies, researchers studied how police agencies implemented COPS in American cities across the nation, and police leaders experienced the political and societal benefits of working with citizens to solve crime problems. Of course, the funding helped. In 1994, President Bill Clinton signed a crime bill, arguing, "Gangs and drugs have taken over our streets and undermined our schools."[3] His solution was to put more police on the streets. With the passing of the 1994 Omnibus Crime Bill, which promised one hundred thousand new police officers on the streets, the link between the level of police protection and resulting crime was solidified. While only about sixty thousand officers were added, a drop in crime was seen nationwide. Despite the falling crime rates, prison populations continued to rise. By 2000, more than two million people were incarcerated, a drastic four times the number that had been locked up in the 1970s. Much of this increase was due to an increased harshness in sentencing, especially for drug crimes.

For these reasons, the 1990s saw an unprecedented hiring trend in policing as departments attempted to become more representative of the communities they policed. This created opportunities for female officers like Heather Noell, Jenny Zimmerman, Rosie Jimenez, Shelly Frank, and the other women featured in this section who joined the police ranks in the 1990s. By 1997, local police departments had an estimated four hundred twenty thousand full-time sworn personnel. Police employment was up by an average of about 3 percent per year since 1993, compared to about 1 percent per year from 1987 to 1993. Women were making steady numerical gains in law enforcement agencies across the country. By 1991, 9 percent of police officers were women. Achieving new firsts, 3 percent of all supervisors in municipal agencies were women by 1990. During this era, women faced the new challenges of promotion and integration into the "all-boys club."[4] In policing, the innovations of zero tolerance and community policing were gaining in popularity. Community policing, which relied more on communication skills and problem solving, seemed a perfect fit for women, who were thought of as more natural communicators and consensus seekers. This section includes the following chapters: chapter 6, "Community Policing"; chapter 7, "Pathways and Entering Police Work"; chapter 8, "Gaining Acceptance and Culture Shock"; and chapter 9, "Making Rank: Glass Ceiling or Escalator?"

6

Community Policing

ON APRIL 29, 1992, A VERDICT WAS ANNOUNCED that shocked the nation. A jury consisting of predominately white members acquitted police officers from the Los Angeles Police Department (LAPD) for their vicious beating of Rodney King, an African American male who was involved in a high-speed chase after police attempted to pull him over for driving erratically. While King initially fled from police, he eventually pulled his 1987 Hyundai Excel to the side of the highway. Immediately, the responding officers pulled King out of the vehicle and brutally attacked him—kicking, punching, and beating him ruthlessly. King wound up with several broken bones and a fractured skull. As a result of the publicity of a video shot by a bystander who had witnessed it all, charges were filed against each of the officers and a trial was held. Based heavily on expert testimony that described King's continued resistance, the jury acquitted the officers. An uproar followed the verdict, and when it was over, more than fifty people were dead, numerous buildings in Los Angeles were burnt to the ground, and looting had taken place all over the city. Many believed that the trial was not fair due to the fact that the trial had been moved out of the city to a small, white, suburban area because of the amount of publicity the case had drawn.[1]

The Rodney King case and the public response to the jury's verdict provide an important lesson on police and community relationships during the 1990s. Of course, there were at least two explanations as to what that lesson was. One explanation was that minority neighborhoods had higher-than-usual crime rates and required increased police presence. The other explanation was that police practices in minority communities were excessive and harassing and contributed to negative police-community relationships. Neither explanation got to the root of the solution: getting community members and police to work together to solve the crime problems facing their neighborhoods. This was the push for community policing, and, for this reason, its potential was very promising during this era.

Community Policing

Prior to community policing, traditional policing emphasized motorized patrol, getting to calls for service quickly, and the successful solving of crimes. These strategies worked for detecting and apprehending criminals but offered little help addressing the root of community problems or the growing tensions between the public and the police in the 1980–1990s. The Office of Community Oriented Police Services defined community policing as "a philosophy that promotes organizational strategies, which support the systematic use of partnerships, and problem-solving techniques, to proactively address the immediate conditions that give rise to public safety issues such as crime, social disorder, and fear of crime."[2] The promise of community policing was that citizens could coproduce crime solutions for their neighborhoods. For example, community members working with the police in their neighborhood had a two-way flow of information about the crime issues relevant to that specific neighborhood. To encourage these relationships, police were challenged to new tasks such as foot patrol, public relations, and problem solving. With community policing, the emphasis of policing shifted from crime fighting to crime prevention, and the public was a key factor in the prevention of crime.

Community policing was wildly popular in the 1990s. By 1999, nearly two-thirds of the county and municipal police departments with one hundred or more police officers had a formally written community policing plan.[3] Heather Noell, a high-ranking police administrator in a large municipal police department, argued that the community policing initiative in her community took a decade or two to take shape, but that community members demanded that they have input into making their communities better and safer places. The greater community input resulted in community surveys, open forums, town meetings, radio and television call-in programs, and citizen advisory boards.

> Interestingly enough, people kind of downplay community-oriented policing because it's a late-eighties idea, but there's very clearly the expectation now that police are going to provide more community service whether they call it community policing or not. The political expectation is that the police department

will be a lot more responsive to different voices in the community. You know, they say change takes a generation, you know, so I think . . . I think [name of department] is pretty close, probably the change started fifteen years ago. We're probably at the point where the older officers would be entrenched . . . you know, opinions are the ones who are retiring. And younger officers who have grown up in the community-policing model, even if they may not love it, there's an acceptance and kind of a knowledge that politically, we have to do this. It's required of a police department unit of a college town, particularly.

Community Policing: A Return to the Nineteenth Century?

The descriptions of the role and responsibilities of the modern community police officer have marked similarities to those of policewomen in the late nineteenth and early twentieth centuries discussed in the introduction. Susan Miller's book *Gender and Community Policing: Walking the Talk* argued that the same feminine-gendered traits that maintained women outside of the traditional crime-fighter model were embraced by the community policing model.[4] Due to the combination of male officer resistance to change and citizen and government demand for community policing, new opportunities for women police were created through community policing initiatives. This is because women and people of color were open to ideas from the community policing approach. For some, this avenue led to opportunities for promotion, but it is apparent that officers were drawn to the approach for reasons other than career advancement. Patrol Officer Jenny Zimmerman believes that her ability to stay calm in the face of aggressive citizens made it easier for her to engage in conflict resolution and de-escalate what could otherwise be violent citizen encounters, a hallmark of community policing. She suggested that these skills have made her and her female coworkers a more natural fit for community policing.

> I'd like to think that my success is due to my ability to stay calm when I need to but assertive when I need to also. Some guys get so assertive they forget to calm down. I talk them down so I don't have to use force. They don't want to fight a woman. Deep down there's a respect for women instilled by their mom. It's not cool to go to their buddies and say, "I beat up a five-foot-one female."

Community policing allows for a revolutionary way to do policing that embodies the principles of social justice. In general, change is tough, and the job of the community policing officer is very different from that of a traditional patrol officer. Building relationships with community members based on trust requires a genuine feeling on the part of the police that community members have something to contribute to police work.

In her book, Susan Miller named four areas in which the role and responsibilities of community police officers are similar to those of policewomen in the late nineteenth and early twentieth centuries: (1) familiarity with community, (2) decentralization of power, (3) prevention, and (4) social work activities.[5] Community policing officers are permanently assigned to a geographical area so they become familiar with the people who live there, the location where calls for service originate, and neighborhood problems. This allows the community members to build rapport and trust with the police in their neighborhoods. Brenda Loggin, a campus patrol officer, described how "beats," or semi-permanent geographical areas, work in her agency.

> We have what are called "focus areas." And what they have done was they divided the campus up into "beats." I mean, when I first got here, it was, "This was your assigned beat and you don't go outside your assigned beat. This is where you're expected to be." Whereas now, we are more community oriented, so you're actually assigned to an area that you're supposed to focus on. It's not necessarily where you're going to spend all your time there, but during your downtime, that's where they'd like you to be. Mine happens to be housing. So, anything that has to do with any type of housing on campus, that's my responsibility. So, if there's a call that comes up in housing, they may not necessarily dispatch me, but it's my responsibility to step up and say, "Hey, that's mine, and I'll take it."

The decentralization of power means that community police officers spend most of their time in their neighborhood assignment rather than in their agencies. This means that the usually hierarchical military structure relied upon in traditional policing is flattened in community policing, reducing the number of layers in the hierarchy and giving patrol officers more independence in crafting solutions to crime problems in their beats. This structural shift also provides the added benefits of improved communication and reduced rigidity and bureaucracy. This independence from the police bureaucracy may have been welcomed by female officers, who felt less than accepted by peers and supervisors.

Community policing relies on foot patrol over automobile patrol to increase citizen and police interaction. In some police agencies, this has led to the creation of police substations, which offer community members an opportunity for increased interaction with police. In others, it is simply an acknowledgment that officers assume a greater responsibility for the crime problems in their beats. They are community experts who do what it takes to help people in their neighborhoods help themselves to reduce crime problems.

Community policing emphasizes the prevention of crime, rather than simply reacting to crime. To do this, officers must be familiar with the happenings in their neighborhood beat in order to be able to identify what is suspicious. Community police officers also pay close attention to the physical and social conditions that give rise to crime. In this way, rather than simply handling incidents, officers seek community cooperation to identify and solve crime problems. County Sherriff's Deputy Rosie Jimenez discussed how community policing requires officers to build relationships with community members and how those relationships allow police to have more information to solve crimes and keep their neighborhood safe.

> I was a community police officer for several years, and citizens let me know what's going on. Because when I built up their trust when something's going on in their neighborhood, they are not going to be afraid to tell me what's going on. They are not going to be afraid to tell me there's a drug dealer at the corner of your house, or that these kids vandalized this person's house, or these guys burglarized it. They may say, "I was out and about and didn't recognize this car." They may not have known that a burglary just happened the night before. And it's like, "I wrote this down, and I figured I'd just give it to you." A lot of times, they don't call the police when certain things are going on. And if they know you and are comfortable with you, they'll say, "Hey, I wrote this number down. Can you check into this?"

Finally, the social work activities of early policewomen are similar to community policing practices. Just as early policewomen had prevention as their major goal as they patrolled pool halls and movie theaters, watching for behaviors that would lead to delinquency and crime, community policing stresses prevention and communication, which requires officers to build a familiarity and trust with community members. These are skills that have not previously been associated with the traditional crime-fighter image of the police. For this reason, community policing has taken some heat for being "social work rather than real police work."[6] Other critics suggest that male officers have been slow to accept community policing due to the perception of it as "women's work." Whatever the reason, clearly not all police departments have embraced community policing. Instead, many agencies have maintained traditional crime-fighting strategies and others have adopted even greater militarized strategies, often called zero-tolerance policing strategies. Others have simply given lip service to the public relations aspects of community policing without making any efforts toward working with their communities. Traditional police agencies with paramilitary organizational structures and strong union representations are often highly resistant to change.

In conclusion, while promising in the 1990s, after almost thirty years of research, there is little empirical evidence to suggest that community policing is effective at reducing violent crime. Instead, what research has established repeatedly is that it is important to successfully engage citizens in coproducing crime solutions. This is because police can't be everywhere all the time. Today more than ever, police must rely on the eyes and ears of citizens to report suspicious and criminal behavior to police. The philosophies and strategies of community policing have had a significant and lasting change on modern police, and the philosophies have given shape to more police innovations, such as problem-oriented policing and intelligence-led policing.

Ironically, at the same time that the popularity of community policing was peaking, another form of policing commonly known as zero-tolerance policing was also growing in popularity, primarily based on the successes of the New York Police Department in reducing crime in their city. Zero-tolerance policing is based on the idea that residents cannot police themselves and that law enforcement officials must use their authority and coercive power to resolve community problems. The debate between these two police philosophies and their resulting strategies dominated the police dialogue during the 1990s, and in many ways, it still does today.

7

Pathways and Entering Police Work

I N 1994, THE *NEW YORK TIMES* FEATURED AN ARTICLE titled "Minorities in Blue—A Special Report: New York Police Force Lagging in Recruitment of Black Officers," calling for the New York Police Department (NYPD) to increase the number of women and people of color in its ranks. Keep in mind that in the 1990s the NYPD had just rolled out its new police strategy popularly called zero-tolerance policing. As a part of this strategy, police officers began to aggressively employ stop-and-frisk tactics. "Stop and frisk" is the practice of temporarily detaining, questioning, and patting down pedestrians based on the reasonable suspicion that the detainee is involved in criminal activity. While stop and frisk was constitutional at the time, it was met with considerable criticism because police had unrestrained discretion to stop and frisk anyone without defining the reasons for the stop. A December 1999 report by the New York State attorney general found that black and Hispanic New Yorkers were disproportionately targeted for stop-and-frisk pat-downs. In fact, of the 175,000 stops engaged in by NYPD officers from January 1998 through March 1999, almost 84 percent were of blacks and Hispanics, despite the fact that those groups comprised less than half of the city's population. By comparison, white New Yorkers, a group that comprised 43 percent of the city's population, accounted for only 13 percent of stops.[1] For this reason, US District Judge Shira A. Scheindlin ruled that the practices of stop and frisk were unconstitutional in 2013. In addition to controversial stop-and-frisk practices, several high-profile police brutality cases, such as the Rodney King case, threw gasoline on the embers, and police departments were publicly under fire to make their departments more diverse.

Making the police department more representative of the city was seen as one possible solution to the perception that police were engaging in racially biased policing. This shift sounded easier than it was, as "New York had been the slowest of the nation's ten biggest cities to open its police ranks to minority groups, especially blacks." For example, "the city, which is almost 29 percent black, is patrolled by a police department that is 11.6 percent black," and, specific to women, "93 percent of the 4,894 officers from sergeant on up were white men of European ancestry."[2] No one debated that being increasingly diverse was a good thing, but many criminal justice experts called into question whether adding more women and minorities would bring about any lasting change in police practice.

Despite these concerns, departments across the nation set out to recruit women and minorities into the world of policing. The NYPD commissioner had a strategy: "You have to get out and beat the bushes. . . . You need a recruitment campaign."[3] Such a campaign is called targeted recruitment, and it is intended to draw a more diverse pool to policing. Shelly Frank, a county sheriff's deputy who entered policing in 1998, argued that departments should seek additional female representation through targeted recruitment for a specific reason: "I think we're looking more at women [for recruitment] because regardless of how we're treated, we offer different things that the men can't offer the community or the department, and I think that's being recognized."

During the 1990s, some agencies were already facing court mandates requiring them to become more diverse based on lawsuits won by officers for discriminated hiring and promotional practices. The Blake consent decree involving the Los Angeles Police Department (LAPD) is an example. Fanchon Blake, an investigator I (comparable to sergeant) with the LAPD, openly objected to policies that prevented her and other women from rising through the ranks. Chief Ed Davis belittled her stance at a meeting of female officers, making it clear that he felt real police work should be done by men, saying, "Women are no longer wanted or needed by the LAPD," and that a drawback to women's representation in policing was their "monthlies."[4] In her unpublished autobiography, Blake wrote in response, "You don't know it, Chief, but war has just been declared between us."[5] She went to war, and she won. Following her successful suit, the courts required the LAPD to find balance in terms of gender in their workforce. Specifically, the Blake consent decree stipulated that 25 percent of all incoming sworn police officers were to be women until the female presence stabilized at 20 percent of all officers. If they failed to impose the plan in a timely fashion, the LAPD could face severe sanction, including fines.

The LAPD was not alone. About 15 percent of agencies were under some form of corrective action (i.e., also known as a consent decree) in 1990. Empirical research suggests that affirmative action litigation significantly impacted the recruitment of female police during this era, but it did little for the retention rates of women. What is the difference?

Female Recruitment in the 1990s

Most programs intended to increase the representation of women in policing focused on either recruitment or retention. Agencies interested in increasing the diversity in their ranks, due to consent decree, political pressure, or inertia, faced a two-staged process: recruitment and retention. Recruitment programs are intended to get more women to apply to be police officers and retention programs are intended to make them want to stay. By the 1990s, departments were recognizing that by eliminating women from their applicant pools, they were missing out on a large part of the skilled workforce. Policing had some work to do to make it an attractive option for women. One interesting question to consider is why women were not attracted to the traditional police recruitment strategies. Concerns about gender bias and war stories about sexual harassment coupled with the "kick butt and take names" stereotypes of police work may have prevented women from applying for police work. The National Center for Women and Policing confirmed that "widespread bias in police hiring, selection practices and recruitment policies keeps the numbers of women in law enforcement artificially low."[6] Regardless of opinion, this much was clear: traditional recruitment programs were simply ineffective at luring women and minorities into policing. Departments interested in increasing diversity in recruitment realized they also needed a change in recruitment practices.

Targeted recruitment strategies have been shown to be beneficial for generating recruits from underrepresented groups. One promising strategy for targeting women included recruiting at events geared toward women, such as women's trade shows, fairs, and fitness clubs.[7] The Albuquerque Police Department (APD) created a targeted recruitment initiative by hosting women and policing career fairs under the "New Workplace Project" funded by the US Department of Labor. They developed flyers, posters, and brochures featuring female officers; the fairs included information about the job, the academy, the application process, and a physical conditioning program designed for women. Their efforts resulted in a significant increase in the number of women applying for officers' positions with the APD, from 10 percent to 25 percent, suggesting a significant payback on their efforts.[8] Another promising recruitment strategy involved highlighting women and people of color in positions of authority in the agency. Using role models from underrepresented groups during recruitment opportunities challenged the stereotype that policing is only for boys.

If you watch any police drama on television, you can see that policing is made up of very masculine, aggressive themes. As the shift toward community policing became a reality in many police departments, a new police image focused on service emerged, which may have been more attractive to women and people of color. Riding on the coattails of the Violent Crime Control and Law Enforcement Act of 1994, which prompted an unprecedented level of support to hire additional police officers, the US Department of Justice Office of Community Oriented Policing Services (COPS) rolled out a program called "Hiring in the Spirit of Service."[9] The idea was for police agencies to market police work as service oriented, seeking recruits who had communication, problem-solving, and leadership skills, rather than the traditional paramilitary skills sought by police agencies. These images were effective in attracting a more diverse recruitment pool.

A more controversial strategy that departments used to increase their diversity in recruits was granting special entry conditions. Departments have granted special entry conditions for women, minorities, veterans, or college students, depending on what group the department is trying to attract. Special entry conditions may include lower fitness or educational standards, exemptions from examinations, faster promotions, higher pay, and waiting list preference. Related to this practice are preference points. Preference points are bonus points added to the test scores of applicants who meet certain requirements. Applicants with prior military service or educational degrees beyond high school graduation may have bonus points added to their entrance examination. For example, the Philadelphia Police Department adds ten points for prior military service and two points for a bachelor's degree to applicants' entrance examinations.[10] In this way, a department can define a preference for applicants with prior experiences. A research study conducted by criminologist Robert Langworthy and his colleagues in 1995 showed that 40 percent of police agencies had special entry condition for minorities, 32 percent for women, and 28 percent for college students.[11] An example of a successful special entry program from the 1990s was the learner-training programs, described by Betty Rossler. Rossler was hired under the learner-training programs utilized at the university police department that she applied to. In Betty's case, she did not have the same educational background as other recruits when she applied. However, due to the special entry conditions requiring lower educational standards for women and minorities, she was given a chance at police work.

Our place certainly has our fair share of minorities and that is due clearly to leadership and the fact that we have a learner-trainee program, which is for minorities, and that is how I got hired. So I didn't have the best test score, but I was given a chance. If you want minorities in this type of field—not everyone's a good test taker, and really to get into law enforcement, you need to take a good test, because that's 40 percent of your score, and then 60 percent of it is verbal but the test scores are all very close after the results come in so it's really five points—makes a huge difference.

After several years on the job, Betty decided to go back to school. Since her entry into policing under the leaner-trainee program in 1997, she has earned both bachelor's and master's degrees through the employee assistance program, which paid for her education at the university where she serves as a patrol officer. Betty gives back by teaching part time at the police training institute housed at the university. Betty cautioned that there was a downside to special entry conditions like the learner-trainee program she came in under, which influenced her reputation, acceptance by colleagues, and eventual opportunities for career progression:

You never get accepted. I knew that when I first was hired. It was very hard because people are like, "Oh she's a learner. She didn't do good on the test," and that's not true. I did good on the test, I was number eight on the list, but I wasn't good enough to get up there. I didn't have any education background, and they look for folks like that.

A successful recruitment strategy is one that works to bring the best police candidates to policing to apply for employment. Interest in police jobs waxes and wanes. Beginning in the 1990s and continuing up into the early 2000s, there was growing concern regarding a "cop crunch," when departments would not be able to attract and hire enough qualified applicants to replace the retirements that were slated to happen during this time. There are several likely factors that made police work less appealing than other occupations, including the improved economy, the lure of private-sector jobs that offered better pay without shift work, and the competition between police departments—especially with small departments losing their recruits to larger agencies with more room for career progression. This contributed to the willingness of police agencies to be more open to nontraditional recruitment strategies.

Female Retention in the 1990s

While recruitment focuses on getting women to apply to police occupations, retention is keeping officers after they have successfully made it through the recruitment phase by mentoring them to promotion and specialized positions. As you recall from the 1980s section, many police agencies employ some sort of field training officer (FTO) programs to formally train recruits after their training academy experiences. These FTO programs help new employees successfully complete their probationary period and establish a foundation for further growth. However, there is some evidence that in the 1990s women struggled with this probationary period at greater rates than men did. Jennifer Miller is a great example. She struggled to pass her probationary field training period and had her time extended because her assessments were not consistent. Her biggest identified deficiency was geography, or being able to remember and physically navigate the streets of her community. Some of her FTOs thought she was doing well and others did not. All probationary officers must receive positive assessments to become full-time sworn police.

> So, I had bad geography. So, you know, you get dinged on that. You normally have three FTOs and then your last two weeks before you get out of the program, you go back to the first FTO and go through your shadow period. I actually had six FTOs because they extended me. So . . . they don't send you back to the first three, they give you another three. So, and I do believe at that time when I did that, that was unique to them because before they did what they could to just get you out. So, mine were not that bad, but my reviews were not that good. And it was up and down, up and down. Some people gave me good ones; some people didn't. To me, you look at it and say, "Is it the student, or is it the teacher?" You know if this person can do well here, but then you get them here, so who's fault is it? So they extended me three more months. "Well, let's see if she can do this." There were things that were being done that were not fair, purposeful things. And luckily, I had some of those people come to me and say, "Hey, this is what they're going to do. It's not fair because they didn't do it to so-and-so. What do you need help on?" And I literally had at least two people who have been here for years who said, "I will make time for you on my time, and I will drive you around geography, and we will learn stuff. We will practice." And that's exactly what we did. And I took them up on it because I knew that was my deficiency. So I said, "Okay, let's do this." I'd meet them after work.

Eventually, she overcame the bad evaluations and passed her FTO program. Today, Jennifer Miller is a successful twenty-three-year veteran serving as a detective with a large municipal police department in the Midwest. Miller's experiences highlight how subjective and discriminatory FTO assessments can feel. These practices may have contributed to the lower pass rate of women during the FTO probationary period reported nationally. In response, departments across the United States began to redesign their recruitment and field training curricula to replace outdated practices and models like the one Jennifer Miller faced. The revised curriculum became more standardized and the evaluative processes for field training became less biased and reliant on the subjective opinions of the FTOs and more grounded in recruits' performance on the job.

Female officers who had made it to leadership positions were encouraging departments to look at ways to increase their retention of women police in addition to recruitment. A great example is the Lansing, Michigan, police department's mentoring program, which was created in the early 1990s by Captain Julie Williams. The Lansing Police Department (LPD) reported that from January 1988 to November 1996 the department hired 135 police officers (108 men and 27 women). Only 83 percent, or 112, successfully completed their FTO program: 87 percent of the men and 67 percent of the women. To address this gap, Lansing adopted a mentoring program. They selected and trained mentors and paired them with those to be mentored. Volunteers were then formally trained via a two-day seminar led by a retired law enforcement officer who had pioneered a mentoring program in her own department, covering the issues of the history of roles of mentors, successful pairing factors, practical suggestions, and general expectations of mentors.[12] To evaluate the success of the program, the LPD focused on employee retention and professional growth as success measures. Both defined the program as a success. The department reported a higher rate of retention since instituting its mentoring program: "The average retention rate from 1992 to 1997 stood at 82 percent, then rose to 86 percent."[13] This is even more significant considering that in 1997 and 1998 the department hired the largest group of minorities and women ever. This is just one example of a program intended to increase the retention of women in policing created in the 1990s.

With improved programs and greater awareness of gender equity, field-training experiences for women improved over previous generations. Jackie Heath described her field training experience as a very positive one: "The guys were great. My field training officers were fantastic. And it wasn't—they didn't ever say, 'Oh she's a girl or she can't.' They wanted to make sure I could prove myself." Departmental participation in programs, like the ones in Lansing and Albuquerque, was voluntary and sparse. These programs were mostly found in large police agencies where the percentages of women were increasing during the 1990s. For example, while women's representation in local police departments increased from about 7 percent in 1987 to 10 percent in 1997, most of this increase was seen in large municipal police departments like Detroit, Philadelphia, and the District of Columbia, in which more than 20 percent of their departments were made up of women.

1990s Pathways to Policing

Women who entered policing in the 1990s can generally be categorized into three career pathways: military, blue-collar roots, and police families. One group entered law enforcement following a tour of duty in the military.

Because of the paramilitary structure of policing, the occupation is often an obvious choice for returning veterans. In fact, this is so common that the International Association of Chiefs of Police (IACP), in partnership with the US Department of Justice, Office of Justice Programs, Bureau of Justice Assistance (BJA), published a guidebook titled *Combat Veterans and Law Enforcement: A Transition Guide for Veterans Beginning or Continuing Careers in Law Enforcement* for service members who are transitioning out of the military and considering a law enforcement career. Some police agencies have shown a preference for veterans in recruitment efforts by giving points for their previous military service, fast-tracking applications submitted by military veterans, waiving education requirements based on training completed while in military service, and offering incentive pay for active members of the reserve or National Guard components. These incentives made policing an attractive career choice for women returning from active duty following Desert Storm.

In December 1991, President George Bush signed the National Defense Authorization Act, which included a provision to repeal the forty-three-year-old legal barriers on women flying combat missions. During that time, women comprised 11 percent of active-duty military personnel and 13 percent of reserve forces. The act suspended gender-based restrictions on sea and land combat roles. This led to a rise in the number of female veterans who served in combat zones—from 7 percent in pre-1990 eras to nearly a quarter (24 percent) among those who served since 1990. These women had already proven that they were physically and mentally fit candidates with good decision-making abilities, common sense, and well-defined morals and who respected the paramilitary chain of command; they were ideal candidates for police work. Brenda Loggin described her pathway into a police career, which started at community college but ended up in the Air Force before becoming a patrol officer in 1993.

> I went to [name of a community college] for two years, but I didn't actually get my Associates degree. I did start studying criminal justice, but then at that point in time I wasn't real sure if that's exactly what I wanted to go to, so then I started taking the general transfer classes. I wasn't real sure where I was going. My brother went into the Air Force, and so I decided . . . maybe that's the direction I wanted to go. So, I actually joined the Air Force. I was in the Air Force for four years. I did law enforcement in the Air Force. It was a lot of fun. I really had a good time. Of course, it's like this profession, mostly male-dominated, but I got along really well with everybody that I worked with.

The military also played a role in Rosie Jimenez's pathway to policing, which began when she was a little girl struggling to find solutions to the constant conflict in her home and in her neighborhood. A conversation with a police officer responding to violence in her home prompted her lifelong goal of becoming a police officer. The birth of her son at fifteen and a tour of duty in the military only strengthened her resolve. Today, Rosie is a sheriff's deputy with a large county sheriff's office.

> The reason I became a police officer was that when I was growing up I had a dysfunctional family and every time something happened the police were always there. And so when I got older, I actually remember this distinctly . . . there was an incident that happened at our home, and I asked him [the officer responding] about being a police officer. He said, "When you turn twenty-one, you can become a police officer. . . . I think you'll be good." That was it. But when you are traumatized and growing up in a certain type of environment it's like, "This is my savior. This is who I want to be. I want to be this for someone else." So when I turned twenty-one, I applied. I went through grade school, went through high school, and it was a struggle. It was a lot of work, and when I got out, my mom, she didn't have enough money. My mom was on welfare. She can't afford for me to go to school. We just didn't have the money, so then I thought, "What is there that I can do? I'll go into the military." My mom said she'd take care of my kid and get the paperwork so she could take temporary custody, and I went into the military right out of high school because "do I want to stay in this environment?" Now, I knew that if I didn't go away, if I didn't do something, meet someone, meet people other than that little group or environment that I was used to, I was going to be in that same circle, and I didn't want to be in that circle. So, the military was the option for me. . . . People always say, "If you go into the military, it opens up doors for you. You get these points for jobs and, you know, they're more likely to hire you. You're going to get money. You'll get money for college." And I was like, "Shoot, why not?" When I had the opportunity I went back to school. I had always wanted to do that; I just didn't have the opportunity to do it. I wound up having my school paid for. The military paid for some and then I took a break because when I started the sheriff's department, school interfered. . . . I went back and I wound up graduating summa cum laude. So, it worked out.

A second group sought out police work due to its steady pay and benefits. Betty Rossler, who grew up in a military family, acknowledged that a career in the military was not a good fit for her. Her story acknowledges how the recruitment of women in the 1990s had improved over the previous era and how the occupation became more open to the recruitment of female police, opening the door for her successful career, which started in 1997. She is currently a patrol officer in a university police department.

> I pretty much grew up in the military. My dad was in the military for twenty-eight years, and I liked the military style but didn't really think the military

was for me. We lived on a little island and within the little compound were the navy security and I was kind of interested in it as a young child, but as a female, I had a hard time getting into it. When I graduated from high school, I got a two-year degree from [name of community college], and after that I started applying for jobs, and in the police world, I didn't realize guys were getting veteran points and so with the little openings that they had, women were never falling in the top ten, because the veteran points were really just enough to teeter you the three to five to ten points that they got. So I got another job and after ten years, I decided that I was going to try in the police world since some women had been getting hired. So I started testing and got hired. I actually could have chosen from quite a few agencies, because all the agencies test at the same time, so I tested with five agencies and was accepted at all but one, so I had to choose which one I wanted, and I picked the university because I'm interested in education. Because of the educational setting, I knew that every year we'd get new people in, so for me, the change in scenery was better. It also gave me the opportunity to go back to school to get my bachelor's and master's because they pay—my education was free. And for me, that was a huge opportunity that I was unable to take advantage of prior to getting hired. Recently I just completed my master's in education and I teach part time at the police-training institute.

Finally, a third group completed their criminal justice degree with the intention of entering law enforcement. Many officers in this group came from law enforcement families and were fully aware of both the sacrifices and the benefits of police work. Shelly Frank entered policing in 1998 following her graduation, majoring in criminal justice, when she was hired into a large county sheriff's office: "My dad was a cop. He was a part-time cop . . . and I later found out, as I got older, that my great uncle on my dad's side of the family was in law enforcement. . . . It's kind of in my blood." Similarly, Roxanne Adler, a twenty-five-year veteran detective with a municipal police agency, graduated from a regional university where she majored in law enforcement. Her dad was her role model, and in a funny twist of fate, she even wore his Kevlar safety vest for a time, until hers, which had to be special ordered, arrived:

> My dad is a police officer. He's retired. And I had a boyfriend in high school; he was a year or two older, and he was in college taking criminal justice classes and that kind of got me really interested. . . . I think I was interested before, but it was about that time I was getting out of high school and trying to decide what I want to do so. Working midnights and taking reports helping victims and making a difference, I guess, and you have all those big aspirations when you're eighteen years old. I am a puzzle kind of person. I like to put things together and look for clues and that part of it. That's why I like what I am doing now.

In conclusion, policy changes in both recruitment and retention made policing more open to women and minorities in the 1990s, and the three general pathways were military service, blue-collar roots, and police families. Interestingly, women who entered policing in the 1990s under a consent decree or special-entry conditions utilized the benefits of employment assistance programs in their departments to better themselves educationally and give back to their departments. Their stories suggest that such programs have helped women to overcome barriers to policing and go on to have successful, decorated careers. The next chapter will explore whether the culture of policing was as open to the potential of female police officers as the recruitment strategies were.

8

Gaining Acceptance and Culture Shock

I learned bitterly during my almost six years in the department, how hard it was to resist this culture, to do the right thing. . . . To get cops to care about doing things right, what needs to change in Baltimore, and in many other cities, is not just policy, but culture. And that's a formidable struggle.[1]

THIS QUOTE CAME FROM BALTIMORE POLICE OFFICER Joe Crystal, who reported the beating of a drug suspect at the hands of his fellow officers to the State's Attorney, stepping beyond the blue curtain and "ratting out" his fellow officers. The blue curtain, or the thin blue line, is the practice of officers closing ranks and refusing to report another officer's wrongdoing, creating a veil of secrecy around police work. Because Joe "ratted out" his colleagues, he was ostracized and even claims that his life was put at risk.

Learning how to do the job and fitting into the culture of policing can be tough. No matter how well prepared a recruit is in the academy, working the streets requires officers to form what criminologist Jerome Skolnick described as a police officer's "working personality." This working personality allows police officers to be ready for violence and willing to assert their authority through their behavior and confidence. They must also learn strategies to communicate effectively with citizens, offenders, victims, and police administrators.

When you couple that with learning to cope with the stress caused by working with victims of crime, as well as the shock at seeing the worst of humanity and the suffering of victims, you can understand why many describe the entrance into policing as a culture shock. Arthur Niederhoffer described the shock as a spike in police cynicism, a distrust of human nature and motives. Cynicism in policing has been defined as a necessary tactic for officers when it comes to surviving the stress of policing. As officers confront the reality of the streets for the first time, the pain, suffering, and criminality of everyday people can make them weary. Shift work and their new role means they may lose friends, as non-police loved ones and acquaintances seem not to understand their struggle. Cynicism has also been shown to be a risk factor for burnout and other physiological and psychological illnesses.

Jennifer Miller described how shocking she found the living conditions of the people who called the police for service and how she struggled early in her career to learn the job of a patrol officer. With the support of her family and coworkers, she made it through.

> When I first came on, it was very hard for me. . . . There are certain expectations, and if you don't quite fit in, or if you're not learning at the same rate as everybody or doing what they think you should be doing, then, of course, people are going to get you down. "Oh, you don't do this." But a lot of that comes from being new and not really knowing and not having experience at the job. Like I said, I came on this job knowing I wanted to do this. But I never knew anybody that was a cop, so I never had anybody to ask, like, "Hey, what is this really like?" Even growing up in Chicago, seeing certain things, I didn't hang out with the criminal element. So, when you first get here and then here you are working patrol and you go in this drug house, you're like, "Oh my God. You live like this?" So it's different.

Another foundation of the police culture is that police officers stick together. They socialize together, go to "cop bars" together, and generally spend their free time with one another, which is why policing is defined as a brotherhood. The danger and cynicism inherent in police work, coupled with shift work and overtime, demands that all contribute to the practice of sticking together. One real question is whether women are accepted into the brotherhood and whether they have the same camaraderie with their colleagues.

Girls Allowed?

During the 1980s the police culture often served as an unofficial "no girls allowed" sign, preventing the integration and acceptance of women in policing. There is considerable evidence to suggest that in many departments this changed during the 1990s. Female police officers who joined policing in the 1990s had a wide variety of experiences with the police brotherhood in their departments. Roxanne Adler, who entered policing in 1992, did not feel like she was a part of the brotherhood: "I guess I was really surprised. When I was reading about it in college and studying it, you always heard about the thin blue line and everybody sticks together. . . . It's not like that at all. At least it hasn't been since I got here." By comparison, Shelly Frank, a county sherriff's deputy who entered policing in 1998, disagreed, arguing that in her department she felt immediately accepted and supported by the police brotherhood: "Everybody knows everybody and we have a tight group of officers. The camaraderie in our department is like nothing I've experience anyplace else."

Female officers who did not feel accepted when they entered policing initially usually found acceptance after a period of proving themselves worthy of the job. When asked about the moment they first knew they had gained acceptance in their departments, almost every woman I interviewed retold a "war story" of when they kicked butt and took names, establishing their legitimacy as strong enough to do the job. Jackie Heath, a campus police officer, remembered the moment she felt accepted following a fight involving hundreds of people on her campus:

> I was six weeks on. I was in the middle of my second FTO, my field training officer. We were on a domestic. I had the female half. He had the male half. We'd split up in a building on campus. And I had the girl. We were going up to her hotel room to get her stuff out of the room. We turned the corner and a fireman said, "What are you going to do about that?" And I'm like, "about what?" And he looked around the corner and there are like three hundred people fighting. It's in a courtyard. I've never seen this amount of people fighting in my entire life. And so I was like, "Oh holy shit!" I didn't have my field training officer with me. He was on the other side of the building. So I stopped. I told the girl, "Stay here." I helped out with a sergeant. I stayed with him and dealt with the problem. And once the guys saw that I was going to jump in and grab ahold of people and handcuff them and I wasn't afraid of that, that was the point when I proved myself. And once they knew that I was not going to run away or be upset, that's the night it happened. And I can distinctly remember it.

It is not surprising that most female officers report greater coworker acceptance following a display of physical strength or authority, given that the greatest concern about female officers has been their ability to handle the physical dangers of policing. Takla Barr, who entered policing in 1991, argued that being a woman in policing was easier as her career progressed, both because her male colleagues and administrators became accustomed to working with women and because the women in her department continued to prove that they could do the job. Male officers and administrators had had positive experiences with the forerunners, those women who entered policing in the 1970–1980s and paved the way for the recruits of the 1990s.

I would say it is easier now and the reason being when I first hired in a lot of the guys were twenty-plus years on. They were in their mid- to late forties, even in their fifties, and hadn't really worked with females in law enforcement and didn't know how to act around you. They didn't think you could handle yourself. "You know on calls if it is a two-man call there is one person that handles it and there's a backup?" If I was the one handling it, they would want to step in and handle it because that is what they were used to. So at the beginning of '91 when I started, '91 and '92, it was kind of awkward.

Tammy Victor, who entered policing in 1985, argued that women who entered in the 1990s were more likely to be accepted upon entering policing without having to prove themselves like earlier generations had to. For her, it was a welcome change.

Oh, my goodness compared to when I came on twenty-two years ago to now it's much better. I mean it's much more accepting to have a female out here than it was when I came on twenty-two years ago. . . . I didn't realize that you had these old goats out here that didn't think that women ought to become police officers. I was like, "Hey, I can do my job. I don't need anybody." I wasn't afraid to do my job and I thought I could handle the job out here. At the time, I had never been exposed to "We just don't think women ought to be out here doing this job." I was just kind of shocked the first few times that I felt that.[2]

Roxanne Adler, who entered policing in 1992, agreed that it was better for women who entered policing after her later into the 1990s: "It just seems like young girls now are much more accepted by the coworkers than they were when I started. When I started they were definitely like, 'You are a girl.'" The salience of the officer's gender and the comfort that administrators and officers had working with women was attributed to the greater gender equality in society and the idea that many officers had grown up with working mothers. The number of working mothers with young children did increase significantly from 49 percent to 75 percent from 1970 to 1990.[3] These socialization experiences, in turn, may have influenced male police officers' views on gender equity and behavior toward female officers. In her commentary on the state of women in policing in 1992, Nancy Herrington, a successful police administrator, argued that discrimination against women in police culture was made less overt through the acceptance of women by a new generation of policemen:

I've talked to other female cops about the way I've felt about the way I've been treated. The harsh treatment seems to be prevalent throughout law enforcement. One woman, I met at a management training school told me that when she started with her department ten years ago [1982], her training officer told her she wouldn't make it through the training program. When she asked why, he said, "Because you are black, you're female and you're a cop. I don't like blacks or females and the district you're working in the people don't like cops. . . ." Today, it's not very likely that those same blatant statements would be made to my friends or me. Instead, they are made in the hallways or locker rooms or in subtle tones and forms of behavior. You can't change attitudes through rules and regulations. Prejudicial feelings run deep and can change through a slowly evolving process of education and generational levels. Young officers are more accepting of women and minorities because they grew up with them and do not view them as differently as the veteran officers.[4]

Male Officer Resistance

Interviews with male officers present a mixed picture of their acceptance of the sizeable increase in women in policing during the 1990s. For example, a 1993 poll of male police officers cited in *Law and Order* magazine showed that only 9 percent of male officers accepted women as officers, leading to what the authors defined as a hostile work environment for women. By comparison, a survey of the perceptions of male officers concerning female officers in city, county, and state police in four northwestern states found that one-quarter of the male officers accepted women police. It is apparent that by the 1990s, compared to the 1980s, male officers were more positive toward women officers, although they still voiced a preference for a male partner backing them for a dangerous call, as an administrator, or as a partner. Female officer interviews also confirmed that discrimination was less overt than in the past, but far from eliminated.[5] Jennifer Miller acknowledged that discrimination was less overt in the 1990s, as it occurred at the individual officer level and was less likely to be as organized and pervasive as the previous era.

> The group I came on with, the people I hung out with, I was accepted then. That wasn't a problem. And you start to work and you work different areas and people see how you work. And if they like how you work, then you don't have too much of a problem. You know . . . you're always going to have the egos of people who just don't think women should do this or do that. They never come out and tell you that, but you don't have to be a rocket scientist to figure it out, but the thing is there are certain people that they don't want to work with.

One reason for the reported decline in overt discrimination may be that 86 percent of police departments had a written gender discrimination policy by 1998 and 81 percent trained their supervisors to respond to allegations or suspicions of gender discrimination.[6] Perhaps awareness that

overt discrimination would not be tolerated and that punishment was possible deterred overtly egregious behavior.

Lisa Ball argued that women's greater acceptance during the 1990s was
due to women proving they could do that job, leading to the decline of seeing
women as "firsts" and tokens.

> I think that a number of people have realized that women can do this job. You
> know, it's not one of those . . . "Oh, she'll outgrow it. It's just a phase she's going
> through." You see more and more women that have been allowed the opportu-
> nity to move up through the ranks, whereas in the past . . . probably when I first
> got into it fifteen years ago, you saw some, but not much. The longer time goes
> on and the more women that do get into policing . . . you're not seeing as many
> firsts. The first police chief. The first captain. The first tactical officer. Because
> women are doing it more and more each day. That's one thing that's changed.
> They're being allowed to get involved in different aspects of it.

Sexism or Canteen Humor?

While overt discrimination was decreasing in the 1990s as women increasingly proved their value to American police departments, the sexism in some
departments appeared to be deeply entrenched. Jennifer Hunt examined the
underlying logic of police sexism among police and found that "sexism . . .
is a deep structure which is articulated in every aspect of the police world."[7]
In a very public example, the Christopher Commission collected comments
in 1991 from computer communications on the Los Angeles Police Department's (LAPD) mobile digital terminals, which emphasized the sexism pervasive in the department's culture in the 1990s. One officer exclaimed, "No but
I left a fourteen-year-old girl that I met yesterday handcuffed nocked o my
chin-up bar wearing nothing but a blindfold and salad oil. . . . I'd like to ck
on her [*sic*]."[8] Another said, "U won't believe this. . . . That female call again
and said susp returned. . . . I'll check it out then I'm going to stick my baton
in her [*sic*]."[9] Whether these are serious claims or just sophomoric banter, it
is illustrative of the sexual climate of the LAPD police culture and it supports
research from the era that suggests that in many departments sexual harassment was still a daily occurrence for female police officers.

How to address the sexualized canteen humor of policing mostly drew
suggestions from women police that the solution was for female officers to
toughen up rather than for any change in male officer behavior. This is remi-
niscent of the *police*women versus police*women* conflict identified by Susan
Martin in the 1980s, where women often critiqued other women for their
femininity or sexuality in policing, rather than confronting discriminating
or harassing male officer behavior. This conflict forced women to carefully

negotiate their gender identity versus their career. For example, Takla Barr agreed that sexual teasing and innuendo were a deep-seated part of policing but recommended that women interested in policing get a tougher skin rather than be offended. She attributed this behavior as just a part of police culture. The de-feminization of the female officers on the job and being just one of the boys seemed to help officers gain acceptance.

> I think some women are just intimidated maybe overwhelmed a little bit with the whole job and maybe the dangers of it and the working with all men. I don't have a problem with it. I have gotten along with men fine in my life, you know. . . . When I first came in if I had walked in this place and I had sat down and if a joke was told, I rolled my eyes or sat there with my arms crossed or something, how willing do you think these people would have been to accept me? I sat and had to listen to some crap that was really nasty. Did it bother me? No, but that's my personality. Did I get into the mix? Did I say the dirty jokes and the bad comments? Yes, and I think it is more of an acceptance thing. I mean I don't want someone to come in here and not be themselves, but my personality and the way I am, it was myself, and I was more accepted, I think, than most would have been.

By comparison, officers who displayed feminine attributes found themselves babied or taken less seriously. Shelly Frank argued that defeminization was important to her acceptance in her department:

> I am successful because I don't play up the "female" part. I'm just one of the guys. . . . We're not treated any differently. We're not babied because that's one thing I hate. I don't want to be babied because I am a girl. You know, I just get in there and do what I need to do, just like any of the guys would. We're just not treated any differently.

One explanation for this continuing theme that women needed to become "one of the guys" to fit in, from the 1980s up into the 1990s, is that despite women's greater acceptance in policing, they were still very much aware of their outsider status.

Female Officers of Color

Another important trend in women in policing is that women of color entered policing in increasing numbers from 1970 to 2000. While black female officers have been represented in policing since 1916, when Georgia Ann Robinson became the first African American female police officer employed by the Los Angeles Police Department, the 1990s saw a consistent representation of women of color in policing. From 1990 to 2000, black women made up about 1 to 2 percent of police and 30 percent of women police in the United States. These token numbers nationwide meant that there were many cities and counties that had never had an officer of color or a female officer of color, even late into the 1990s. In her study of the experiences of black female police, Susan Martin found that black women reported experiences with both race and sex discrimination, but, due to their societal experiences with racism, they did not believe that the discrimination in the police world was any different from the discrimination they faced in the larger society. In fact, they were drawn to policing because it provided occupational opportunities not available in the private sector, including the detailed job hierarchy, civil service approach to hiring and promotion, and the higher blue-collar pay.[10] Policing also saw the entrance of Hispanic and Asian American women during this era. From 1990 to 2000, policing saw an 80 percent increase in the representation of Hispanic female officers. One reason for the increased minority representation of female police is that communities were also becoming more diverse. Research consistently suggests that the increase in minority officers is positively associated with increases in minority populations in cities.[11]

The stories of minority women surviving and thriving in the police profession are important, as they become role models for future generations. In 1993, a popular Latin American magazine publicized the promotion of Ramona Arroyo, Kansas City's first Mexican American female sergeant.[12] Sergeant Arroyo discussed in the interview how she felt considerable pressure to live up to the role-model status she achieved when she was promoted.

As a county sheriff's deputy who entered policing in 1994, Rosie Jimenez talked about how surprised she was that her race and gender stood out so saliently to citizens as the first African American officer in her department.

> I remember when I first started [in 1999] working, I was working out in [name of small town], and there was this huge fight. Now, I was the closest car there, and I got there and . . . they stopped fighting. The lieutenant thought it was the funniest thing he'd ever seen in his life. It was a ball of people fighting. I get out and I say something to them and this guy turns and looks. He was like, "It's a black officer." Because they had seen it on television but had never seen a female, black officer. Then it's like, "Wow, the fight has stopped." I didn't even have to do anything.

Rosie Jimenez defined her token status in her department and the visibility of both her gender and her race to citizen interactions: "I am the first black female they've ever had and the fifth female overall." Her token status added to the difficulties she already faced, defined as the "double marginality" women of color negotiate in policing.

The Dynamics of Acceptance

Acceptance in policing is not a one-time deal. Female police officers of the 1990s described acceptance in their respective departments as a dynamic status that had to be negotiated on a day-to-day basis. In other words, acceptance was not something that, once attained, could be stored: "Acceptance in a police department when you are female is something that you never completely obtain but you kind of strive towards it to some extent."[13] Once gained, acceptance had to be nurtured.

I led the crowd-control team, of all things, and we were at a KKK rally. It was a mess. I was the crowd-control supervisor of the team of forty officers in full riot gear and I was calling the shots. I was able to lead that unit and it was successful. We got the two groups separated because the KKK haters wanted to kill them, and the KKK, you know. We got in between them and were able to separate them and the KKK got in their bus and left. My boss was like, "Wow!" I felt that that night when I went home, I had finally arrived. And I was a lieutenant with eighteen years on the job. They acknowledged that I led them, but it's a continual process. You are never accepted based on your merits. . . . And I'll tell you, I felt like I couldn't call in sick. Because it's "There she goes, she is probably having her period." Yeah. I couldn't do things that men didn't think a thing of. Like this whole year, I have had no sick days. For many years because I, like, I couldn't even take a sick day because it would be looked upon as a female problem.

There were several events mentioned by female officers that put their feeling of acceptance in jeopardy, like hiring new officers and seeking promotion. Roxanne Adler told how early in her career she worked as hard to impress the new recruits as they did to impress her: "You had to work for acceptance, and they would hire somebody new, and it's like you had to work for acceptance from them too because they automatically assumed that, and I just got tired of always having to prove myself, and finally I'm just, like, 'I don't care what they think,' you know."

The good news is that the women I interviewed felt accepted in their respective police departments despite early resistance they faced. This acceptance was accompanied by less overt discrimination and harassment, opportunities for promotion and specialized training, and greater camaraderie in the departments. In examining female officers' experiences in gaining acceptance, it is clear that the evolution of police culture involved more "enlightened" male officers and weakened "boys club" attitudes of the 1980s.[14]

In summary, a great deal of progress was made in the status of women in policing during the 1990s, but there were clearly still some lingering issues that inhibited the ability of women police to be accepted on the job. There are several reasons that this matters. Thomas Whetstone and Deborah Wilson suggested that the ability of women to gain the support and acceptance of their coworkers and administrators influences how rapidly and fully they learn the job and grow confidence in their ability to do the job.[15] Several studies have shown that women police officers report having less confidence in carrying out certain tasks than male officers.[16] Because women feel less support, they may be less empowered to carry out police tasks and more concerned with making mistakes.[17] This can turn into a self-fulfilling prophecy in which women perform poorly due to their perceived lack of support and that performance is used as a reason to discourage the expanded recruitment of women.

Because acceptance is something that is constantly negotiated and renegotiated throughout their careers, rather than a level of achievement, women are hesitant to draw attention to themselves in the form of promotion or specialization. Officer Nancy Stiles of the Ventura Police Department critiqued the idea that the only way women can prove themselves worthy is to have a "fistfight with a man," calling it the "John Wayne syndrome." The idea that women officers must "out-smoke, out-drink and out-cuss" men to be accepted denies the potential individuality that each officer brings to police work.[18] It also leads to heightened self-monitoring, which has implications for officer health and well-being in the form of increased officer stress, burnout, and turnover.

In conclusion, both research and female officers' reported experiences point to the fact that, while still a problem, sexism, discrimination, and sexual harassment were less overt during the 1990s than in previous generations. These improvements in the culture of policing led to a consistent increase in the numbers of women and women of color during the 1990s. Even more important, women were increasingly accepted and integrated into the police brotherhood, overcoming the no-girls-allowed attitude of many departments in the 1980s. In the next chapter, women challenge this newfound acceptance by attempting to move up the ranks. Due to the mass entry of women into policing in the 1980s, by the 1990s many were interested in seeking promotional and specialized position opportunities. It's one thing to find acceptance in an entry position, but quite another to compete for the very few promotional opportunities available in policing.

9

Making Rank

Glass Ceiling or Escalator?

Eᴌɪᴢᴀʙᴇᴛʜ M. Wᴀᴛꜱᴏɴ, ᴡʜᴏ ᴊᴏɪɴᴇᴅ ᴘᴏʟɪᴄɪɴɢ ɪɴ 1972 in Houston, Texas, as one of the first women allowed to patrol the streets as an equal to the men in her department, was named police chief of the Houston Police Department in 1990. Watson came from a family of police officers and was considered an insider candidate for chief, as she pledged to continue the city's community policing efforts. Watson's remarks on the occasion focused on her dedication to the field: "I am deeply committed to policing, and if in the course of doing that I serve as a role model to other women, I am doubly honored."[1] Her progression to chief was a gradual one, starting with her 1976 promotion to detective followed by lieutenant in 1981. She was promoted as the first female captain on the force in 1984 and the first female deputy chief in 1987. In response to the question of what resistance Chief Watson would face because of her gender, Mark R. Clark, president of the Houston Police Officers Association, responded that there would be muted resistance: "The police officers from time to time have their surges of machoism. I'm guilty of it too. But they will fall in line. This is 1990, not 1960."[2] This quote shows how much had changed from the early history of women in policing to 1990s but also how the undercurrent of discrimination and sexism still existed covertly, waiting to rear its ugly head.

Only five years earlier, Penny Harrington had made history when she was appointed police chief in Portland, Oregon, the largest police force ever led by a woman. These events were noteworthy in the 1990s, as women and especially women of color were increasingly accepted into policing but were severely underrepresented in the supervisory and command ranks. While women made up about 9 percent of police officers by 1991, they only made up 3 percent of supervisors in municipal agencies. By 1999, 2 percent of African American women, compared to 16 percent of African American men and 30 percent of white men, had attained a rank above the entry-level rank of patrol officer. So what was keeping women from leadership positions in American police agencies?

The Police Promotion Process

To understand the underrepresentation of women in leadership in policing, it is first important to understand how promotion works. Borrowed from the military, the occupation of policing is a hierarchically structured bureaucracy signified by uniform, rank structure, and the legal authority to use deadly force. The police organizational structure, a conglomeration of military and bureaucratic models, is characterized by an authoritarian command structure that adheres to a strict subordination, a rigid chain of command, and a formal provision for moving up the ranks.[3] In municipal departments, the hierarchical command starts at the bottom with patrol officer, followed by the corporal, sergeant, lieutenant, captain, deputy chief, and chief.[4] One of the major ways that policing differs from other careers is that administrators work up through the ranks to become leaders of their organization. To become a police administrator (captain, deputy chief, chief, colonel, and lieutenant colonel), an officer must have started as a patrol officer and usually held a middle-management position previously (commander, sergeant, and lieutenant).

Achieving rank in a paramilitary organization like policing depends on the civil service testing process. Police administration requirements vary from agency to agency but usually consist of a written assessment, an oral interview, and a review of past job evaluations. The first stage is based on self-selection. The reasons why a person would seek promotion are varied, but generally the reasons for participation are to accomplish a personal goal, career opportunity, increased salary, and desire to assume a leadership role. Generally, the process starts when an agency posts a vacancy announcement. This announcement states the qualifications for the position or positions the agency is hiring for as well as the process for applying. Officers who apply for promotion are required to pass a written and oral examination similar to the one that recruits pass for employment. Modern police agencies utilize an assessment center as an important part of the police promotion process to increase the objectivity, reliability, and fairness of the process. An assessment center utilizes trained observers to evaluate candidates' communications skills, command presence, technical and professional knowledge, decision making, judgment, planning, and problem analysis.[5] Agencies that do not utilize an assessment center usually use a committee to evaluate these skills.

The vast majority of police supervisors are promoted from within the ranks of their own department. Lateral entry (e.g., the practice of transferring from one department to another without losing seniority) is the exception rather than the norm but is more common in smaller police agencies. While the usefulness of evaluations of past performance is not clear, most departments utilize them when considering applicants for promotion. For example, whether street performance is indicative of the potential to be an excellent administrator is not well defined. Past performance often comprises 20–30 percent of the total score of the promotion. Seniority is also an important part of the promotion process. Many departments give credit for years of service in the total score of the promotion. Other departments make a certain number of years of service mandatory to apply for promotion. For example, to become lieutenant, an officer might be required to have served at the rank of sergeant for three years. The written assessment and oral interview make up the rest of the total score. Scores on the assessments are ranked and placed on an eligibility list. The scores for promotion are listed by assessors in rank order, but the final selection is usually made by the personnel department, police chief, city manager, or mayor. In the selection stage, the decision maker(s) may choose any candidate from the top 10 percent of the list or may choose the top scored, depending on department practice or policy. Regardless of the department particulars, gaining promotion always requires strong testing capabilities along with administration support.[6]

The reality is that in most municipal departments opportunities for promotion are rare, making the progression up the ranks slow.[7] A study by the Police Executive Research Forum suggested that civil service regulations that require officers to serve a certain number of years at each rank (typically between two and five) before becoming eligible for promotion to the next rank are partly responsible for the lack of upward mobility in police agencies. This is exacerbated by the offering of promotion exams at irregular intervals based on department needs and fiscal health. Combined, these practices make promotion an irregular and competitive process. However, these factors alone may not explain the underrepresentation of women in leadership.

The Brass Ceiling

Dorothy Moses Schulz, in her book *Breaking the Brass Ceiling: Women Police Chiefs and Their Paths to the Top*, documented how women seeking promotion in the 1990s bumped into a "brass ceiling," causing them headaches every time they attempted the climb up. Despite early gains, the average police department in the 1990s had no women in top or command positions. A couple of surveys on the status of women in leadership in policing conducted in the 1990s provided a snapshot of the nature of women in leadership during this time. First, in 1999, the International Association of Police Chiefs surveyed eight hundred police executives about the state of women in police leadership. They found that 91 percent of the police departments surveyed had no women in policy-making roles, which limited young officers' access to role models. Based on their additional finding that gender bias was an obstacle to promotion for women, they recommended that police departments implement fairer screening procedures and more rigorous sexual harassment policies.

Second, that same year, the Bureau of Justice Statistics released a survey that reported that women were most likely to be serving in leadership positions in sheriff's offices, where they served in jails rather than patrolling the streets. County sheriff's offices are unique in that their deputies can be employed either working in the jail as a correctional officer or working in patrol as a police officer. These findings suggested that the actual representation of women in policing may be much lower, based on the findings that female sheriff's deputies were actually being employed as correctional officers and not as police. Women were needed at the jail to assist with female inmates, which may have limited their promotional opportunities.

Finally, the last survey conducted by the National Center for Women and Policing presented the rates of women in leadership in policing as of 2001 as alarmingly low. They found that women made up about 10 percent of lieutenant and sergeant positions in large police agencies and 5 percent in smaller agencies. Among the top command positions of captain and above, women made up 7 percent of large agencies and 3 percent of smaller agencies. As the 1980s generation of token female police executives retired, many questions remained about the future legacy of women in police leadership. Many factors have been suggested to explain the lack of proportionate representation of women in the administrative ranks of policing, including sexism and discrimination, tokenism, lack of role models and mentoring, and conflict with familial responsibilities.

Sexism, Discrimination, and Tokenism

A 1998 survey suggested that police administrators still had some concern regarding females' competence to perform in police patrol. Twenty-eight percent of those surveyed reported concerns that women lack sufficient physical strength, capacity for confrontation, size, strength, and force to patrol.[8] This presents a quandary from an administrator's standpoint. Police administrators must encourage female officers' integration with male colleagues and the public, appreciate female officers' "unique skills," and deal with work issues specific to female employees while most are still concerned about their effectiveness. When women first entered policing in the 1970–1980s, women in leadership positions were often tokens and failed to make it to the top of the organizational police chart. Kim Centra, who joined policing in 1988, discussed her mind-set toward promotion and her regret at not challenging the framework of the time: "Always a bridesmaid, never a bride. And I think part of that was my mind-set and part of it was the department's mind-set. I would settle for the second position instead of the top position. And I am not sure why I did that."[9] In her book *Men and Women of the Corporation*, Rosabeth Moss Kanter suggested that women's token status causes them to lower their work expectations and develop different work patterns from their male counterparts who have more power and greater opportunities for advancement.[10] In policing, these differences discourage administrators from giving recognition, rewards, promotions, and transfers to officers who do not do police tasks that are valued by the policing culture. The police culture emphasizes and rewards arrests and crime control. Despite the fact that the police organization has shifted focus to combine social control and social service functions under the guise of community policing, Susan Miller argued in her book *Gender and Community Policing: Walking the Talk* that policing made this shift while also refusing to acknowledge this response as "real police work."[11]

Ideas about the proper placement of women in leadership into the 1990s had many arguing that there were areas of policing that were still off limits for women. While women made great strides in their integration in American police agencies, gender discrimination was found in the absence of women in special units and administrative offices. In Gossett and Williams's 1998 study of female officers' perceptions of discrimination, women reported that supervisory discrimination was the most detrimental because supervisors were seen as the key to recognition, rewards, promotions, and transfers.[12] A 1991 report of women's experiences in the LAPD confirmed that supervisory discrimination may also include race, as more than 40 percent of African American women and more than one-third of Hispanic women reported receiving racial slurs from their supervisors and/or peers.[13] Supervisors start as line officers. The negative and discriminatory way male officers view and treat women simply continues as they advance to higher positions.

Citizens' interactions with female police officers can be a shock for the citizens too. Female police officer researcher Susan Martin pointed out that interactions between female officers and male citizens can be tough due to the culturally mandated rules governing interaction, such as "acting like a lady" and "being macho."[14] Officers humorously retold stories filled with sexual innuendo:

> There're some people where as soon as you get out of the car, they'll whistle or say, "Hey baby!" or "You look good in those pants." We got a new female that just started—I'm not her training officer—but when her training officer was gone, she was with me for several days, and so she and I would show up for calls and when we got out of the car together, we would just get tons of inappropriate comments, because—I think our community is slightly above the national average for female police officers—but it's not very often you see two females getting out of a car together, so we do get comments.

Perhaps the more progressive view of women police preferred that police primarily perform stereotypical roles. In other words, citizens were most comfortable with male officers handling violent calls like bar fights and female officers handling rape cases and child abuse situations.[15] Roxanne Adler joked about an inherent preference from citizens for male colleagues when in need of driving directions.

> I would always laugh that I would be sitting and like talking to a male officer and on night shift and someone would come up needing directions and I am there with seven or eight years on and they're there for like six months and they would come up and always go to the male officer for directions. . . . One time I was at the front desk and I was in uniform and somebody came in and the lady just like looked right past me and one of the detectives came around the corner and was using the computer and he was in plain clothes and the lady she's like, "Excuse me." She kept yelling at him and he's like, "What!" And she's like, "Can you give me directions?"

While citizens in the 1970s voiced some concerns about the ability of female police to do the dangerous job of policing, by the late 1990s, citizens were expressing strong support for female patrol officers even in their ability to handle violent encounters. In her 1997 analysis of Kentucky citizens' perceptions of female police, Kristen Leger argued, "Citizen endorsement of female patrol officers signifies the public's changing attitudes towards women."[16] In other words, women found acceptance in patrol but found it harder to break through to traditionally male roles like SWAT (Special Weapons and Tactics) or SRT (Special Reaction Team), patrol, and others. Instead, women who sought out these positions were often told there were no vacancies or that they lacked the experience for these male-only units. In some ways, this was a throwback to the days of the women's bureau, when women's tasks were specialized and based on their natural abilities as nurturers and communicators. Rosie Jimenez identified specialized positions and ranks that were considered off limits to women and how belonging to the "old boys club" benefits men and not women.[17]

I don't think they've ever had a woman lieutenant. They have never had a woman detective. Never had a woman in DARE. Never had a woman in the lab. Never had a woman in canine. None of us has ever gotten it. I've put in for the lab. I've put in for detective three times, and I put in for community police and I got that. I think it's a good-ole-boy thing, personally. I think that we got a lot of nepotism, so that's an issue. I think it's a really big issue. I'll tell you this, I applied for the detective position that just opened up, and they said that this position may or may not open up, but they wanted to get the interviews out of the way. So we had the interview, and this interview, out of the other past interviews I've had, was an actual real interview with people, with the Lieutenant Detective, the Chief, and the Captain. They asked questions specific to the job, specific crime-related issues. I was told that I gave the best interview and that the person they recommended was not the person that the Sheriff chose. My questions were, "Why even have the interview if the Sheriff is going to make the final decision?" And he chose a guy that had less seniority than everybody that had applied and this person also had just been assigned to the M.E.G. [Metropolitan Enforcement Group, a multijurisdictional unit that deploys proactive strategies on specific crimes problems like guns and drugs], but the Sheriff's son wanted to be in M.E.G. And the Sheriff was upset. He wanted his son to be in M.E.G., so the Sheriff cut a deal. The captain's son works there, the sheriff's son works there, a Lieutenant's son works there, and my understanding is the same Lieutenant, his other son may also be working there soon. He may be going through [the local police training academy] in August. And then you have this good-ole-boy group. I mean, so there's a lot of good-ole-boy, and that's why. Because we don't play by the rules, but I think women are outspoken and, unfortunately, I think sometimes we wear our emotions and that may hinder us. And we're not out drinking with them. You know, we're not out golfing. We have families. We're women. With those guys, their wives are doing all that stuff, you know what I mean? So they're hanging out, golfing, and fishing, and that's what happens. They become friends.

It is in these informal settings that career advice is given and that police administrators and officers build a common ground, which helps for promotional experiences.

Lack of Role Models and Mentoring

Role models and mentors are integral to the integration and career progression of female officers. Without the guidance of seasoned veterans to teach rookies the ropes, female officers fall behind.[18] One solution for dealing with both the isolation and the lack of available role models is a mentoring program. The Charlotte-Mecklenburg Police Department's Women Network started as a group of sworn female officers informally socializing with recruits over lunch breaks, but as the program became more formal, the goals of the program expanded. Today, the Women's Network works in three important areas to make its mentoring program successful: executive support, clear goal definition, and front-end mentors. Specific to promotion, the Women's Network "shared advice on preparing for the process, study techniques, presentation skills, appearance issues, and other helpful suggestions for successfully completing a promotional process."[19] Since the program was created, the department reported that sixteen women had been promoted, including its first female deputy chief. This almost doubled the women in leadership positions in the department. As the number of women in leadership increased, they focused their efforts on policy changes such as uniform issues, duty belts, physical fitness standards, and part-time policies, all directly affecting the recruitment of women. "Because policy making occurs only at the top management levels in any paramilitary organization, it is essential that women reach these positions in order to have a role in influencing policy."[20]

Mentoring programs, like the one in Charlotte-Mecklenburg, are unique. Barbara Raffel Price reported an effort to keep women separated, which she defined as a "divide and conquer" strategy carried out by individuals and institutions to keep women from banding together. One female police administrator, who faced censure by her chief for hosting a social women's night at her home with coworkers, defined this as fear of the "estrogen mafia."[21] Her belief was that her gathering prompted insecurity and fear of competition if the old boys club turned into a girls' night out.

That may also explain the low participation in groups dedicated to women in policing. As mentioned in this book's introduction, "The History of Women in Policing: Matrons to Patrol Officers," the International Association of Women Police (IAWP) is a longstanding organization dedicated to giving voice to the interest of women in policing. In the 1990s, two new groups emerged: the National Association of Women Law Enforcement Executives (NAWLEE) and the National Center for Women and Policing (NCWP). NAWLEE focuses on helping women to strengthen their leadership roles in policing, and NCWP focuses on "increasing the numbers of women at all ranks of law enforcement as a strategy to improve police response to violence against women, reduce police brutality and excessive force, and strengthen community policing reforms."[22] Jackie Heath argued that her male colleagues perceived her friendship with her female chief as an unfair advantage to her career. In return, her accomplishments were downplayed as being a result of that advantage rather than something she earned.

I think when you come up there's a huge deal. Guys can go and have drinking nights and go on golf tournaments and go on fishing trips, but if you are
friends with a female—specifically I am friends with my chief. We have social
lives together. It's never been an issue about that. But when the guys found out
that I was friends with her it was a major deal. When I came on the FBI's Joint
Terrorism Task Force there were a lot of people that were very upset about that
also. The same type of deal. The only reason she got this job position at the FBI
is because of her relationship with the chief. Not because of any of the things I
have already named.

Conflict with Familial Responsibilities

Women are still primarily responsible for the majority of childcare and
household tasks in American families. Due to the increasing numbers of
women in the workplace in the past decade, much attention has been centered on how motherhood influences the career paths of young women. In
1989, Felice Schwartz coined the term "mommy track" to describe two diver-
gent paths to leadership: a fast one for those who are childless and a slower
one where mothers pause or stay in middle-level management. While no
research to date has explored how motherhood influences the career trajec-
tories of police executives, several recent studies have suggested that familial
obligations influence officers' decisions to take the important first step of promotion exams.[23] In their study of officers eligible for the promotional exam,
Thomas Whetstone and Deborah Wilson argued that family and childcare
issues played a large role in women's decisions to forego promotional opportunities, reflected in a preference to stay in their current assignment and
job shift.[24] Confirming this finding, Christine Cooper and Samantha Ingram
reported that the most often cited reason female officers gave for leaving their
posts was domestic responsibility.

For the women I spoke to, the primary reason for not seeking promotion
was based on the security of their current schedule for childcare. Due to civil
service systems, union influences, and police tradition, officers bid for shifts
based on seniority within rank (i.e., patrol officers bid against other patrol
officers and sergeants bid against other sergeants). So, as strange as it may
sound, a patrol officer with fifteen years on the job could bid for a more
desirable schedule than a first-year sergeant or lieutenant because they have
greater seniority at that rank.

Promotion means a change in work schedules, which means a change in
childcare and availability for school duties. This meant that most women found
ways to be satisfied with their current assignment. This satisfaction was often
linked with the officer's ability to manage childcare and familial responsibilities

along with her professional duties. This was the case for Denise White, who was married to a police officer in the same department. Between the two of them, they chose different work shifts so that their childcare needs were met. If she sought promotion, it would mean a change for all of them.

> I am happy in patrol. Right now, I have had so much time on as far as seniority that I can bid. Right now, I am on day shift with Sundays and Mondays off, which are the best days you can get, other than Saturdays and Sundays. So if I went through the promotional process, you go back to the bottom of the totem pole as far as seniority goes. The bottom of the sergeant, and you would be on midnights with Wednesdays and Thursdays off, so if you work overtime to make up the difference, it is not really worth it.

In other words, the perceived benefits of promotion were not great enough to exceed the risk to be taken in giving up their current assignment, which Denise was happy with.

Overnight childcare options are scarce, especially for single parents. In focus groups conducted by Thomas Whetstone and Deborah Wilson, single-parent fathers reported many of the same concerns with promotion and often chose to sacrifice upward professional mobility for a more "normal" family life. While this problem is not exclusive to women, female officers have consistently reported childcare as a reason to opt out of the promotion process.[25] In sum, the priorities for women were family and children, and because the requirements of promotion did not allow them to meet both familial and professional goals, they chose family and opted not to seek promotion. Takla Barr, a single parent following her divorce from a fellow police officer, avoided promotional opportunities because she could not be the primary caregiver to her daughter if her shift changed.

> Reason number one: I have fifteen years on, almost sixteen, and right now, I am on the street I am top patrolmen so I have day shift with weekends off. Reason number two: I have a four-and-a-half-year-old daughter, and with daycare to change the shift right now would about be impossible. She is settled in the daycare and she is not going to start school this year because her birthday is not until the middle of September. So if I did get a promotion to a sergeant, if I took the test and did get a promotion more than likely I would go to swing shift and you would go to like three seconds and two-thirds. With my child, I cannot. Yes, there is a pay increase but it is not enough for me to try to juggle everything with daycare and everything else because I am a single mom.

In addition to the difficulties of balancing childcare and work, many women police officers feel underutilized and frustrated with a lack of promotional opportunities. Jackie Heath voiced this concern in relation to the civil service system in her department, which prioritized seniority in promotional opportunities. She was an officer with ten years on the job, but that was not enough to be at the top of her promotional lists. Waiting became very frustrating for her.

> I want to do other things and I want to make policy and want to set a standard for police officers that come into my department. I want to be in charge and I want to have that ability to lead others and to have a professional police department. I have applied with the [name] State Police. I have applied for NCIS. There is also a position down in Atlanta Georgia that I have applied for. I would leave in a heartbeat. If I could go work at Hooter's tomorrow, I would probably do it. I think I am really getting burnt out. I want to go to the next level. I am ready. I need to go to the next level.

Because women are isolated from informal structures within departments, they are deprived of important contacts, information, and professional relationships to guide their confidence in promotional experiences. Sometimes this is a purposeful decision made by the female officer due to familial responsibilities. Other times, it's an attempt to protect her reputation against being defined as a "badge bunny" (i.e., a women who is attracted to a police uniform) or "get around girl."[26] Because of the isolation, women sometimes lack the guidance needed to fully understand the promotional process, and they miss out on the advantage of "knowing the ropes." Lisa Ball argued that a "guidance counselor" for the police career path would be very helpful for female officers. This is because women often miss out on the informal situations (i.e., golf tournaments, fishing trips, guy's nights out, and baseball games) when these discussions often take place.

> You know . . . when I go to college, I sit down with a guidance counselor, and I'm guided in whatever direction I want to take it, but here are your choices. This is what you can do and this is what's offered. That's the one thing that I see lacking is the support in an officer's career path. Now, I had a guy sit down with me who's now retired. He retired as a lieutenant, and he sat me down. He got out a piece of paper, and he drew a line and says, "This is where you are now. Where do you want to be in five years? Where do you want to be in seven, eight, ten, fifteen, and twenty?" That was the breakdown that we did. And I'm where I want to be with the exception of promotion. I've not attained that, but when it gets to a certain point, you know you have to reevaluate, reassess. Where am I at now and where am I going to go? And with me, different things that were brought into the picture was, when I came on, I was single. Now I have children. You know, you don't have anybody that's supporting you by saying, "This is where you can or should go."

The expansion of formal mentoring programs like the one featured in Charlotte-Mecklenburg may provide much-needed guidance in these areas.

1990s Summary

In conclusion, as Susan Martin said in her 1990s update on the status of women in policing, "There is good news and bad news."[27] On the one hand, women made steady gains in policing in the 1990s. Female representation in policing steadily improved during the 1990s and women increasingly took on leadership roles, accomplishing new firsts. For example, Dorothy Moses Schulz found that by the 2000s, there were 175 female chiefs in multiple departments, making up 1 percent of police chiefs nationwide. This is especially true in the nation's twenty largest cities, where the representation of women increased exponentially. The voice of this cohort of women and their legacy is heartening. Female officers' integration into policing has forced police officials to "rethink traditional practices in selection, training, and performance evaluation, and has improved the quality of police services for the community."[28] Further, female police executives have the potential, through their administrative policies and statutes, to enact change in how police "do" justice and gender. The potential for enduring change in the field of policing is great, as women continue to make strides in achieving high ranks, breaking down assignments barriers, and ensuring just opportunities for future generations of female police officers.

The bad news is that women entering law enforcement in the 1990s continued to face obstacles in their integration into the "all-boys club" of policing.[29] While women police gained in terms of their representation within police agencies, they were still underrepresented, especially within supervisory and command ranks. Police organizations miss out on qualified and viable candidates for supervisory and command positions when women are systematically discouraged or opt out of promotional opportunities. While the debate of whether men and women actually bring different qualities to the job is discussed in the next chapter, there is the potential that each person brings something unique to the job. One way of overcoming the overwhelming preference of women to opt out is to incorporate flexibility into the process. The reason that the Fortune 500 world has increasingly lured women back into the workplace, especially following starting a family, is the flexibility offered in on-site childcare, work sharing, part-time work, and alternative paths to leadership that are more conducive to the ability to balance family obligations with professional obligations. As men and women increasingly share family responsibilities, this flexibility benefits men too. These factors have consistently been shown to increase the upward mobility of parents in an organization. In 1998, more than 75 percent of police administrators believed that the number of women officers and administrators in their departments would increase in the next five years.

Would the 2000s see the predicted increase in female police? According to the tokenism framework, if the numbers of women in police increase and gender loses its visibility in police agencies, which appeared to assist women in obtaining promotional opportunities, the next generation of female police executives may have very different promotion experiences. It is difficult to predict how those potential changes will affect the future of female police executives. Recent research suggesting that women are opting out of the promotional process will further exacerbate the lack of female executives in policing due to the civil service regulations that require officers to serve a certain number of years at each rank combined with the practice of offering promotional exams at irregular intervals. Timing is important. Crucial decisions that may affect one's ability to move into management must be made early in one's career. Since women are likely to postpone early promotional opportunities for family and childcare reasons, they may simply miss those early opportunities. In addition to the loss of early promotion, behaviors such as having kids and taking time out of the workplace constitute career risks because they are perceived as a lack of organizational commitment.[30] The next section, "Female Police Officers of the 2000s: Career Minded and College Educated," will take a close look at how the landscape changed for women in the 2000s.

Section III

FEMALE POLICE OFFICERS OF THE 2000s

Career Minded and College Educated

O FFICERS WHO LIKE MARY NAVARRO AND SARA DECKER joined the police ranks in the 2000s saw a dramatic shift in the role of the police, based on the increased militarization of policing, 9/11, and increasing and public unrest between police and communities of color. Mary Navarro noted, "It's gotten more violent, more dangerous. . . . We get a lot of warrants, a lot of drugs. . . . I learned from other officers that it never used to be that way." Sara Decker noted that she "entered police work at a time when the environment was becoming a lot more hostile toward police officers—the law and the community." This shift has dramatically influenced how police do their jobs. Of course, it did not happen overnight but across a series of events that shaped the role of modern police.

Marking the almost thirty-year commitment to the war on drugs in the United States, President Clinton provided $1.3 billion in aid to Colombia to decrease the amount of cocaine trafficked into the United States in 2000 through the aerial spraying of coca crops. The war on drugs officially started in 1971, when President Nixon declared drug abuse "public enemy No. 1."[1] When it became clear that the United States was not winning the war on drugs, the 1033 Program of the National Defense Authorization Act upped the ante. It authorized the Department of Defense to transfer military-grade weapons to local law enforcement agencies.[2] Thousands of police agencies have received weapons and equipment to police American streets. For some, winning the US war on drugs was not worth the cost. In 2000, Human Rights Watch published "Punishment and Prejudice: Racial Disparities in the War on Drugs," arguing that the war on drugs was overwhelmingly a war against black Americans. They cited fifteen states where "black men were admitted to prison on drug charges at rates that are from twenty to fifty-seven times greater than those of white men." Their recommendations called for the elimination of racial profiling tactics utilized by police agencies.[3]

All of this occurred in 2000, the year before 9/11. Following the coordinated terrorist attacks by the Islamic terrorist group al-Qaeda on the morning of Tuesday, September 11, 2001, everything we knew about policing changed. Several changes quickly went into effect to restore safety and to combat this new threat. The Department of Homeland Security was created to coordinate domestic antiterrorism efforts. Congress passed the US Patriot Act, granting the federal government greater powers, including the authority to detain foreign terror suspects for a week without charge; to monitor telephone communications, e-mail, and Internet use; and to prosecute suspected terrorists without time restrictions. Years later, reports that assessed the response to the attacks argued that first responders, including firefighters, emergency medical technicians, and police officers, needed much more information and coordination to successfully combat future terrorist attacks. These findings ushered in a new role for local law enforcement officers in intelligence gathering and terrorism prevention, defined as intelligence-led policing. Intelligence-led policing trains police officers to identify and reduce risk through understanding crime threats and developing proactive information sharing.

By the 2010s, this new counterterrorism role, coupled with the war on drugs and the military-grade equipment provided by the 1033 Defense Act, led to a growing concern that police departments had overly militarized. A recent ACLU investigation into police raids found that not only have police become excessively militarized in the 2000s, but this militarization has also occurred with almost no oversight. They studied more than eight hundred paramilitary raids and found that almost 80 percent were for ordinary law enforcement purposes like serving search warrants in people's homes; only 7 percent were for genuine emergencies, such as barricade or hostage situations. Most compelling, the raids disproportionately targeted people of color.[4]

In 2014, the police were involved in several well-publicized shootings, including Eric Garner, Michael Brown, and John Crawford III. The public responded with outrage, resulting in protests, sit-ins, and the popularization of an interactional activist group, Black Lives Matter. Violence between police and citizens of color has consistently made national headlines. In response, the *Washington Post* sought to compile a record of every fatal police shooting in the nation in 2015. What they found was that the types of incidents that have ignited protests in many US communities—white police officers killing unarmed black men—were rare.[5] Despite that fact, police face a new crisis of legitimacy as citizens, news commentators, experts, and even the president of the United States have called for increased accountability for police behavior. This issue is far from decided in American policing and the reestablishment of trust between the police and the communities they protect will be the major issue facing police in the immediate future.

Female police officers like Mary Navarro, Sara Decker, and the others featured in this section will likely play an important role in the resolution of this conflict, as the positive benefits that women bring to policing are well established. Recently they have caught the attention of the media. In 2016, the *Atlantic Monthly* asked the question, "Why Aren't US Police Departments Recruiting More Women?" and the *New York Times* featured an article titled "Female Police Officers Save Lives" in reaction to the increasing violence between police and male officers.[6] To do so, the representation of women in American policing must be maintained. In the 2000s it has become apparent that the progress that women were making in increasing their representation in American police agencies in the 1990–2000s has stalled. Perhaps the emphasis on militarization has deterred women from considering policing as a profession, or maybe departments, overly concerned with safety, have put more focus on hiring officers armed with brawn rather than communication skills. Whatever the reason, the representation of women in policing has decreased slightly from 14 percent in 1999 to 12 percent in 2013.[7]

However, their declining representation has not diminished their mark on policing. Today female officers hold high ranks in police agencies and have achieved new firsts, including breaking into stereotypically masculine assignments such as SWAT (Special Weapons and Tactics) and CSI (Crime Scene Investigation). Often unaware of the struggles of previous generations, equality is assumed for this generation of women police. This generation's struggle is about finding a work and life balance and struggling to find a niche in the highly masculine world of policing. This section includes chapter 10, "Doing Policing Differently?"; chapter 11, "Women's Work"; chapter 12, "Motherhood"; and chapter 13, "Work and Life Balance."

10

Doing Policing Differently?

D O MALE AND FEMALE OFFICERS bring inherently different skills and talents to policing? As discussed in the introduction to this book, "The History of Women in Policing: Matrons to Patrol Officers," the role of women in policing has changed significantly in the past hundred years. Women were first employed in the male-dominated occupation of policing as prison matrons, entrusted with the task of guarding juveniles and women inmates. Later, policewomen would continue to fulfill stereotypically feminine jobs, primarily focused on the "protection of young girls and the suppression of social evils, including dance halls, liquor sales, and gambling."[1] It was not until women began encroaching on typical male police duties in the late 1960s and early 1970s that the debate on the skills and abilities of female officers as police officers began. This debate peaked in 1972 with the expansion of the Civil Rights Act, which legally unlocked the door to patrol for female officers. Research was conducted at this time to determine whether female officers could adequately perform the stereotypically masculine job of patrol. Police administrators, fellow officers, and the public as a whole were concerned with the physical and emotional abilities of policewomen to do the dangerous job of patrol. Research consistently found that women were up to the task of patrol work, but doubts lingered.[2]

With the advent of community policing, the police were challenged to new tasks, such as foot patrol, public relations, and problem solving. Several feminist researchers have argued that women may be *better* suited than men to these particular police tasks because of their unique abilities and skills. For example, female officers have been assumed to have a greater commitment to public service, to have a calming and beneficial effect on police-citizen interactions, to be more effective at diffusing potentially volatile situations, and to provide comfort to crime victims more often than their male peers.[3] In settling this debate there is surprisingly little empirical research to rely on. This chapter will review the question: Are there special skills or talents that are unique or essential to being male or female, and do any of these make better police?

Biology/Essentialism

The biological/essentialist viewpoint suggests yes. Gender essentialism is the idea that men and women act differently and have different options in life because of *inherent* differences between men and women. Biological or essentialist theorists commonly suggest that differences between the sexes are natural. For example, males have a penis and XY chromosomes, whereas females have a vagina, more prominently developed breasts, and XX chromosomes. Biology and the resulting physical differences have dominated discussions of women and work. Early on, the 1872 court case *Illinois vs. Bradwell* clearly defined women as being prized for the skills in the home, which naturally enhance their biological roles of being mothers and nurturers: "The constitution of the family organization, which is formed in divine ordinance as well as the nature of things, indicates the domestic sphere as that [to] which properly belongs the domain and function of womanhood."[4] In other words, women are suited to occupations that allow them to use their natural skills as nurturers. *Muller v. Oregon* later reaffirmed this assumption:

> The two sexes differ in structure of body, in the functions to be performed by each and the amount of physical strength, in the capacity for long-continued labor particularly when done standing, the influence of vigorous health upon the future well-being of the race, the self-reliance which enables one to assert full rights, and in the capacity to maintain the struggle for sustenance. This difference justifies a difference in legislation and upholds that which is designed to compensate for some of the burdens that rest upon her.[5]

In more modern research, the differences between men and women focus on cognitive patterns. Research suggests that men outperform women on a variety of spatial tasks, with the largest difference occurring on tests of spatial rotation and manipulation. Men also excel at tests of mathematical reasoning. Some of these differences are found early in development and most endure throughout the life span. The sex differences in verbal memory and in spatial orientation and math reasoning have been found across cultures.

Most researchers attribute the differences to our long evolutionary history as hunter-gatherers in which the division of labor between men and women was quite marked.[6] Men traveled farther from the home base during hunting and scavenging, whereas women gathered food nearer to their homes. The proximate mechanisms for differentiating these cognitive patterns appear to rely heavily on early exposure to sex hormones. Nonhuman studies show unequivocally that masculinization of both genitalia and behavior depend on the presence of androgens prenatally or early in postnatal life.

Recently, the biological/essentialist viewpoint has seen a resurgence in interest based on Louann Brizendine's 2007 book *The Female Brain.*[7] In response to the lack of information on the female brain that Brizendine discovered while a medical student, she established the first clinic in the country to study and treat women's brain function. In her book, she shows how the structure of the female brain differs from men and how this change determines how women think, what they value, and how they communicate.

In policing, this manifests in the debate over the physical ability of women to do the dangerous job of patrolling the streets. Men, on average, are physically stronger than women are. Many female officers identified the physical strength of men as an advantage to them in doing police work. However, women also argued that female officers are trained to use the tools of the trade to equalize any differences in physical size between officers and criminals. Danielle Lund, a state police trooper, pointed out that the tools of policing are the ultimate equalizer in policing: "In most cases, we [women] are not as physically strong as most of our male counterparts, but we are given all sorts of tools to remedy that. We've got OC [pepper spray] and our asp [baton]." Naomi White, a patrol officer at a small municipal department, agreed:

> I'm not small, but I have worked with females five-foot-two and they handle themselves. You are taught to deal with things and then your own personality. I have been able to talk down other people that I know, had another officer been there, probably would have been a fight. It's more communication than physical ability. People don't understand that when dealing with the public, mostly they want to tell you their problems. I may have to arrest them, but you get them to talk first and they respect that much more. They are willing to cooperate.

Socialization

Of course, as tempting as the argument is that men and women have "different equipment," in everyday life, physical characteristics such as brain structure and genitalia are rarely used to distinguish men from women. According to the socialization perspective, children are not biologically gendered; rather, they learn gendered behavior from their environment through a variety of processes, including imitation and modeling.[8] Through these processes, children learn at a very young age to adopt gender as a basic organizing principle for themselves and the world they are learning about. They learn to conform to the norms in society regarding masculinity and femininity. These gendered differences, such as a preference for same-sex playmates and gender-appropriate toys, clothes, and activities, are believed not to be essential but rather the result of social and cultural forces.[9] Most telling is that when researchers began to consider the social contexts in which the sex differences in math and spatial tasks, spatial rotation, and manipulation occurred, the differences all but disappeared. In one study, social factors such as the perceived importance of math classes for future careers, as well as the actual number of math classes taken, provide a more accurate explanation for the observed differences than do the natural math and spatial abilities of girls and boys.[10] Mary Navarro, a patrol officer with a large university police department, defined how her socialization as a woman has benefited her:

> I think what makes me a very good street cop is that I have really good instincts and I can read people well. . . . And women, really more than men, are able to pick up more. . . . When I am out on the street, most of the things I've gotten into [good arrests] have been because I noticed someone just walking down the street and being able to build on something so small into something bigger just based on things people are doing when they shouldn't be doing. Human behavior is pretty fascinating to me.

Kathy Geiger, a patrol officer in a small municipal department, argued that how men and women are socialized to see the world impacts their responses to belligerent suspects: "The guys just want to beat someone. They do not have it in their makeup. Men have three emotions: happy, horny, and pissed off. Women have many." The idea that women see the world differently than men has recently been confirmed by the work of Carol Gilligan, who suggested that we, as a society, accept and celebrate the different strengths men and women possess. In 1982, Gilligan wrote a book arguing that there are two types of moral reasoning: care thinking and justice thinking. Care thinking is guided by emotions and is context sensitive. By contrast, justice thinking emphasizes impartiality and rights. She wrote her book in response to Lawrence Kohlberg's moral development scale, arguing that Kohlberg's scale only focused on one type of moral reasoning, which essentially favored the ways men were socialized. Instead, Gilligan work's emphasizes that how we socialize men and women matters to understanding how they see the world, and both should be prized.

Biology and Socialization: Same Result

Today, most theorists have conceded that biology as well as socialization play some role in sex-specific behavior. This is generally referred to as the difference between sex and gender. Sex refers to the biological characteristics and gender refers to the culturally determined behaviors and personality characteristics that are associated with, but not determined by sex. However, environmental causes are not easily detangled from natural or biological ones, and in reality, they have the same result—there are physical, emotional, and behavioral aspects that are maintained as significant differences between the sexes: "Every individual is legally classified at birth as a biological male or female and a whole set of gender expectations are mapped onto this primary sex distinction."[11] These clearly defined sex expectations define what appropriate behavior is for men and women.

Defining gender characteristics in this way still does not answer the question as to whether there are skills that are essential or unique to women. There is an inherent danger in making broad generalizations about the abilities and skills for either sex. Within-group variation (i.e., differences among women, rather than between men and women) makes it very difficult to assign certain traits or skills essential to women. What about the differences, for example, between "girly girls" and "tomboys"? Clearly, both men and women display a whole range of behaviors and attributes, and differences within each sex are frequently greater than those between men and women. If there are no essential features to being female, then how can researchers ever hope to study and understand their experiences? If the existence of characteristics that categorize a group is denied, it eliminates the possibility of capturing the importance of that group experience.

So here is my stance: Regardless of the origin or explanation, femininity is very specifically and narrowly prescribed by culture and has often been understood simply as the opposite of masculinity. We all know what it means to act like a lady. A multitude of studies over the past forty years have found a 75 percent agreement on traits that were masculine—such as dominant, aggressive, independent, objective, and competitive—and feminine traits, which are defined as affective traits and include such characteristics as emotional, subjective, tactful, and aware of the feelings of others. These gender stereotypes appear to have changed relatively little in recent years. In sum, sex role expectations, regardless of where they come from, define expected behavior for both men and women (i.e., men act like men, and women act like women). So the final question is: Do female traits make women well suited to police work?

Female Officer Studies

Interestingly, much of the research on female officers analyzes the opinions of experts regarding the possible benefits or detriments of female officers' stereotypical feminine attributes to policing, without empirically measuring the skills of men or women in the profession. For example, in 1998 the International Association of Chiefs of Police did a survey to assess police administrators' views of female officers. Top responses of where women possess exceptional skills included communication, verbal, and interpersonal skills. In comparison, 28 percent of those surveyed reported concern that women lack sufficient physical strength, capacity for confrontation, size, strength, and force.[12] In these analyses, sex role stereotypes provide "commonsense" or anecdotal proof that women are either well or ill suited for police work. Recently, researchers have moved beyond opinions to apply the scientific method to studying differences between men and women, empirically. Let's start with the most hotly debated issue regarding female police officers: their ability to use the force and authority necessary for police work.

Use of Force

In March 2016, a Florida deputy sheriff shot a man in a parked car when he raised his gun at the deputy as she approached his car. She discharged her weapon, and the suspect was pronounced dead at the scene.[13] Six months later, Tulsa, Oklahoma, police officer Betty Shelby shot Terence Crutcher, age forty, while responding to a call of a vehicle abandoned in the middle of the roadway.[14] What makes these stories so unique? Female officers were involved in these deadly incidents with citizens. According to the Bureau of Justice Statistics, officers involved in justifiable homicides with citizens are almost always male (98 percent).[15] Only a handful of the police shootings every year involve female police. Why are women so underrepresented in police-involved shootings?

There are two major, diametrically opposed explanations about female police and force. The first, embodied by critics of women police like the one shown in the preface of this book, is the belief that women cannot perform the job as well as men due to their lack of physical strength and authoritarian presence. Critics argue that women who are unprepared to go "hands on" will rely on deadly force rather than scuffle with criminals. For example, in his study on the relationship between police diversity and negative community and departmental outcomes titled "Does a Helping Hand Put Others at Risk? Affirmative Action, Police Departments, and Crime," John Lott argued that increasing the representation of female officers would lead to more assaults on police officers. The reason that he gave is that, in compensating for their weaker strength, women will substitute other ways of controlling criminals—by shooting them.[16]

The other diametrically opposed position is that women utilize communication skills to an expert level, eliminating or reducing the need for deadly force. One argument for hiring more women as police officers is that they utilize a style of policing that relies more on communication skills and less on physical force. By using techniques that de-escalate potentially violent situations, female officers often successfully resolve situations that might otherwise lead to violence. In 1981, Katharine Van Wormer stated female officers were less likely to provoke citizen complaints, violence, or brutality, instead being likely to avoid assaults and produce a calming effect. The calming effect has been explained as follows: "In our society, the word cop is synonymous with ruggedness, toughness, and masculinity. . . . We are conditioned to expect violence from the police. This expectation may cause us to behave in ways that will produce the events we expect."[17] Femininity, on the other hand, is associated with softness, sympathy, and understanding. For this reason, women evoke less fear and antagonism from citizens. Sex norms may also dictate that "potentially violent citizens may feel it is heroic to attack a policeman but cowardly to attack a policewoman."[18] The National Center for Women and Policing recently published a report summarizing several previous studies of excessive force, suggesting that women officers were less likely to be named in excessive complaint suits, less likely to have allegations sustained against them, and more likely to have smaller payouts for the alleged suits. Women only accounted for 6 percent of the dollars paid out in court judgments and settlements for excessive force among these large agencies, despite the fact they make up 12 percent of officers. Based on these results, the authors encouraged departments to hire more female officers.[19]

Early in my career, I set out empirically to settle the debate of whether women use more or less force than male officers. In 2005, Amie Schuck and I analyzed the use of force by police in one- and two-person cars between 1996 and 1997 in several police departments.[20] What we found was that female officers and same-gender female-female officer pairs used less force in their police-citizen encounters than male officers and male officer pairs. Later, in 2009, I examined the controlling behaviors of male and female officers in the Indianapolis, Indiana, and St. Petersburg, Florida, police departments, and, once again, I found that women were less likely to use extreme controlling behaviors such as threats, physical restraint, search, and arrest. Since 2009, my colleagues and I have repeatedly measured the ability of female officers to use force under every condition we could conceive, and we have always found that women use less force than male officers do. In fact, no empirical study to date shows women use more force than male officers do in their interactions with citizens or when making arrests. These findings support the assertions that women and men perform policing duties differently and that hiring more women as police officers may help to reduce the excessive force in some police departments.[21]

When considering this information, it is important to remember that police and citizen encounters rarely end in physical force. Estimates of encounters that end in *any* force being utilized range from 1 to 20 percent. For this reason, it is interesting to consider that even if women possess skills different from those of their male counterparts, it may make little or no difference in police response. The idea that "blue is blue" and that the "job shapes the officer, not the other way around" argues that all officers police the same "masculine" way because it's the culture in policing. For example, in her study of women police, Patricia Remmington found that female officers' behaviors were co-opted by the strong policing subculture. She noticed that on routine "report" encounters with the public, female officers manifested an abrupt behavior style and unsympathetic attitude toward the public, similar to their male colleagues. Interestingly many women's voices actually took a deeper and gruffer tone during police-public interactions. In other words, women may become "one of the boys."[22]

That being said, almost all of the female officers I interviewed described themselves as having a unique style of policing that relied less on physical force. Naomi White, a patrol officer in a small town, argued that she wished that people understood:

> We are not any less of an officer. I have strengths that others don't; they have strengths that I don't have. As far as being because I am female, I have never seen that. I might be thankful that I have a bigger person to help me, I have weapons. I have tools that if I have another female with me, I would feel comfortable. One night, there were five of us in uniform surrounding a guy. I felt no less comfortable than if male officers would have been there. We have been trained; we all know what we are doing. It was so cool looking around because there are not that many women in law enforcement and to have that many show up, that guy was probably like, "What the hell did I get myself into."

With the issue of force being settled, the next chapter analyzes the idea that women are "sex specialists" who are best prepared to handle cases where women are often victims, such as sexual assault and domestic violence. Does women's contribution to the profession mean doing women's work in policing, responding to crime victims and juveniles girls? The idea that women are sex specialists sounds dangerously similar to when women were separated into women's bureaus rather than doing general police duties.

11

Women's Work

BECAUSE OF WOMEN'S EMPATHY and communication abilities, there is an assumption that they are more comforting to victims of crimes.[1] Similar to the question tackled in the last chapter regarding women's ability to use force, it is hard to determine whether this is true or just reaffirming the feminine stereotypes that women are natural caregivers. In other words, it is possible that our assumptions that women are good at comforting crime victims are simply colored by our expectations of what we consider normal gender roles. This sounds a lot like a throwback to the idea of women being sex specialists in women's bureaus. Remember that women first entered the world of policing as police matrons, responsible for the social welfare of girls and women, and then moved into separate women's bureaus. This practice of segregation was renounced in the 1970s when women joined the world of patrol work, but it seems to continue to influence women's roles and responsibilities in policing today.[2]

Today, when women are pushed into traditionally female roles, such as writing reports or working with juveniles, it is called sex-stereotyped job assignments. In policing, what are the consequences of sex-stereotyped job assignments? It should not be surprising that a woman who joined one of the most masculine professions available did so not because of her desire to display overly feminine caretaking behaviors but because she was drawn to policing for other reasons—like because of the strength and authority inherent in police work. In this chapter, we will review the relevant research and practices in having women respond to victimization to answer the question: Are women more comforting and helpful than men in their response to crime victims?

International

Violence against women is a global epidemic. In the United States a staggering, one in four women face violence daily. The rates are even higher in countries like Bangladesh, Ethiopia, Peru, and Tanzania, where more than 50 percent of women report living in physical and sexual violence.[3] Sadly, violence is the leading cause of death for women ages sixteen to forty-four in most places in the world.[4] The United Nations leads the international efforts to reduce and respond to violence against women globally, and female police officers are important to this fight. The United Nations found that when female police officers respond to domestic conflicts, women and children receive greater protection. Ann-Marie Orler of the Department of Peacekeeping Operations at the United Nations believes this is because "women sometimes fear turning to male uniformed personnel for assistance."[5] For this reason, they are trying to increase their female representation in international police and peacekeeping forces.

In the United Kingdom, Canada, and Australia, researchers have found that female officers were more likely to take domestic violence calls seriously than male officers. Specific to Canada, they found that female officers demonstrate more concern, patience, and understanding than male officers when responding to domestic violence calls. In the United Kingdom, they found that increased representation of women police in England led to higher arrest rates for domestic violence. In some countries, police agencies have hired women specifically to respond to female victimization.[6] For example, the inspector general for Rwanda argued that "women trust female officers when it comes to investigating gender-based violence cases."[7] For this reason, women's bureaus have been created recently in Afghanistan, Dubai, Croatia, Albania, and Moldova. In these countries and others, female officers' talents are being sought to handle gender-related violence.

In August 2016, Public Radio International (PRI) featured a story titled "US Spending Millions to Train Women Police Officers Worldwide. What about at Home?" It argued that international women's organizations have long recognized the connection between increased women police officers and a range of other improvements, such as "less violence against women, stopping rape, preventing terrorism." It also points out that while the United States will spend $133 million in 2017 to increase the presence of women in peace and security forces in places like Afghanistan, Pakistan, and Nigeria, "policy experts and advocates are at a loss as to why this idea falls on deaf ears domestically."[8]

United States

While violence against women in the United States is also epidemic, our organizational responses to the violence have not overtly involved the increased representation of women in policing. One of the reasons for this is that unlike many of the countries discussed earlier, female police have integrated into general police duties, rather than staying in women's bureaus. However, female police officers often report being called to respond to crime victims, due to their "natural caretaking skills." In their 1985 study of police perceptions of domestic violence, Robert Homant and David Kennedy found that female police officers showed more concern, patience, and understanding in handling domestic violence situations than male officers.[9] Mary Navarro, a patrol officer with a university police department, argued, "With some of the guys wearing black and white . . . they miss slowing down and being patient. I think some of the guys are real quick to just jump on somebody right away. You know, not physically, but not patient enough to allow them to tell their story, whether it's a victim or a criminal." Navarro believes that her ability to communicate gives her an advantage when investigating crimes.

Citizens also believe women have an advantage in responding to crime victims. In a 2014 study that used hypothetical scenarios of domestic violence incidents, researchers found that the gender composition of the law enforcement team was associated respondents' perceptions of job performance and quality of policing. In the experiment, respondents rated the team with more female officers (six women and four men) handling the situation more fairly than the team with fewer female officers (one woman and nine men).[10] These studies suggest that there may be a citizen preference for female officers when reporting a victimization experience. In her 1985 article on female police officers, Barbara Price suggested that female police officers help victims avoid a secondary victimization, which may result from a less empathetic police interviewer:

> Because raped women frequently are in severe emotional crisis following their victimization, an especially sensitive police response is required. Public policy should support the hiring of female officers not only for the symbolic value that they represent by assuring the community that the police are committed to serving all citizens but also for practical reasons. Women's voices are needed in influencing how police conduct themselves.

Susan Schneider, a patrol officer in a large municipal department, argued that secondary victimization was a likely risk if the wrong officer responded to a victim of violence: "I prefer those calls to protect the victim. I don't want the guys to tell the girl she deserved to be raped."

Secondary victimization refers to behaviors and attitudes of police and social service providers that are "victim blaming" and that traumatize victims of violence. Recent research on police officer attitudes found a sizeable minority of police officers who adhere to rape myths. Rape myths are stereotypical and incorrect statements about rape, such as "only bad girls get raped," "women ask for it," or "women cry 'rape' only when they have been jilted or have something to cover up."[11] Police were especially likely to apply rape myths to victims who did not adhere to stereotyped victim characteristics. These involved cases that veered away from stranger rape toward acquaintance rape, which incidentally is the most common form of rape.

Interestingly, Jan Jordan argued that the preference for female police officers following a victimization is reflective of the idea of consumerism. Her article, which aptly asks the question "Will any woman do?" makes the point that empathy and compassion in responding to crime victims are not essentially female skills. Both men and women can display these qualities. Her prediction is that as men and women increasingly challenge sex role expectations in policing, the expectations will evolve and all officers may be more open to listening to a survivor's story. For these reasons, as my colleague Amie Schuck pointed out, there may be a greater danger in assuming that female officers bring something unique or better than male officers to the policing occupation—namely, unrealistic expectations:

> There could be tremendous individual and group consequences for women if policymakers and the public have unrealistic expectations of what woman can do as police officers. Just as women's progress has been hampered in the past by expectations of what women *cannot do*, expectations about what women *can do better* are potentially just as harmful.[12]

Catch-22?

It is also important to mention that the preference for a female police officer following victimization presents a catch-22 for female police officers. By emphasizing women's unique attributes, women are defined as "gender specialists" and shuffled into tasks that highlight their gender. While altruistic, these tasks come at a cost. One cost is the emotional labor that it takes to respond to crime victims. Naomi White, a patrol officer in a small municipal department, identified the stress that comes with handling sex crimes: "If they are the victim and they've had a sexual assault . . . they would rather talk to me, which can be a good thing but it can also be stressful." In a recent survey of police stressors, responding to family disputes and battered children were at the top of the list for most frequent and highly rated stressors.[13] While stress is discussed more fully in chapter 13, emotional labor or the idea that police work "requires the officer to induce or suppress feelings to sustain the outward countenance that produces the proper state of mind in others" takes a tremendous toll on officer well-being.[14] Another cost is that displaying overtly feminine skills is not a pathway to promotion. Masculine, aggressive crime fighting is viewed as real police work and is associated with leadership potential and promotion. Having women respond to the cases regarding victimization and service opportunities channels them into the least desirable jobs within policing and those least likely to lead to promotional and leadership opportunities. Of course, internationally researchers have pointed out that by doing policing differently, women are challenging the acceptable ways to do police work. D. J. McCarthy and Marisa Silvestri have both found examples in the United Kingdom where female representation in policing is stronger, where the "role of female officers is highly active" and "largely dominant," thus changing how officers display leadership and transforming police agencies.[15] This issue is far from settled in policing.

Almost 60 percent of female police officers may become pregnant during their employment. Given that the most common reason women give for leaving police work is the needs of their families, the next chapter explores the experiences of pregnant police officers. Through the lens of safety, chapter 12, "Motherhood," also explores the policies and practices that departments have in place.

12

Motherhood

Consider "Jane Doe" who is a police officer in a small city in the mid-west. Jane gave birth to a daughter two years ago and is expecting another one later this year. Because her agency denied her a light duty assignment during her pregnancy, she was forced to not only use all of her accumulated sick time, vacation, and compensatory time; she also lost a year of seniority. Unless the chief of police permits her to work light duty during this pregnancy, she stands to lose even more of these same employment rights. . . . The chief of police denied her request, noting that "the law does not require me to make any provision for you." He also expressed a concern that granting light duty to Jane during her pregnancy would set a precedent that he would be "stuck" with—apparently forgetting that she is the only female police officer in the department. . . . Nevertheless, in the fourth month of her pregnancy, the department forced Jane to take leave—leave that the department charged against her FMLA [Family Medical Leave] allotment. She will therefore exhaust the twelve weeks to which she is entitled before her baby is born, and will have to cope in a "leave without pay" status until she is able to return to full duty. She hopes that the department will preserve her position for her, but understands that it has no legal obligation to do so. Jane describes her situation as "the pregnancy penalty."[1]

BEING PREGNANT CAN BE A VERY EXCITING TIME in a person's life—picking out names, preparing the crib, and anticipating the changes that will come with a new family member. For female police officers, this excitement is complicated by their concerns for psychological, physical, and financial safety. The job of a law enforcement officer is a complex one, and almost every aspect of the more than six hundred essential functions of police work poses risk to pregnant police.[2] Common risks include violence by offenders, contact with diseased populations, exposure to lead, heavy materials, and unsafe levels of noise during firearms training and discharge. Despite these potential dangers, light-duty accommodations that allow officers to do less dangerous deskwork are not guaranteed, adding stress and worry during pregnancy. This chapter explores the experiences of pregnant police officers and the policies and practices that departments have in place to maintain the safety of officers and their unborn children while also maintaining a strong police roster and the financial costs that accompany pregnancy and maternity accommodations.

Dangers for Pregnant Police

Recall from chapter 5, "The Dangers on the Beat," the various potential dangers of police work, such as violent encounters with combative and diseased citizens, car accidents, and physical injury while doing the job, just to name a few. Officers face these same dangers when policing while pregnant. Sadly, in January 2008, a pregnant female police officer was shot in a fight with an armed suspect.[3] While this is an isolated and rare event, it highlights the need for a closer look at the safety of pregnant officers. No research to date has explored the risk of pregnant officers. For most people, violence during pregnancy is rare, estimated to be between 1 and 20 percent with a majority of the perpetrators being intimate partners.[4] However, the increased risk of violence associated with police work may also increase the potential for violence during pregnancy.

Police employment also poses unique risks to pregnant employees through the increased risk of transmission of several infectious diseases, including HIV, viral hepatitis, and tuberculosis through close contact with infected populations.[5] While the Centers for Disease Control reports on-the-job exposure ranges of 2–10 percent for hepatitis and less than 1 percent for HIV, researchers recently documented a case of seroconversion from a single bloody arrest incident. A fifty-two-year-old police officer punched a suspect in the teeth, causing two wounds on his knuckles, resulting in his contraction of HIV and hepatitis C.[6]

Finally, motor vehicle crash exposure occurs in tens of thousands of pregnancies every year and is directly responsible for at least hundreds of fetal deaths annually.[7] Police work makes up about 50 percent of fatalities in which the automobile was the primary source of injury.[8] Of the 670 officers killed accidentally in 2005, more than 80 percent involved an automobile and 65 percent were due to motor vehicle accidents, again suggesting a higher potential risk for officers.[9] While little is known about the prevalence of these risks while pregnant, these are the most common dangers that police face.

Accommodations: Light Duty

Because of the increased risks inherent in police work, departmental policies and practices allow for the potential for injury and the need for a light-duty accommodation. Light-duty accommodations continue the employment of officers who, because of injury, pregnancy, or illness, are temporarily unable to perform their regular assignments but are capable of performing alternative duty assignments.[10] However, each of these conditions—on-duty injury, off-duty injury, and pregnancy—have different laws that govern them.

On-Duty Injury

The American Disabilities Act of 1990 mandates that departments make reasonable accommodations for employees disabled from on-the-job injury who are otherwise qualified to perform the essential functions of the job. The light-duty assignment is a common accommodation. Officers injured on the job may otherwise claim worker's compensation benefits under the Federal Employees Compensation Act.[11] Therefore, the light-duty assignment is a cost-saving alternative to worker's compensation payments for officers injured on the job.

Off-Duty Injury

By comparison, the creation of light-duty policies for officers who become injured or sick while off duty have been much more controversial. There are no cost savings to departments or legal requirements that departments provide accommodations to injuries sustained off duty. Because of the physical nature of police work, officer's injuries can be financially devastating. The establishment of light-duty policies for officers' injuries off duty provides reassurance for police employees that they are valued employees and that they can reestablish full duties once able. The rub is that the establishment of light-duty positions may create a legal expectation of continued light-duty assignment. What if an officer's injury goes beyond a reasonable period, or if the officer is malingering? These issues make light-duty policies controversial and expensive. Departments cannot hire new employees to take the place of officers on light duty because the idea is that the injured officer will return to his/her position once able. Therefore, to maintain strong rosters, police administrators often have to make the costly decisions to use overtime pay or to stretch their rosters carefully to maintain the safety of their communities.

Pregnancy

The Pregnancy Discrimination Act of 1978 (PDA) governs light duty related to pregnancy accommodations and requires that employers treat employees affected by pregnancy, childbirth, or related conditions the same in employment as other persons not so affected but similar in their ability to work. Defined as the "equal-treatment" model, when a law enforcement agency provides light-duty assignment to temporarily disabled officers, the PDA requires that the agency offers the same opportunity to officers temporarily disabled by pregnancy and childbirth.[12] For example, if an employee recovering from a major stroke was permitted light-duty assignment, as a function of an expressed policy or implied practice, the agency is required to provide the same consideration to employees who are disabled by pregnancy.[13] The equality clause of the PDA has been challenged in the courts repeatedly in the last few decades. In fact, a recent Equal Employment Opportunity Commission report shows a 40 percent increase in charges related to pregnancy from 1997 to 2007, on top of a 10 percent increase between 1992 and 1996. Specific to policing, two 2006 court cases, *Lochren v. Suffolk County* and *Tysinger v. Police Department of the City of Zanesville*, inform the practice of light duty for pregnant employees.

In the 2006 case *Lochren v. Suffolk County*, a jury awarded six officers between $5,000 and $23,000 in damages from their employer, the Suffolk County New York Police Department. In April 2000, the police department had changed its policy to disqualify pregnant officers from light-duty assignments while still maintaining light-duty assignments for officers injured off duty. The American Civil Liberties Union filed the lawsuit on behalf of six female police officers, arguing that a light-duty policy that disqualified pregnant officers from desk and other non-patrol jobs violated federal law because of the policy's disparate impact on women. During the trial, one of the officers testified that the policy forced her to choose either working unsafely as a patrol officer while pregnant or not working at all. The jury agreed. However, in that same year, in the case *Tysinger v. Police Department of the City of Zanesville*, the court sided with the police department, noting that agencies are not legally required to make light-duty accommodations if the department does not have light duty available to anyone or available only for certain workers—such as those injured on the job.[14] In sum, the legal requirement for light duty depends on how an employer's light-duty policy is designed.

One critique of the PDA applied to pregnancy in policing is that, by definition, neutrality ignores gender differences, and pregnancy is a biological issue that only affects women, so these seemingly neutral rules may potentially yield biased outcomes for women. As one female administrator pointed out, "When your chief legal advisor tells you that being pregnant is actually no different than someone breaking their ankle, we figure we might have a problem. I never did quite see his philosophy."

To get around these legal details, many agencies have light-duty practices but lack formal, written policies. In her report *On the Move: A Status Report on Women and Policing*, Susan Martin voiced concern over the lack of policy and consistent practice in the care of pregnant police. She argued that while departments have light-duty policies that permit officers who are temporarily disabled to work in non-contact positions, they lacked uniformity and common practice on three main points: (1) defining the point in time when a pregnant woman becomes unfit for her regular duties, (2) who is in charge of the reassignment decisions and what factors lead to officers being forced to take extended leave while pregnant, and (3) what assignments are suitable for a pregnant officer on light duty. She concluded with a plea for more articulated and consistently applied policies to assure the rights of pregnant police.[15]

In a recent update of light-duty and maternity policies, it appears little has changed. To explore the prevalence of maternity policies in police agencies in the United States, my colleague and I did a research project titled "A Survey of Maternity Policies and Pregnancy Accommodations in American Police Departments." We found that more than 80 percent of agencies queried had a written maternity leave policy; however, about one-third of the policies were discretionary, meaning that whether a person would be eligible was up to an administrator. Regarding light-duty or disability accommodations, only 28 percent of agencies reported having a formal light-duty policy, with 82 percent reporting discretionary policies. Almost 85 percent of agencies surveyed had no one requesting a maternity assignment in the past three years.[16] There is no uniformity in police policy regarding pregnancy in policing, leaving the more than 18,000 law enforcement agencies in the United States to enact their own unique policies regarding pregnancy. The low rates at which police agencies employ women of childbearing years, coupled with the infrequency in which female officers are pregnant on the job, make police pregnancy rare. For this reason, agency accommodations for pregnancy are dealt with on a case-by-case basis. This was true for officers' perceptions as well. Many officers I interviewed were unaware of their department's accommodations for pregnancy and maternity because they had not experienced them. Sometimes they knew of officers who had been pregnant. For example, Peg Joseph, a young municipal officer, described her knowledge of her department's accommodation based on her female colleague's experience: "I have to base this off [officer's name] experience. She got pregnant and all I know is that she had to take care of evidence during that time [for her light-duty assignment]."

Based on a 2010 survey of women police officers, Corinne Schulze concluded that the uncertainty of accommodations, or, more specifically, paid accommodations, was a source of stress for women police. The lack of well-defined policies may also inadvertently encourage female police officers to limit disclosure to police administrators.[17] When faced with the decision to disclose pregnancy and lose employment and benefits, officers often choose to remain silent, opening themselves up to the risk of harm to themselves and their unborn children.[18] As one officer stated, "I worked until the day before I delivered for both of my pregnancies, but there wasn't a day that went by that I didn't question the safety of my baby."[19]

Mary Navarro, a pregnant officer concerned about the certainty of light-duty accommodations, delayed reporting her pregnancy to administrators for many of these same reasons: "I was worried because . . . the issue was, 'we are not sure if something is going to be available [for light-duty assignment].'" For this reason, Mary made the decision to hide her pregnancy from her department until she was physically showing. There were a couple of reasons why she made this decision. First, Mary "heard a female officer at [neighboring police department] who had been pregnant and when she told them she was pregnant, they immediately sat her down and said, 'You're not going out on the street. You are going to stay here. We will find something for you to do.'" While the law is clear that a law enforcement agency cannot remove a pregnant officer from her assignment or compel her to assume a light-duty assignment unless she is unable to perform the essential functions of a police officer, employers can encourage female officers to report their pregnancies.[20] The result is that unless a pregnant officer reports her condition, department administrators cannot alter her work assignment unless the officer is unable to perform it.[21]

While the neighboring department required their pregnant officer to immediately leave street work, they guaranteed her a light-duty assignment via a written light-duty policy for pregnancy. By comparison, Mary's department had told her there might not be a light-duty assignment available to her. They had a discretionary practice, meaning that the availability of the light-duty position was not guaranteed but instead left up to her administrators. She feared that she wouldn't be able to pay her bills if she was required to take unpaid time off before her baby was born: "I was afraid because I didn't have the time, and if I used up all the time, then I wouldn't have any left when I had my baby. When I have my baby, what—I am supposed to go to work the next day?"

Family Medical Leave Act of 1993

This is where the protections in the PDA for pre-baby and the protections for after the child is born in the Family Medical Leave Act interact. The FMLA of 1993 requires employers with fifty or more employees to allow eligible employees up to twelve weeks of unpaid leave within any twelve-month period of the birth or adoption of a child. FMLA is a guarantee that one's job will be there when one gets back to work, but it is not necessarily a paid leave. What generally happens is that women save up their time so that they can be paid during FMLA leave. Mary wanted to work in a light-duty capacity as long as possible before her baby arrived, so she could spend the full twelve weeks protected by FMLA after the baby's birth.

Mary hid her pregnancy until her control tactics training was coming up. Officers must occasionally update their training. Control tactics training generally includes instruction on techniques used in controlling suspects, weapon recovery, and arrest techniques using empty-hand arrest and control tactics, baton, and OC spray. This hands-on training is physically demanding, but Navarro was most concerned about the training taking place at the shooting range, where toxic levels of lead are common.[22] The ingestion and inhalation of lead have been linked with spontaneous abortion, minor malformations, preterm birth, and delayed cognitive development of offspring.[23] In addition, there is no real protection from noise levels from firearms, which all register above Occupational Health and Safety's recommended 140 dB for the threshold of pain (140 to 150dB for rimfire pistols and 150 to 160 dB for centerfire rifles, pistols, and shotguns).[24] To avoid these risks, Mary Navarro reported her condition to her department: "I ended up talking to [a female officer] from a [neighboring department] and she told me about lead and . . . the development of baby's ears even with shooting rifles, so I didn't want to be a part of that." Once Mary reported her pregnancy before her control tactics training, her department required a doctor's note to verify her condition. During the two-week lag between submitting the paperwork and having it approved by her department, Navarro realized how much was really at risk while policing the streets pregnant.

> I had to go through the process of first getting a doctor's note saying I was pregnant and second what my restrictions were. And at a certain point, I was able to do that and wrote a letter to the chief. . . . So, eventually, I was able to not go to the training, but it took a lot of work, and then when I finally gave them the note, I had to write a letter requesting light duty and the reasons why. So I wrote a letter saying, "Because I was pregnant, I was requesting to go to light duty, blah, blah, blah." In that time, it took, I want to say two weeks, and it was not until I realized how stupid my choice was, until we went to a call and I was driving

around wearing the belt because my fear was, I could not not work. I needed the money. . . . We had gone on this call, a shooting with an armed suspect and I was driving the street and I slowed down a little bit when I was going. I am like, "Well, that's probably not good. You know, it's probably not safe for me to be on the street." I slowed down a little bit, because I was in the lead, and everybody started to pass me, and was like, "Why are you slowing down?" I think it was that moment I realized . . . I could just tell or maybe I could feel like the flutter-ing and the movement—that's when it became real. I thought, "What the hell I am I doing here?"

Mary's struggle to keep up when chasing a suspect is not unusual for preg-nancy. Pregnant officers, especially in the later months of their pregnancy, may have difficulty physically or psychologically performing some of the usual police duties.[25] Bodies undergo unique physical changes during pregnancy in-cluding increased size and weight, fatigue, nausea, impaired equilibrium, and reduced muscle strength, making physical movements difficult to perform.[26] The next hurdle for Mary was staying busy on light-duty assignment:

One of my sergeants suggested that when I write this letter requesting light duty to give them a list of ideas that I think could be done, which I did. Well, appar-ently, that offended them because they did not want me to give the ideas; they wanted to come up with them on their own. Well, eventually they came up with some stuff, and I did do it. And, it was hard for me. You know, I want to say I got the feeling that they thought I was lazy, that I just wanted to do nothing and get paid for it. But light duty was probably the hardest thing ever because I am a worker and I hated it. I hated to sit around. . . . I was still married and we thought about trying for a third baby . . . but there's no way we would want to go through that again.

Light Duty: Finding Something to Do

Administrators have previously reported that one challenge to a light-duty assignment is finding something meaningful for officers to do.[27] In her study of pregnancy policies, Schulze contended that the prestige and flexibility of the reassignment significantly affect the satisfaction of reassigned officers. Menial, boring work reinforces the message that the officer on light duty is being punished. Danielle Lund, a state trooper, described the difficulties her department faced in finding meaningful tasks for officers to complete while on light duty for pregnancy:

I know that, as far as light duty goes, we are limited on what we have available. . . . I ended up doing a lot of piddle stuff like erasing our in-car videotapes that we no longer needed to keep on file, and erasing and rewinding them so we could use them again. We actually were doing some rearranging in the office, so I worked on that.

In a similar situation, Isla Thomas, a patrol officer in a large municipal department, requested light duty after sustaining an injury that she feared would be dangerous to her child: "I was seven weeks pregnant when I got kicked in the gut and I almost lost that child. . . . The doctor told me I had caused the placenta to tear, so the city obliged it [light-duty assignment]." Sadly, shortly after she returned to work a scuffle with a drunken citizen left her injured:

I went back to work and I was messing with a drunk person who ripped out my shoulder. Totally ripped it out. Tore everything. I wound up going to take the pre-op test and they did a blood test. I was two weeks pregnant, so they could not fix my shoulder. I said, "Okay, I'm not going to tell the department anything about the pregnancy because it's not really any of their business. I'm just going to let the pregnancy go on the coattails of being injured." I told the doctor. The doctor wrote a letter to the chief that said, "She can't get surgery right now because of an existing circumstance." Oh, my God, that opened up an enormous problem because he cannot understand why I cannot get surgery. Finally, it comes out that I am pregnant. Okay, he flips a switch. "Why is she pregnant? When was she pregnant?" We had to go get the gynecologist to go get an expert ovulation to prove that I was pregnant prior to the shoulder being ripped out. I ripped out my shoulder two weeks ago. I am seven weeks pregnant. That really should be a no-brainer. . . . We gave him all the paperwork because he was saying that I should have an MRI, but my doctor said, "No because the magnetic fields of an MRI have been known to damage a child." I am like, "Oh no, I'm not going to hurt my kid. I already almost lost my first kid because of the department. I'm not going to do this again." Because I was injured, I went on light duty.

Remember that because Isla was injured on duty in her scuffle with an intoxicated suspect, the American Disabilities Act protected her right to light-duty accommodation, and if her department did not make a reasonable accommodation, or she was unable to perform light duties, she would qualify for worker's compensation payments. Her condition as a pregnant officer did not guarantee her light-duty accommodations and would require her to take unpaid leave unless she had some accrued time.

The chief had told me, "You're not going on light duty again for your baby." "Okay, that's fine, because I'm not asking for light duty for my baby. I'm asking for it for my arm." Well, we went back and forth. HR kept classifying my light duty as pregnancy and the chief would deny it, so I wouldn't get paid for two weeks. Then we would go back again and they would flip-flop, and then I would get paid. Then we would flip-flop again, and I wouldn't get paid. We went through that for a while until I wound up getting a lawyer. And the lawyer put the kibosh on that and said, "Look, get your paperwork straight. This is a work comp claim, and she will be on light duty because she cannot have the surgery due to the growing baby. You will continue to pay her; otherwise, we will sue you." I had a meeting with the chief. . . . He said, "You know, I wanted to let you know that it's kind of fortunate with the shoulder thing because you weren't going to get light duty for this baby." I said, "That's kind of funny you say that because the woman before me had two kids and you gave her light duty for both. And you told me when I had my first one that I would get past practice." Past practice is two light-duty assignments. "Where's mine?" He goes, "Well, we're done with that; we've washed our hands." I said, "That's because you won't put anything in writing so I couldn't hold it to you." He goes, "Well, it's a good thing it's that way." I said, "You know what, with all due respect, when this is all said and done, you're going to give me $40,000 for my shoulder." "Yep." "Okay, what are my options if I'm pregnant and I work pregnant and I lose my baby. How much are you going to pay me for my baby?" "Well, none. That is your fault. You got pregnant, you deal with that." I said, "So, wait a minute. What are my options? If I didn't get injured, what would my options be if I'm pregnant, which I am right now?" He said, "You can go on family leave, which is twelve weeks unpaid." Well, we all know that is not the gestation period for a human, it is a puppy.

In both of these stories, female officers had to fight to get a light-duty as-signment in order to ensure their safety and that of their unborn children, even when women in their organization had previously received light duty. It is not clear how many women leave policing when facing these obstacles, but the research suggests that many do. In her article "Pregnant Officer Policies," Carole Moore found that a large number of female police leave following the birth of their children because they felt unwelcome once they became pregnant.[28] An unseen tax accrues when female officers take time off to have children. Women interviewed by Renee Cowan and Jamie Bochantin in 2009 argued that pregnancy was a risky business and could "hurt and possibly end their police career."[29] Women in their study described how pregnancy highlighted their female status and called into the question their legitimacy as real police and their dedication to their profession. Isla Thomas was told that she was ineligible for promotion at her large municipal department due to the time she took off to have children. Departments in agencies with written light-duty policies did not report the same level of uncertainty. These women had very little difficulty in negotiating their needs regarding pregnancy and maternity. Rita Larkin, a patrol officer with a municipal police department, summarized her department's practice: "Once the belt doesn't fit you, there's light duty." Another patrol officer in a large municipality discussed light duty in her department: "They are guaranteed light duty." This assurance alleviated some financial and physical stress on police officers during pregnancy.

Family Leave: Future Directions

There is considerable evidence to suggest that police policy makers are facing political pressures to adopt family-friendly policies. In January 2012, the International Association of Chiefs of Police (IACP) announced a revised model policy regarding pregnancy and maternity in American police agencies, which encouraged agencies to make every reasonable effort to "accommodate the needs of pregnant employees to allow them to remain gainfully employed during their pregnancies."[30] They recommended nondiscretionary light-duty policies to help alleviate the financial considerations of female officers who would otherwise have to take extended leaves without benefits and to increase officer safety by not putting pregnant officers in the line of fire. Although exploring policy and its implementation does not provide a complete solution to the dangers pregnant police face, it does provide a starting point for a model policy that "supports officer well-being without compromising police operations or community safety, without unfairly burdening other police employees, and without violating anti-discrimination laws, thus protecting departments from liability."[31] The IACP contends that the formalization of light-duty policies for pregnancy is the best way of reducing the risks of policing while pregnant, arguing for an "equal-results" model, rather than the "equal-treatment" model. The equal-results model legally protects agencies that make accommodations specifically for pregnant women, such as flexible scheduling, sick days without going on disability leave, and formal light-duty policies.

Important to the adoption of family-friendly policies, there is evidence that police fathers are increasingly claiming paternity leave rights, reducing the stigma associated with family medical leave. Our study on the use and perception of family medical leave in policing showed that paternity leave was significantly related to maternity leave and light-duty accommodations for pregnant officers. Sam Long, a patrol officer in a small rural police agency, mentioned that although she was unaware of an official policy in her department regarding maternity, she was aware "that one of the male officers that I am working with, his wife is getting ready to have a baby, and I know that he is taking leave." These results suggest that maternity leave is increasingly turning into family leave. This is good news, as police dads, especially those in supervisory and top command positions, may have an impact on the policies and culture surrounding family-friendly policies in policing.

While the revision of IACP's outdated maternity policy and the shift in thinking of maternity leave as shared family leave represent a shift in the direction of family-friendly policies, there is still significant work to be done. In her work for the International Association of Chiefs of Police, Karen Kruger described the potential of pregnancy-friendly policies, such as "adequate maternity leave, light-duty assignments, maternity uniforms and body armor, deferral of in-service training, continuation of benefits and seniority credits while on leave, and flexible schedules upon returning to work."[32] Many departments have already begun adopting these policies and practices. In 2006, the Santa Fe Department of Transportation became the first state-sponsored childcare center in the United States. At the federal level, the Federal Law Enforcement Training Center in Georgia; the National Security Agency Police in Fort Meade, Maryland; and several of the US Customs and Border Protection offices have on-site day care. These governmental entities have just learned what the Fortune 500 companies already knew, which is that on-site childcare programs increase the retention and recruitment of both male and female employees.

At their heart, all of these solutions acknowledge that a diverse workforce is a valuable asset, and pregnancy is a temporary physical condition, unique to women, which may or may not affect her ability to perform her usual duties. We know that in the future, a national paid policy for maternity leave would have a significant impact on internal police policy adoption and implementation. However, the United States continues to be woefully behind other industrialized nations in providing federal policies for the well-being of working families.[33] In comparable countries, paid maternity, paternity, and parental leave policies function much like unemployment benefits. For example, working mothers may receive approximately two months of paid maternity leave, and several more months of paid childcare leave.[34] No such paid system exists at the federal level in the United States. Until those changes are made at the federal level, how departments handle pregnancy and institute safe and family-friendly policies communicates a message to employees about the value of women in police organization and the organization's dedication to a work-family balance. To competitively recruit and retain quality police officers, departments must focus attention on employment practices that ensure the safety of pregnant officers.

The next chapter explores the work-life balance of female police officers, the unique strengths and struggles of police families, and the strategies female police officers utilize to stay physiologically and physically strong in the face of demanding police work.

13

Work and Life Balance

In testifying to Congress, police psychologist Dr. Ellen Scrivner argued that the average police officer would see more human tragedy in the first three years of his or her career than the average person would see in a lifetime. Police officers see, hear, and experience some of the most difficult moments in people's lives as they respond to car crashes, violent crime scenes, and heinous victimizations. This makes law enforcement one of the most stressful occupations in the United States.[1] Adding to this stress is that when responding to calls, police officers have to control their own emotional reactions to manage the needs of citizens who are upset, injured, and angry.[2] The stress does not end there. Police have shift work, administrator's priorities, and families to deal with. Police stressors can generally be divided into four areas: stress from the work environment, bureaucratic characteristics of police agencies, availability of peer support and trust, and the availability of coping mechanisms. Theses stressors take a toll on police, producing numerous negative outcomes, such as broken relationships, excessive alcohol use, cardiovascular disease, depression, and violence. How officers cope with these stressors has serious implications for their physical, mental, and psychological well-being.

Many studies suggest that female police officers face unique stressors in police work.[3] These findings reflect a national trend in employment in which levels of stress-related illness are nearly twice as high for women compared to men.[4] In addition, women who work in predominately male-dominated occupations tend to report even higher levels of stress than those who do not. The higher levels of stress may be due to experiences of harassment, discrimination, and tokenism that influence women's work environment. It may also be due to attempts to balance family and work, which may create stress in both places.

Stress from the Work

Critical incidents, such killing someone in the line of duty and experiencing a fellow officer being killed in the line of duty, are incident-specific forms of stress. They are rare circumstances capable of generating considerable psychological discomfort for a couple of days to a couple of weeks following the incident. For some officers, these events may trigger posttraumatic stress disorder (PTSD), which is a mental disorder that manifests in substantial and disruptive changes in an officer's life. Like Teresa Bosch, whose experience of being in a police-involved shooting was discussed in chapter 5, "The Dangers on the Beat," officers who face PTSD can be treated and return to duty, but for many, it is a difficult path to tread.

Losing a fellow officer is another form of incident-specific stress. Naomi White, a patrol officer in a small rural community, discussed how losing her mentor in a violent standoff with a citizen was the most stressful experience in her career. Following the shooting, she faced a heightened sense of constant awareness, called hypervigilance, along with other emotional, physical, behavioral, and cognitive reactions.

> We had a [neighboring] county shooting, and [officer name] was shot in [town]; she was my mentor. That's been a lot recently. It's been so hard. It makes you think about what you would do, and I know my husband was softer with the situation than I was. They worry even in a small town—never would have thought something like that would happen. We have to be on guard as much as everyone else, even when the crime rate is really low. If I am having a bad day, I'm not going to break down and cry as much as I may want to and I feel like it. I am still in a man's world. When I found out about my mentor's shooting, I was on duty, and I broke down in front of the chief, and he didn't know what the hell to do. He was like, "You can go home."

While these events are rare, the potential for danger is always there. The dangerousness of the work environment of policing, coupled with responding to crimes in progress and seeing gruesome crime scenes, led one officer to famously described police work as "three hours of boredom, followed by two minutes of terror, concluding with six hours of report writing."[5]

Police expert Susan Martin argued that the day-to-day repression of police officer emotions, coupled with the management of the emotions of citizens and coworkers, is just as stressful. She explained that when workers manage, interpret, and experience feelings publicly, they are doing emotional labor. In policing, there are organizational and professional norms that dictate that police severely limit expressing their emotions. Their ability to remain in control, knowledgeable, and unafraid, hides the strain and pressure of the situation behind a "public face." Danielle Lund, a state police officer, shows her detached "public face" in her discussion of an armed incident with a citizen that had occurred just days before I interviewed her:

> Even in stressful situations, it does not get me too much. I just had a mini-standoff the other day with this guy. He had committed a hit and run and I went to his door because he had passed us as we were sitting there. He only lived a few houses down. Anyway, I get there and he comes to the door but doesn't open it and then he's acting like he's reaching for something under his shirt, and so I stepped back and got back a bit, but I mean that was just a moment, and it was kind of like, it didn't really bother me that much.

The practice of detachment or being unemotionally involved can be difficult to shut off. While emotional detachment is necessary to get the job done, it can cause hurt and alienation if applied to family and friends. Kevin Gilmartin, author of *Emotional Survival for Law Enforcement*, argued that while this is an important skill for surviving police work, hypervigilance and detachment wreak havoc on officers' well-being and must be carefully managed by officers to strike a balance between their professional and personal lives.

Police Bureaucracies

While police may not face a critical incident every day, they do face the police bureaucracy and all the agency politics that go with it. A bureaucracy is a system of administration distinguished by its (1) clear hierarchy of authority, (2) rigid division of labor, (3) written and inflexible rules, regulations, and procedures, and (4) impersonal relationships.[6] What makes police work unique is that patrol officers, who are the least powerful in the chain of command, have the most discretion or decision-making power and are the most visible to citizens. By comparison, patrol officers have very little input regarding the policies and procedures of the organization, which dictate everything from the length of their hair to how much force they may use in their interactions with citizens. Because they have considerable discretion or decision-making authority, officers must work around the policies but face disciplinary actions when they skirt those policies. In his 2006 examination of stress in policing, researcher Ni He found that a tension exists between the high level of discretion that police have in doing their job and the endless amount of rules and policies that constrict their behavior.

In some agencies, the leadership style of administrators is another source of stress. Administrators may "treat their employees like demanding, willful, impulsive adolescents who can't be trusted."[7] Mary Navarro, a campus police officer, argued that how her administrators ignored the poor work of underperforming officers and then overworked high-performing officers was frustrating to her:

> The administrative level . . . instead of talking to the people who have low standards, they kind of reward the hard workers with more work, and that's frustrating to the officers who are workers. I would consider myself a worker. . . . You get kind of burnt out because I know supervisors can depend on you to get something done, but there is not accountability for the other people. . . . It's your job as a supervisor to get them up to that level. Don't give them work and then decide to give it to an officer that will get it done. . . . The more work you take away from them, the lazier they are going to be. . . . Most of the struggles are not with the population. It is with the people that are here at the department.

Other aspects of the police job such as poor pay, long hours, and shift work also cause stress in police families. The reality is that most police miss family holidays, birthdays, and their kids' games and performances at school. Non-shift-working friends and family members may not understand this reality, and police administrators, used to this reality, may or may not be able or willing to make accommodations for family events. Police who consistently ask for time off are perceived as having problems at home or unable to handle the job.[8] In sum, policing as an occupation rewards long hours, as overtime is common in court appearances, training, and calls that extend well beyond the scheduled workday. This can result in stress, especially in police families.

Availability of Peer Support

Having the support of your coworkers and a sounding board for those aspects of work that are troubling has been consistently shown to reduce perceived levels of stress.[9] Sam Long, a patrol officer with a large municipal police department, discussed the important of peer support:

> I have a couple of friends that are also in law enforcement, so I call them especially if I have a call that I handled and I want a different aspect of it. . . . Different ideas are great, so it's just kind of a release. I can talk to them. They can talk to

me. Because I think that if you go home and unload on whoever is at home, they tend to get scared or worry a little bit more.

However, women may lack the same social support that male officers rely on. A 2012 study called "Men Rule: The Continued Under-Representation of Women in U.S. Politics" argued that the reason why women face more stress in the workplace and are less likely to be represented in leadership is because they lack role models that would make that possible.[10] The authors pointed out that only eight of the nation's one hundred largest cities have a woman as mayor, only around 17 percent of US senators and members of the House of Representatives are women, and about 12 percent of state governors are women. Compared to our international counterparts, the United States comes up short. In fact, there are ninety nations and fifty democratic countries that rank higher than the United States in female representation in their countries' legislatures. Interestingly, the report suggests that the low ranking is not due to discrimination. Instead, Val Van Brocklin, a federal prosecutor and law enforcement trainer, argued that it's because female candidates are less likely to receive the peer and administrative support that makes coping with police work less intimidating. Historically, the solidarity of the working-class, white-male environment has been integral to understanding police culture. While that has clearly eroded over the past forty years, women are not always included in the opportunities that police have to "blow off steam." Police often feel that they can only trust other police to share things that are troubling or bothersome. The opportunity to recount experiences to others, as well as participate in these aspects of informal police culture, builds trust and camaraderie. Mary Navarro mentioned that having friends in law enforcement was especially important because often the friends from before police work disappear after joining the force: "At some point, you are so focused in that the friends you used to have, they don't understand, or maybe they think it's you who have changed, and then there's the issue of talking about work information. It's nice to have people who understand what you do."

Do Female Officers Face More Stress?

There is a debate about whether female officers face more stress than male officers do. In their seminal piece on female officer stress, Merry Morash and Robin Haarr found that while women did face unique stressors that men did not, they did not face more overall stress.[11] A more recent article found the same: The rates of stress and burnout that men and women face are similar.[12]

Another found that female police officers who are married with children have the highest stress levels. There are actually several reasons why.

Police families do face unique struggles in balancing family and work. This is especially true because women are disproportionately responsible for the caregiving and household tasks in most American families. Defined by Arlie Russell Hoschschild as the "second shift,"[13] to denote the domestic and childcare labor required of full-time employed wives and mothers, the bulk of household labor still resides with women. This makes it difficult to compete in policing organizations that are "highly structured, paramilitary organizations" adhering to a "traditional, albeit unrealistic orientation, which assumed that familial and work responsibilities are distinctive and independent."[14] Interestingly, Carol Archbold and Kimberly Hassell published an article in 2009 titled "Paying the Marriage Tax: An Examination of the Barriers to the Promotion of Female Police Officers," exposing how marriage in "cop couples" deters women from the promotional process.[15] Dubbed the marriage tax, they learned that female police officers married to other police face a variety of restrictions regarding their decisions to seek promotion, including scheduling, shift work, and anti-nepotism programs.

Taken together, it is not surprising that more than half of the women who left policing cited their primary reason for leaving as wanting to spend more time with their families and caring for their children. Jessie Pritts left a large municipal department to work at a smaller agency that provided a better work-life balance for her and her children.

> I don't regret any of it. I mean, if I didn't have the kids, I would still be over there. But I wanted to be a part of their lives. Why would I have them and not? When my daughter was really little, I kept having to send her here and here. Then, I would get held over and eventually I was like, "This is ridiculous! I have not seen her for a day."

Jessie did admit that her move came at a major cost to her career: "I started at a place I would have loved to stay forever and I would have been way up in the ranks by now. Here I have moved down." Mark Pogrebin and colleagues remind us that women are pressured to choose between fulfilling society's expectations for marriage and motherhood and those defined by their career.[16] While social expectations of men and women are becoming less traditional, women today still comprise the vast majority of childcare givers and nurturers. The strain felt by all working mothers of trying to meet both career and family demands may add to the stress that women face in policing, especially when coupled with the irregular work hours and shift work inherent in policing.

One influential theory of the 1990s, career development theory, suggests that while men and women have similar career aspirations and motivations, women make alternative career choices based on their conformity to societal expectations and their personal upbringing. Women have more constraints on their time, based on spousal attitudes and support and childcare responsibilities, favoring men who have fewer draws on their time. This is tough because women who opt out of the workforce for a short time period may be demonized as not being willing to make a long-term commitment to police work. When women resign, it also endangers efforts to increase female representation within police agencies, leading to greater tokenism. The amount of visibility and isolation of today's women officers appears to depend on the legacy of previous generations of women police. Becky Boutt discussed how important her mentor was in her success:

> I have a sergeant who is female and who has, through the hard times of being ostracized in the department or going through a challenging situation, has always been there to motivate me, to put confidence in me that I am doing the right thing. . . . She gives me a lot of tasks to do and expands my responsibilities and gives me a pat on the shoulder. . . . I think she is one of the biggest contributors to my successful career so far.

Many women I interviewed in the 2000s worked in agencies that had previously only had a few women. Their experiences were very different from women who worked in agencies that had always hired women. In fact, their experiences were similar to women who entered policing in the 1980s. This idea has not been explored in policing previously. Instead, researchers have looked at the percentage of women currently in the agency to gauge visibility and isolation. In sum, the question about men and women in policing and who has more stress is moot; in reality, both men and women who do the job face considerable stress, both on and off the job. Coping with it and balancing the needs of family and work is important to the modern law enforcement officer.

Availability of Coping Mechanisms

Police have a reputation for having dark humor following traumatic calls and events. It is important to recognize that this is a form of coping with stress by displacing the emotion through cursing, joking, or escaping after the fact. It is also a learned way of expressing emotion in police work. In her analysis of officer reactions to the stressors of police work, Susan Martin found that male officers "guard themselves for the emotionally wrenching situations they face with slogans like 'don't let it get to you' and seek acceptable manly outlets such as heavy drinking, cursing, sexual exploits, fast driving, and other dangerous sports, and displacing anger onto others."[17] In her article "10 Ways Law Enforcement Ruined Me as a Woman," Kathryn Loving humorously describes how becoming a police officer changes a woman emotionally:

> Being a police officer changes our entire way of thinking and affects our psyche. It transforms us for life, not just for the duration of duty. Sometimes this projects a hard edge. At times, our femininity gets lost in the equation. My mother would say the job has hardened me and I have lost all refinement. How does that song go—conceal, don't feel? Maybe she is right, but I am still fighting to keep my womanhood. . . . Kicking and screaming all the way.[18]

Coping mechanisms can be divided into positive and destructive strategies. Positive strategies strengthen relationships or create a plan of action for dealing with stressors in the work environment. Psychological counseling services and reliance on the family are positive coping mechanisms. While balancing family and work can be very stressful for officers with families, having family support also reduces stress among officers. Rita Larkin, a patrol officer, mentioned that having her father as her police mentor has been really helpful: "You have to have those people that you can trust and that you can throw ideas off of. My biggest one has actually been my dad because I can call and just vent it out."

Others rely on their police spouses and intimate partners. Being a police officer married to another police officer may have distinct advantages. You always have someone who will understand your work and the challenges of shift work. They have the same friends and understand police humor. You have a built-in supporter who can give you advice and feedback without overreacting. Kathy Geiger argued that not talking about the stressors of policing is dangerous, as she watched her husband battle with silence. She argued that either it will "eat at you or it will make you crazy."

Officers working in stressful work environments long term may benefit from counseling to deal with the negative emotions and outcomes that are inherent in this work. To counter the stigmas in policing associated with help seeking, researchers have suggested requiring periodic counseling for all police officers.[19] In the article "Mental Health and Peer Support in Law Enforcement," Officer Jeff Watson supported this idea, arguing that "integrated mental health services and appropriate peer support programs for all law enforcement officers" is necessary to help police officers survive their careers.[20] One of the major obstacles to police seeking counseling and other mental health services is trust. Watson explains, "The law enforcement profession does not hold mental health professionals in high regard. Historically speaking, mental health professionals were the last stop before a law enforcement officer was fired, suspended, or had their firearm officially taken from them."[21] For this reason, he recommends the training and utilization of peer counselors to help with the stress of police work.

Physical exercise is another way that police respond to stress in a healthy way. Danielle Lund discussed how working out made her mentally and physically stronger: "I work out all the time. I go to the gym six days a week. That is huge for me. . . . It's a great release for me; it's something that really gets me motivated, wakes me up, gets me started for the day. I am the only police officer you know who does yoga."

Another way of coping was keeping policing in perspective. Rita Larkin, a patrol officer with a medium-sized municipal department, discussed the importance of a separation between work and personal time: "A lot of the people at work, policing is all they do. They eat, breathe, sleep, and live law enforcement." Isla Thomas, a patrol officer in a large municipal police agency, described a similar process in avoiding taking police work home with her:

> I try to just take every call. Start the call. Finish the call. End it, and not think about it. If you dwell on things, then you are going to think, "Oh, I did this wrong or this could have happened," or, "Oh my God, I almost got shot." Then you start getting nervous and worried, and then as you are driving, you hit poles because you are thinking about other things. If you just drop what you are doing for that call and be done with it, it seems to help me. . . . You have to take the job off here. If you wear the clothes home, you are still a cop.

Destructive coping strategies involve isolation from friends and family and increased substance abuse, such as smoking and drinking. Officer Mary Navarro admitted that smoking helps. Denise White, a patrol officer, casually responded that how she copes with police stress is "alcohol." Truthfully, alcohol has been commonly found to be a coping mechanism used by police officers to respond to the demands of the job. In their study of officer stress, the National Institute of Justice reported that officers admitted increased anxiety and alcohol use within five years of police employment.[22] Of course, this may have just as much to do with shift work as it does with coping. Officers who work unpredictable shifts, especially midnight shifts that disrupt sleep patterns, often use alcohol and other sedatives to sleep and caffeine and legal stimulants to stay awake. The concern is that officers who employ destructive coping mechanisms like drinking are more likely to burn out and withdraw altogether.[23] Burnout is defined as "a prolonged response to continual emotional and interpersonal stressors at the workplace."[24] Mary Navarro, a campus police officer, described how she knew she was struggling to manage the stress associated with police work: "Some days I will be motivated on my days off and I will do stuff and then there are other days I'll just sleep and think about having a different job." Whether stress leads to burnout has a lot to do with the individual officers' perceptions of the stressors and their ability to manage it.

Domestic Violence

The stress of police work can also affect family life at home in police families. A very recent study published in the *Brigham Young University Law Review* found that domestic violence is more common in police families and that as a result of their training, it is more difficult to prosecute and potentially more dangerous to victims.[25] According to the National Coalition against Domestic Violence, domestic violence is willful intimidation, physical assault, battery, sexual assault, and/or other abusive behavior as part of a systematic pattern of power and control perpetrated by one intimate partner against another. It includes physical violence, sexual violence, psychological violence, and emotional abuse.[26] In one study, about 29 percent of law enforcement officers reported that they had been physically violent with a partner or family member in the past.[27] Another study put the percentage closer to 9 percent of officers who had perpetrated violence against their partner.[28] Calling it the "best-kept secret shame of policing," Ellen Kirschman, author of *I Love a Cop*, explains that when police confront struggles in their family lives, they attempt to solve them with the same level of control and authority that they do police work.[29] Faced with a lack of compliance, they may respond physically or through orders, intimidation, and commands. In 2003, the International Association of Chiefs of Police wrote a model policy for handling domestic violence perpetrated by police officers, but policies are only as good as their enforcement. A study of police officer–perpetrated violence in Baltimore found that 80 percent of cases that were referred to Internal Affairs for investigation were dropped, suggesting that there is more work to be done in improving the police response to officer-perpetrated domestic violence. Some agencies have specific interventions such as requiring officers who have allegations of domestic violence against them to attend mandatory counseling or to put them on light duty while investigating the charges. Others require that command staff or Internal Affairs units be notified of any allegations of officer-involved domestic violence. It is important to note that family violence in a problem in every segment of the world, and the research is not clear regarding whether the stressors of policing contribute to family violence. What is clear is that any domestic violence is too much.

In conclusion, work-life balance is important. The nature and structure of police work coupled with long hours and shift work contribute to the stress police face. This stress, when not properly managed, leads to alcoholism, heart disease, divorce, and many more negative outcomes. Police agree that one avenue of change is reducing the stigma of coping through healthy mechanisms, including counseling. Mary Navarro, a patrol officer for a university department, had this advice:

> When I was on a ride-along and I wanted to be a cop, the cop said, "You know this is really hard if you want to do this, besides the stuff on the street." I never knew what they were getting at . . . and now that I have gone through, its like, "Dang, I wish I would have known. . . . I probably would not have ended up divorced." . . . I wish I had read the book, *Emotional Survival for Law Enforcement*. I'm an FTO now and one of the things I have done . . . is make them read that book . . . or you will end up looking around and all you'll have left is your job. I wish someone had said that to me. . . . Now I understand.

2000s Summary

Today female police officers have broken almost every barrier that existed since their integration in the 1970s. Their representation is strong at nearly 4,000 state police, 19,400 sheriff's deputies, and 55,300 local police officers. Coupled with 18,200 federal agents, that means there were more than 100,000 female law enforcement officers in the United States by 2010. These women have also knocked down leadership barriers. Anne Kirkpatrick, chief of the Oakland, California, police department, is one of 169 women leading the nation's top fifteen hundred police agencies. The representation of women at the top spot in major police agencies across the nation suggests a leap forward in the progression for women. However, female representation nationwide is slipping from its high mark and the climb up the ladder in police agencies is still slowed by the brass ceiling. Only four of the very largest municipal departments (Detroit, Philadelphia, District of Columbia, and Chicago) have more than 20 percent of their sworn ranks as women in blue and many smaller police agencies have never hired a female police officer.[30] This suggests that agencies have more work to do to recruit a diverse pool of applicants representative of the communities they police.

As law enforcement agencies attempt to keep strong, diverse rosters, family-friendly policies are increasingly important provisions to millennial recruits, who so far spend more time with their children than previous generations of parents. Much of the current research suggests that relationship building and familial time is much more important to employees of this generation than material wealth.[31] For example, today's millennial fathers spend an average of 4.3 hours per workday with their children under thirteen, significantly more than their age counterparts in 1977, who spent an average of 2.4 hours per workday with their children. Mothers are also spending considerably more time with their children.[32] Policing is way behind the Fortune 500 companies in making family-friendly accommodations, and the next generations of employees are increasingly opting for agencies that allow for a healthier work-life balance.

The question of whether women bring something unique or different to policing than men is the question that has not yet been settled. A recent article published by the Associated Press titled "The Growing Number of Women Leading US Police Departments" exemplified this debate. Dawn Layman, the president of the National Association of Women Law Enforcement Executives, argued, "I think females bring something different to the table. The goal is to diversify the table. We don't want a cookie-cutter. We learn more, we bring more to the table when it is diverse." In response, Dorothy Moses Schulz argued, "They [women] are supposed to be the healers. It's a terrible burden. I don't think it's based on any solid research; I think that's based on a feeling that it is going to set a different tone."[33] These two quotes perfectly sum up the debate of modern female officers. If women do bring something unique to policing, we have to ask at what cost. This debate will have to be settled by the next generation of female police officers.

What has been settled is that women are as capable of doing police work as male officers. Women who entered policing in the 2000s refuse to accept the idea that they are incapable of doing the job. Empirical research and officers' experiences have repeatedly confirmed that women make an important and meaningful impact in the field. The conclusion of this book, "The Current Status of Women Police and Future Directions," takes a look at the current trends and gives the reader some ideas about what the future holds for female police officers.

Conclusion

The Current Status of Women Police and Future Directions

W̲HEN CONSIDERING THE FUTURE DIRECTION of women in policing, it is important to take a moment and reflect on the crisis of police legitimacy. In the past several years, the law enforcement community has faced considerable scrutiny about how they do their job. At no other time in history has society placed such emphasis on the accountability of police behavior. Even the president of the United States publicly addressed the violence between police and citizens of color, suggesting body-worn cameras as a way of holding police accountable for the violence:

> When all this takes place, more than fifty years after the passage of the Civil Rights Act, we cannot simply turn away and dismiss those in peaceful protest as troublemakers or paranoid. We can't simply dismiss it as a symptom of political correctness or reverse racism. To have your experience denied like that, dismissed by those in authority, dismissed perhaps even by your white friends and coworkers and fellow church members, again and again and again, it hurts. Surely we can see that, all of us. We also know what Chief Brown has said is true, that so much of the tensions between police departments and minority communities that they serve is because we ask the police to do too much and we ask too little of ourselves.[1]

The conflict between police and communities of color must be settled, as the United States population is increasingly diverse and police-community relationships are necessary for safe communities. According to the United States Census Bureau, slightly more than one-third of the population reported their race or ethnicity as something other than non-Hispanic white in

2010. In addition, people of color increased from 86.9 million to 111.9 million between 2000 and 2010. That is a 29 percent increase.[2] Those numbers are likely to continue to increase. It is apparent that law enforcement is not keeping up with the diversification of communities in the United States. One police administrator argued that when it comes to diversity, many departments are guilty of "failing to understand many of these changes, and still trying to conduct business as usual, we find the tools and rules that worked before don't work now."[3]

Looking to the future of policing, one solution is to make police departments more representative of the communities they police. This solution is embedded in the recommendations of the 2015 President's Task Force on 21st Century Policing: "to create a workforce that contains a broad range of diversity including race, gender, language, life experience, and cultural background to improve understanding and effectiveness in dealing with all communities."[4] While the idea of making police departments more representative of the neighborhoods they police is not a new solution or one without critique, the diversification of police departments along with police reform has the potential to transform modern police agencies. In many places this shift has already begun and women have played an important role in this transformation.

The positive benefits that women bring to policing are evident. Women are strong communicators and less likely to use force against citizens, especially excessive force; their increased representation in policing means more peaceful police-citizen relationships.[5] They are also less likely to be named in citizen complaints and lawsuits, which saves agencies and taxpayers millions.[6] Female officers are more likely to take reports of domestic violence and sexual assault seriously and to follow up with reports, preventing future violent attacks for victims. In other words, they are less likely to dismiss reports of domestic violence and sexual assault from survivors.[7]

In addition to the positive benefits women bring to the communities they police, there is growing evidence that women serve as change catalysts inside police organizations. Their presence destabilizes the monolithic male working-class culture, resulting in agencies that are more open to change and reform.[8] As change catalysts, women have the potential to challenge the way things have always been done by integrating diverse ways of knowing based on their socialization experiences. In response, organizations are forced to rethink how they do their work and make changes accordingly. This may involve innovation in policy, increased creativity in problem solving, and improved decision making within the organization.[9] Agencies with female leadership and greater female representation benefit from innovative recruitment and retention policies, the establishment of family medical leave and light duty, maternity policies, and more inclusive leadership styles.[10]

After reading the stories of the women in this book, one thing is clear—despite the struggles that women face to survive in the "all-boys club" of policing, not only do women survive, but most also thrive in this almost exclusively male occupation. That is evidenced by the 58,000 female police officers nationwide. Several factors have contributed to the increased representation of women in policing in the past two decades, including the strong leadership and professionalism of forerunners who blazed the way, the strengthening of discrimination and harassment laws, and a push toward diversifying police departments to make them more representative of the communities they police.

It is important as we consider the future of women in policing that we do not take past efforts for granted, as progress has recently stalled. The most current figures suggest that the representation of women in police agencies has actually declined from 14 percent in 1999 to 12 percent in 2013.[11] This decline has also been seen in supervisory and command positions.[12] The most recent Law Enforcement and Management Statistics Survey points out that the percentage of females working in first-line supervisory positions (9.5 percent) was less than that among sworn personnel overall (12.2 percent).[13] How do we explain this recent halt in progress?

Several factors are likely contributors to the underemployment of female police officers. These issues need to be addressed to ensure future generations of female leadership. First, recruitment practices of police agencies tend to overemphasize upper-body strength and the traditional crime-fighting image of the police.[14] The overemphasis in the testing process on upper-body strength physiologically disadvantages women. One of the major frustrations with this obstacle is that we really don't know what the necessary physical requirements are to predict successful policing. Researchers analyzed the physical ability of recruits in a Midwestern police agency and concluded that while women did fail the physical ability test more often than men, the physical ability test used did not depict the actual physical tasks that police officers perform on the job.[15] Why require police recruits to test for tasks they won't really do? This is an issue in policing that is still not settled. Many departments have opted for more modern tests that account for age and gender in the requirements without any negative consequences in job performance, leading many to argue that the outdated emphasis on upper-body strength used by some agencies is for the express purpose of excluding women. Testing requirements need to be carefully examined by agencies interested in expanding their recruitment of female police as the Justice Department has begun filing suits against agencies whose tests exclude women. For example, the Corpus Christi police department settled with a group of eighteen women who alleged that the physical fitness test discriminated against them and the US Justice Department sued the Pennsylvania State Police for the same reason.[16]

The National Center for Women and Policing argues that another reason for the underemployment of women in policing is that the media stereotype of the police conveys the message to potential recruits that the only response to fighting crime is through the use of force and that skills, such as communication and mediation, are not as highly valued. Research has found that women are most likely to apply for jobs where they have the opportunity to help others.[17] One way of combating the myth that policing is only crime fighting is through a targeted recruitment strategy that clarifies what real police work entails. Targeted recruitment strategies, such as using a diverse recruitment team and materials, recruiting from women's colleges or liberal arts colleges, and citizen outreach classes that invite citizens to attend classes taught by police officers, have been successful in increasing the number of women and minorities who apply for police work.[18] Agencies interested in becoming more diverse should consider a targeted recruitment strategy.

The expiration of consent decrees in large, urban departments may be another reason why we are seeing decreases in female officer representation. Once police agencies were no longer required to hire women and minorities, they stopped. However, we must acknowledge that consent decrees only get female officers in the door of policing, and they are usually put into effect after an agency has engaged in a discriminatory pattern of behavior to trigger a consent decree ordered by the courts. This focus on getting them in the door (i.e., recruitment) may be masking the problem of retention.[19] Research confirms that agencies under a consent decree have learned to hide their high female turnover rate by quickly replenishing their female roster.[20] This gives the illusion that the agency has taken consent decrees seriously in the recruitment phase without making any real changes in their long-term employee retention patterns. The reality is that being forced to hire diverse recruits does not force an agency to retain a diverse workforce.

To retain a diverse workforce, agencies must address the continued resistance to women in the police culture. Harassment and a glass ceiling regarding promotion both contribute to the underrepresentation of women in policing. In a recent survey, three-quarters of female police officers agreed that "the culture in police agencies is male-dominated and not very woman friendly."[21] There is considerable evidence that the harassment and discrimination that was once blatant, malicious, and widespread has become less overt and the exception rather than the rule.[22]

The increased representation of women in the workplace, coupled with the elimination of overt sex discrimination and harassment, has created additional opportunities for women in policing. Women are accomplishing new "firsts" every day, as exhibited by the 2016 headline, "Growing Number of Women Leading US Police Departments."[23] In 2015 alone, women headed the

Drug Enforcement Administration, Secret Service, DC Metropolitan Police Department, US Park Police, the FBI's Washington Field Office, US Marshals Service, and Amtrak Police Department.[24] In her 2003 book *Breaking the Brass Ceiling: Women Police Chiefs and Their Paths to the Top*, Dorothy Moses Schulz found 175 female chiefs in myriad departments, making up 1 percent of police chiefs nationwide. Within large police agencies, sworn women currently hold 7 percent of top command positions, 9 percent of supervisory positions, and 14 percent of line operation positions. These are all indicators that women are making great strides in promotion. However, with more than half the agencies surveyed reporting no women in top command or supervisory positions, it is clear that more work needs to be done. Without the guidance of seasoned veterans to teach rookies the ropes, female officers will continue to be excluded from informal networks important to securing promotion. For many women, the biggest obstacle to promotion is the ability to balance the needs of their families with their professional goals.

This leads us to the last major contributor to the underrepresentation of women in policing: the high turnover rate of women in police agencies. When faced with male officer resistance, shift work, and the difficulties of balancing their family and professional lives, there is considerable evidence that women simply opt for other forms of social service work or for police work in agencies that are more family friendly. Agencies must consider more family-friendly policies, including the formalization of light-duty and maternity policies, flexible scheduling including part-time police work, and childcare options such as on-site daycare. The fact that some police agencies have beaten the odds, with much higher percentages of female officers than the national average (between 10 and 13 percent) because of their supportive work environment (i.e., Tucson, Arizona, 29 percent; Miami Beach, Florida, 28 percent; Madison, Wisconsin, 26 percent), proves that departments can be family friendly while also balancing the needs of officer safety, overtime pay to cover officers' shifts, and the struggle to meet mandatory strength minimums.

In looking at future directions for women in policing, the obstacles discussed are no match for the women who wear the uniform every day. Progress has slowed, and it is apparent that there is work that still needs to be done before the rank and file and supervisory structure in policing represent the diversity of the communities that they serve. The brave officers whose stories are represented in this book have more than laid the groundwork. They have fragmented the once monolithic police culture and infused it with new ideas about how to do policing, including greater empathy for crime victims and more peaceful police-citizen relationships. They have challenged the ethos that policing requires nothing but brawn to get the job done while proving that women have what it takes to do the job.

Looking toward the future of policing, the profession needs the positive benefits that the next generation of female police will provide. (For those interested in becoming a police officer, see the box of advice below.) Despite falling crime rates, fear of crime is high, and, more important, the legitimacy of police is being challenged with increasingly strained relationships between the police and citizens, prompting the Black Lives Matter movement and protests against the police in a dozen major cities in 2016. The next generation of police officers faces considerable challenges to reestablish trust with the public.[25] I have no doubt that the efforts of women police nationwide will play a large role in this process, and I will use a story to tell you why: A female police officer I interviewed recently told me about her best day on the job. She was at an elementary school doing a program for the children, and, as Halloween was coming up, she chatted with the kids about their costumes and trick-or-treating plans. One of the kids asked if she was going to dress up, and she replied by asking the children what they thought she should be. One suggested a cat. Another suggested a zombie. Finally, one little boy excitedly suggested a superhero. A little girl sitting next to him scoffed, saying, "She is a superhero every day. She is a policewoman!" Simply by doing police work every day, female officers are changing the concept of what police do and they are encouraging the next generation of female police superheroes.

Interested in Becoming a Female Police Officer?

My advice to those of you interested in law enforcement as a career is to do your homework. Find an agency that does not overemphasize upper-body strength as an entrance requirement. That is likely the agency's nice way of saying "no thank you" to women. Agencies with more modern tests that account for age and gender are likely more progressive and female friendly. Also take a look at how women are utilized in the agency. Are they confined to women's work such as specializing in women and children's victimization, or are women represented in most bureaus and specializations in the agency? Finally, the advice that female officers and administrators always ask me to relay to women interested in policing is this: Policing is a great profession that is rewarding and exciting, and offers great benefits, but it comes at the cost of requiring shift work, missing holidays and birthdays, and being self-motivated and willing to get your hands dirty.

Appendix

Additional Resources

National Center for Women and Policing
http://www.womenandpolicing.org/

National Association of Women Law Enforcement Executives (NAWLEE)
http://nawlee.org/

International Association of Women Police (IAWP)
http://iawp.org/

National Organization of Black Women in Law Enforcement
http://www.nobwlenational.org/

Women in Federal Law Enforcement
http://www.wifle.org/

Notes

Preface

1. Diane Diamond, "More Female Officers, Please," *Diane Diamond* (blog), March 30, 2015, http://dianedimond.net/more-female-police-officers-please/.

2. Brian Reaves, *Local Police Departments, 2013: Personnel, Policies, and Practices* (Washington, DC: Bureau of Justice Statistics, May 2015), accessed August 15, 2016, http://www.bjs.gov/content/pub/pdf/lpd13ppp.pdf; United States Department of Labor, "Traditional and Nontraditional Occupations" (Washington, DC: Census, 2014), https://www.dol.gov/wb/stats/Nontraditional%20Occupations.pdf.

3. Cara Rabe-Hemp, "Survival in an 'All Boys Club': Policewomen and Their Fight for Acceptance," *Policing* 31 (2008): 257.

4. Rabe-Hemp, "Survival," 257.

Introduction

1. "Police Matron's Job Is Not a Sinecure—What with Preventing Suicides and Lodging Vagrants Her Life's a Busy One," *New York Times*, February 16, 1908, http://query.nytimes.com/mem/archivefree/pdf?res=9802E7D7173EE233A25755C1A9649C946997D6CF.

2. "Police Matron's Job Is Not a Sinecure."

3. "Police Matron's Job Is Not a Sinecure."

4. "Want Naughty Plays Stopped," *Los Angeles Times*, March 15, 1911, I15.

5. "First Woman Policeman," *Los Angeles Times*, September 14, 1910.

6. Robert Snow, *Policewomen Who Made History* (Lanham, MD: Rowman & Littlefield, 2010), 2.

7. Sheila Rothman, *Women's Proper Place: A History of Changing Ideals and Practices 1870 to Present* (New York: Basic Books, 1978), 68.

8. Nicole Hahn Rafter, *Partial Justice: Women, Prisons and Social Control* (New Brunswick, NJ: Transaction, 1990).

9. "As to the Affairs of the South Prison," *Journal of the House of Representatives for the State of Indiana*, April 14, 1869, 227.

10. Enoch Wines and Theodore Dwight, *Report on the Prisons and Reformatories of the United States and Canada* (Albany, NY: Van Benthuysen and Sons, 1867), 123–24.

11. "Police Matron's Job Is Not a Sinecure."

12. Joseph Balkin, "Why Policemen Don't Like Policewomen," *Journal of Police Science and Administration* 16 (1988): 29–38.

13. Frank Morn, *Forgotten Reformer: Robert McClaughry and Criminal Justice Reform in Nineteenth-Century America* (Lanham, MD: University Press of America, 2010).

14. Dorothy Moses Schulz, *From Social Worker to Crimefighter: Women in United States Municipal Policing* (Westport, CT: Praeger, 1995).

15. Marie Owens, "Enforcement of the Child Labor Laws," *Chicago Daily Tribune*, July 28, 1901, https://www.newspapers.com/newspage/28521967/.

16. "The Only Woman Detective on the Chicago Police Force," *Chicago Tribune*, October 28, 1906, http://archives.chicagotribune.com/1906/10/28/page/59/article/the-only-woman-detective-on-the-chicago-foree.

17. Schulz, *From Social Worker to Crimefighter*.

18. Peter Horne, "Policewomen: Their First Century and the New Era," *Police Chief* 73, no. 9 (2006): 23–32, accessed August 15, 2016, http://policechiefmagazine.org/magazine/index.cfm?fuseaction=display_arch&article_id=1000&issue_id=92006.

19. Schulz, *From Social Worker to Crimefighter*.

20. Alice Stebbins Wells, "Personal History of Los Angeles's First Policewoman," *Los Angeles Police Association's Bulletin* (October 1940): 5.

21. Catherin H. Milton, *Women in Policing* (Washington, DC: The Police Foundation, 1972).

22. Bertha H. Smith, "The Policewoman," *Good Housekeeping* 52, March 1911, 296–98.

23. "Portland to Ban Public Dances," *Oregonian*, November 1912, 15.

24. Mary Hamilton, *Policewoman: Her Service and Ideals* (New York: Frederick A. Stokes, 1924), 4.

25. Los Angeles Police Department, *Annual Report, Police Department, City of Los Angeles, California for the Fiscal Year ending June 30, 1914* (Los Angeles: Los Angeles Police Department, 1914), 26, 40–49.

26. Milton, *Women in Policing*, 23.

27. Schulz, *From Social Worker to Crimefighter*.

28. Chloe Owings, *Women Police* (Montclair, NJ: Patterson Smith, 1969).

29. August Vollmer, "Meet the Lady Cop," *Survey Graphic*, March 15, 1930.

30. Owings, *Women Police*, 100–112.

31. Josephine Nelson, "On the Policewoman's Beat," *Independent Woman*, May 1936, www.sameshield.com/press/sspress112.html.

32. "Good Housekeeping Finds Out What a Policewoman Does," *Good Housekeeping* 113, December 1941, 26–28.

33. "Good Housekeeping Finds Out What a Policewoman Does," 26.

34. "Some Cops Have Lovely Legs," *Saturday Evening Post*, December 24, 1949.

35. Schulz, *From Social Worker to Crimefighter.*

36. Schulz, *From Social Worker to Crimefighter.*

37. Theresa M. Melchionne, "Report of Committee 'A' Organization and Administrative Considerations," in *Proceedings of Workshop for Policewomen*, ed. Nelson Watson and Robert Walker (Washington, DC: International Association of Chiefs of Police, 1966), 1.

38. Milton, *Women in Policing.*

39. Alice Fleming, *New on the Beat* (New York: Coward, McCann, and Geoghegan, 1975), 221.

40. Felicia Shpritzer, "A Case for the Promotion of Policewomen in the City of New York," *Police* 5 (July/August 1961): 50–57.

41. Title VII of the 1964 Civil Rights Act, 42 USC 2000a, 2a (1972).

42. *Griggs v. Duke Power Company*, 401 US 424 (1971).

43. *Harless v. Duck*, 619F2d 611 (1980).

44. Daniel J. Bell, "Policewomen: Myth and Reality," *Journal of Police Science and Administration* 10 (1982): 112–20.

45. George L. Kelling and Mark H. Moore, *The Evolving Strategy of Policing* (Washington, DC: National Institute of Justice, 1988).

46. Schulz, *From Social Worker to Crimefighter.*

47. President's Commission on Law Enforcement and Administration of Justice, *The Challenge of Crime in a Free Society* (Washington, DC: US Government Printing Office, 1967), 125.

48. Snow, *Policewomen*, 48.

49. Susan Martin, *Breaking and Entering: Policewomen on Patrol* (Berkeley: University of California Press, 1980), 46–47.

50. Harold W. Bartlett and Arthur Rosenblum, *Policewomen Effectiveness* (Denver, CO: Denver Civil Service Commission, 1977); Peter Bloch and Daniel Anderson, *Policewomen on Patrol* (Washington, DC: Police Foundation, 1974); California Highway Patrol, *Women Traffic Officer Project: Final Report* (Sacramento: California Highway Patrol, 1976); Lawrence Sherman, "Causes of Police Behavior: The Current Police State of Quantitative Research," *Journal of Crime and Delinquency* 17 (1980): 69–100; Joyce L. Sichel, Lucy N. Friedman, Janet C. Quint, and M. E. Smith, *Women on Patrol: A Pilot Study of Police Performance in New York City* (Washington, DC: National Institute of Law Enforcement and Criminal Justice, 1978).

51. Snow, *Policewomen.*

52. "Women on Patrol?" *Indianapolis News*, September 16, 1968.

53. Susan E. Martin, *On the Move: The Status of Women in Policing* (Washington, DC: Police Foundation, 1990).

Introduction to Section I

1. Brian Reaves, "Campus Law Enforcement, 2011–12, NCJ 248028," Bureau of Justice Statistics, January 2015, accessed March 13, 2017, https://www.bjs.gov/index.cfm?ty=pbdetail&iid=5216; Brian Reaves, *Local Police Departments, 2013: Personnel, Policies, and Practices* (Washington, DC: Bureau of Justice Statistics, May 2015), accessed August 15, 2016, http://www.bjs.gov/content/pub/pdf/lpd13ppp.pdf.

2. Dan Balz, "24 States Face Orders to Relieve Overcrowding," *Washington Post*, June 16, 1983, accessed August 15, 2016, https://www.washingtonpost.com/archive/politics/1981/06/16/24-states-face-orders-to-relieve-overcrowding/e8bd2eb8-33c9-4684-a255-21eece40939d/.

3. Samuel Walker, *Sense and Nonsense about Crime, Drugs, and Communities* (Stamford, CT: Cengage Learning, 2015), 107.

4. James Q. Wilson and George L. Kelling, "Broken Windows: The Police and Neighborhood Safety," *Atlantic Monthly*, March 1982, 3.

5. Peter Horne, *Women in Law Enforcement*, second edition (Springfield, IL: Charles C. Thomas, 1980).

6. Juanita L. Wehrle-Einhorn, "Gender, Stress, and Self in the Work-Family Role System," PhD diss., University of Kansas, 1980.

Chapter 1

1. Hollie McKay, "Angie Dickinson 'Felt Exploited' in '*Police Woman*' but Says Women's Roles in Crimes Dramas Have 'Evolved,'" *Fox News Entertainment*, June 23, 2014, accessed August 15, 2016, http://www.foxnews.com/entertainment/2014/06/23/angie-dickinson-felt-exploited-in-police-woman-but-says-womens-roles-in-crimes.html.

2. "Obama Marks 1972 Law Lifting Education Barriers to Girls," Reuters, June 23, 2010, accessed August 15, 2016, http://www.reuters.com/article/us-usa-obama-sports-gender-idUSBRE85M0I720120623.

3. Susan E. Martin and Nancy C. Jurik, *Doing Justice, Doing Gender: Women in Legal and Criminal Justice Occupations* (Thousand Oaks, CA: Sage, 2007).

4. Susan E. Martin, *On the Move: The Status of Women in Policing* (Washington, DC: Police Foundation, 1990), xii.

5. Virginia Armat, "Policewomen in Action," *Saturday Evening Post*, July 1975, 87.

Chapter 2

1. Patricia Lunneborg, *Women Police Officer: Current Career Profile* (Springfield, IL: Charles C. Thomas, 1989), 36.

2. *Smith vs. the City of East Cleveland*, 363 F. Supp. 1131 (1973).

3. Illinois Law Enforcement Training and Standards Board, *Peace Officer Wellness Evaluation Report (POWER)*, 2016, accessed August 15, 2016, http://www.nemrt.com/downloads/POWERTEST.pdf.

4. Belton Texas Police Department, "Police Officer Agility Test," accessed August 15, 2016, http://www.beltontexas.gov/DocumentCenter/Home/View/428.

5. *Thomas v. City of Evanston*, 881 F.2d 382, 1985, 485.

6. *Thomas v. City of Evanston*, 432.

7. Catherine Milton, Ava Abramowitz, Laura Crites, Margaret Gates, Ellen Mintz, and Georgette Sandler, *Women in Policing: A Manual* (Washington, DC: Police Foundation, 1974), 67.

8. Susan E. Martin, "The Changing Status of Women Officers," in *The Changing Roles of Women in the Criminal Justice System*, ed. Imogene L. Moyer, second edition (Prospect Heights, IL: Waveland, 1992), 293.

9. Robin N. Haarr, "Factors Affecting the Decision of Police Recruits to 'Drop Out' of Police Work," *Police Quarterly* 8 (December 2005): 431–53; Anastasia Prokos and Irene Padavic, "'There Oughtta Be a Law against Bitches': Masculinity Lessons in Police Academy Training," *Gender, Work & Organization* 9 (2002): 439–59.

10. Cara E. Rabe-Hemp, "Survival in an 'All Boys Club': Policewomen and Their Fight for Acceptance," *Policing* 31 (2008): 257.

11. Rabe-Hemp, "Survival," 257.

Chapter 3

1. Rosabeth M. Kanter, *Men and Women of the Corporation* (New York: Basic Books, 1977).

2. Cara Rabe-Hemp, "Survival in an 'All Boys Club': Policewomen and Their Fight for Acceptance," *Policing* 31 (2008): 262.

3. Rabe-Hemp, "Survival," 259.

4. Susan E. Martin, *Breaking and Entering: Policewomen on Patrol* (Berkeley: University of California Press, 1980); Catherine A. Riordan, Tamara Gross, and Cathlin C. Maloney, "Self-Monitoring, Gender, and the Personal Consequences of Impression Management," *American Behavioral Scientist* 37 (1994): 715–25.

5. Diane L. Pike, "Women in Police Academy Training: Some Aspects of Organizational Response," in *The Changing Roles of Women in the Criminal Justice System: Offenders, Victims, and Professionals*, ed. Imogene L. Moyer (Prospect Heights, IL: Waveland Press, 1985), 264; Susan Miller, *Gender and Community Policing: Walking the Talk* (Boston: Northeastern University Press, 1999), 70.

6. Rabe-Hemp, "Survival," 261.

7. Rabe-Hemp, "Survival," 261.

8. Rabe-Hemp, "Survival," 261.

9. Rabe-Hemp, "Survival," 261.

10. Rabe-Hemp, "Survival," 261.

11. Rabe-Hemp, "Survival," 259.

12. Rabe-Hemp, "Survival," 262.

13. Martin, *Breaking and Entering*, 219.

Chapter 4

1. Courtney A. Franklin, "Male Peer Support and the Police Culture: Understanding the Resistance and Opposition of Women in Policing," *Women and Criminal Justice* 16, no. 3 (2007): 1–25.

2. Malcolm Sparrow, Mark Moore, and David Kennedy, *Beyond 911: A New Era for Policing* (New York: Basic Books, 1990).

3. Philip Bonifacio. *The Psychological Effects of Police Work: A Psychodynamic Approach* (New York: Plenum Press, 1991), 39.

4. Victor E. Kappeler, Richard D. Sluder, and Geoffrey P. Alpert, *Breeding Deviant Conformity from Forces of Deviance: The Dark Side of Policing* (Long Grove, IL: Waveland Press, 1998).

5. Franklin, "Male Peer Support and Police Culture," 7.

6. Susan E. Martin, *Breaking and Entering: Policewomen on Patrol* (Berkeley: University of California Press, 1980); Jennifer Hunt, "The Logic of Sexism Among Police," *Women and Criminal Justice* 1 (1990): 3–30.

7. Peter Horne, *Women in Law Enforcement*, second edition (Springfield, IL: Charles C. Thomas, 1980), 71.

8. Peter Bloch and Daniel Anderson, *Policewomen on Patrol* (Washington, DC: Police Foundation, 1974); Lawrence Sherman, "Causes of Police Behavior: The Current Police State of Quantitative Research," *Journal of Crime and Delinquency* 17 (1980): 69–100.

9. Claudia Dreifus, "People Are Always Asking Me What I Am Trying to Prove," *Police Magazine* 3 (1980): 19–25.

10. Lesli K. Lord, "A Comparison of Male and Female Peace Officers' Stereotypic Perceptions of Women and Women Peace Officers," *Journal of Police Science and Administration* 14 (1986): 85.

11. Cara E. Rabe-Hemp, "Survival in an 'All Boys Club': Policewomen and Their Fight for Acceptance," *Policing* 31 (2008): 263.

12. Ralph Weisheit, "Women in the State Police: Concerns of Male and Female Officers," *Journal of Police Science and Administration* 15 (1987): 137–44.

13. Joanna Bunker Rohrbaugh, "Women in the Workplace," in *Crisis in American Institutions*, ed. Jerome H. Skolnick and Elliott Currie (Boston: Little, Brown, 1976), 215–30.

14. Weisheit, "Women in the State Police."

15. Rabe-Hemp, "Survival," 258.

16. Rabe-Hemp, "Survival," 258.

17. Patricia W. Remmington, "Women in the Police: Integration or Separation," *Qualitative Sociology* 6 (1983): 118–35.

18. Rosabeth M. Kanter, *Men and Women of the Corporation* (New York: Basic Books, 1977).

19. Rabe-Hemp, "Survival," 262.

20. Juanita Wehrle-Einhorn, "Gender, Stress, and Self in the Work-Family Role System," PhD diss., University of Kansas, 1980.

21. Remmington, "Women in the Police."

22. Martin, *Breaking and Entering.*

23. Martin, *Breaking and Entering,* 290.

24. Marty L. West, "Sexual Harassment Complaints: A Growing Concern for Police Management," *Journal of California Law Enforcement* 20 (1985): 55–58.

25. Rabe-Hemp, "Survival," 257.

26. California Highway Patrol, *Women Traffic Officer Project: Final Report* (Sacramento: California Highway Patrol, 1976), 69.

27. Lincoln Fry, "A Preliminary Examination of the Factors Related to Turnover of Women in Law Enforcement," *Journal of Police Science and Administration* 11 (1983): 149–55.

28. "Jury Awards $900,000 to Black Female Officer in Detroit Police Case," *Jet* 72 (April 27, 1987): 33.

Chapter 5

1. *Cops,* "Season 3, Episode 24, Pittsburgh, PA2," accessed August 15, 2016, http://www.pogdesign.co.uk/cat/Cops/Season-3/Episode-24.

2. New York City Police Department, *New York City Police Department Annual Firearms Discharge Report, 2012,* accessed August 15, 2016, http://www.nyc.gov/html/nypd/downloads/pdf/analysis_and_planning/nypd_annual_firearms_discharge_report_2012.pdf.

3. William Wilbanks, *True Heroines: Police Women Killed in the Line of Duty throughout the United States* (Paducah, KY: Turner Publishing Company, 2000), 29–31.

4. Wilbanks, *True Heroines.*

5. Jackie McElroy, "Officer Gail Cobb," http://www.mcjackie.com/cobb.html.

6. Virginia Armat, "Policewomen in Action," *Saturday Evening Post,* July 1975, 87.

7. Federal Bureau of Investigation, *Law Enforcement Officers Killed in the Line of Duty* (Washington, DC: FBI, 1971).

8. Federal Bureau of Investigation, "About *Law Enforcement Officers Killed and Assaulted,*" 2010, accessed August 15, 2016, http://cdn.ca9.uscourts.gov/datastore/library/2013/02/26/Mattos_LEOK.pdf.

9. Lorie A. Fridell and Antony M. Pate, *Death on Patrol: Felonious Homicides of American Police Officers, Final Report,* NCJ 159609 (Washington, DC: Police Foundation, 1995).

10. United States Department of Labor, Occupational Safety and Health Administration, "Critical Incident Stress Guide," accessed August 15, 2016, www.osha.gov/SLTC/emergencypreparedness/guides/critical.html.

11. Dan W. Clark and Elizabeth K. White, "Clinicians, Cops, and Suicide," in *Police Suicide: Tactics for Prevention,* ed. Dell L. Hackett and John M. Volanti (Springfield, IL: Charles C. Thomas Publishers, 2003), 16–36.

12. Laurence Miller, "Practical Strategies for Preventing Officer Suicide," *Law and Order* 3 (2006): 90–92.

13. Teresa T. Tate, "Police Suicide, What Can Be Done?" *Tears of a Cop*, accessed August 15, 2016, www.tearsofacop.com/police/articles/tate.html.

14. Anthony V. Bouza, *The Police Mystique: An Insider's Look at the Cops, Crime, and the Criminal Justice System* (New York: Plenum Press, 1990).

15. Armat, "Policewomen in Action."

16. Catherine Milton, Ava Abramowitz, Laura Crites, Margaret Gates, Ellen Mintz, and Georgette Sandler, *Women in Policing: A Manual* (Washington, DC: Police Foundation, 1974).

17. Lawrence Sherman, "An Evaluation of Policewomen on Patrol in a Suburban Police Department," *Journal of Police Science and Administration* 3 (1975): 434–38.

18. "Incident at the Airport," *Courier-Journal* (Louisville, Kentucky), January 21, 1973.

19. Cara E. Rabe-Hemp, "Survival in an 'All Boys Club': Policewomen and Their Fight for Acceptance," *Policing* 31 (2008): 263.

20. Peter Horne, *Women in Law Enforcement*, second edition (Springfield, IL: Charles C. Thomas, 1980), 40.

21. Armat, "Policewomen in Action," 87.

22. Rabe-Hemp, "Survival," 263.

Introduction to Section II

1. John J. Dilulio Jr., "The Coming of the Super–Predators," *Weekly Standard*, November 27, 1995.

2. Laurie Garrett, "Murder by Teens Has Soared Since '85," *New York Newsday*, February 18, 1995.

3. Carrie Johnson, "20 Years Later, Parts of Major Crime Bill Viewed as Terrible Mistake," *Morning Edition*, National Public Radio, September 14, 2014, accessed September 12, 2016, http://www.npr.org/2014/09/12/347736999/20-years-later-major-crime-bill-viewed-as-terrible-mistake.

4. Cara E. Rabe-Hemp, "Survival in an 'All Boys Club': Policewomen and Their Fight for Acceptance," *Policing* 31 (2008): 263.

Chapter 6

1. "Rodney King 1965–2012," *Biography*, accessed October 26, 2016, http://www.biography.com/people/rodney-king-9542141#acquittal-and-resulting-riots.

2. COPS, *Community Policing Dispatch*, January 2008, https://cops.usdoj.gov/html/dispatch/january_2008/nugget.html.

3. Bureau of Justice Statistics, *State and Local Law Enforcement Statistics, 1999* (Washington, DC: NIJ, 2000), accessed October 2016, http://www.nrc.uscg.mil/insum2005/facilityfire1.html.

4. Susan Miller, *Gender and Community Policing: Walking the Talk* (Boston: Northeastern University Press, 1999).

5. Miller, *Gender and Community Policing.*

6. Robert Green, "Police as Social Service Workers?" *Journal of Sociology & Social Welfare* 3 (1976), accessed March 2017, http://scholarworks.wmich.edu/jssw/vol3/iss6/9.

Chapter 7

1. Office of the Attorney General, *The New York City Police Department's "Stop and Frisk" Practices: A Report to the People of New York from the Office of the Attorney General* (Albany: Office of the New York State Attorney General, December 1999), 94–100, 106.

2. Peter Kilborn, "Minorities in Blue—A Special Report: New York Police Force Lagging in Recruitment of Black Officers," *New York Times*, July 17, 1994, accessed September 2016, http://www.nytimes.com/1994/07/17/nyregion/minorities-blue-special-report-new-york-police-force-lagging-recruitment-black.html?pagewanted=all.

3. Kilborn, "Minorities in Blue."

4. Lawrence C. Trostle, "LAPD Successful in Recruiting Minorities and Women," *Alaska Justice Forum* 7 (Fall 1990): 1, 6–8, accessed September 2016, http://justice.uaa.alaska.edu/forum/07/3fall1990/a_lapd.html.

5. David Colcker, "Fanchon Blake Dies at 93; Lawsuit Broke LAPD's Glass Ceiling for Women," *Los Angeles Times*, May 2, 2015, accessed September 2016, http://www.latimes.com/local/obituaries/la-me-fanchon-blake-20150503-story.html.

6. National Center for Women and Policing, *Equality Denied* (Washington, DC: Feminist Majority, 2001).

7. Robert Langworthy, Tad Hughes, and Beth Sanders, *Law Enforcement Recruitment, Selection, and Training: A Survey of Major Police Departments in the US* (Highland Heights, KY: Academy of Criminal Justice Sciences—Police Section, 1995).

8. Joseph Polisar and Donna Milgram, "Recruiting, Integrating, and Retaining Women Police Officers: Strategies That Work," *The Police Chief* 65 (October 1998): 42–52.

9. Ellen Scrivner, *Innovations in Police and Hiring in the Spirit of Service Recruitment Hiring* (Washington, DC: US Department of Justice, Office of Community Oriented Policing Service, 2001), accessed September 2016, http://ric-zai-inc.com/Publications/cops-p090-pub.pdf.

10. Philadelphia Police Department, *Preference Points*, 2012, accessed September 2016, www.phillypolice.com/careers/preference-points.

11. Langworthy et al., *Law Enforcement Recruitment.*

12. Julie Williams, "Mentoring for Law Enforcement," *Law Enforcement Bulletin*, March 2000, 19–25.

13. Williams, "Mentoring for Law Enforcement," 24.

Chapter 8

1. "Culture Shock," *Simple Justice* (blog), August 15, 2016, accessed September 2016, https://blog.simplejustice.us/2016/08/15/culture-shock/.

2. Cara E. Rabe-Hemp, "Survival in an 'All Boys Club': Policewomen and Their Fight for Acceptance," *Policing* 31 (2008): 263.

3. United States Department of Labor, "Facts Over Time," 2014, accessed October 2016, www.dol.gov/wb/stats/facts_over_time.htm.

4. Nancy L. Herrington, "Female Cops," in *Critical Issues in Policing*, ed. Roger Dunham and Geoffrey Alpert (Prospect Heights, IL: Waveland Press), 364.

5. Jennifer Gossett and Joyce Williams, "Perceived Discrimination among Women in Law Enforcement," *Women and Criminal Justice* 10 (1998): 53–73.

6. International Association of Chiefs of Police, *The Future of Women in Policing: Mandates for Action* (Washington, DC: IACP, November 1998).

7. Jennifer Hunt, "The Logic Underlying Police Sexism," *Women & Criminal Justice* 1 (1990): 26.

8. Christopher Commission Report, *Report of the Independent Commission on the Los Angeles Police Department* (Los Angeles: Independent Commission on the Los Angeles Police Department, 1991), 87.

9. Christopher Commission Report, *Report of the Independent Commission*, 88.

10. Susan E. Martin, "'Outsider within' the Stationhouse: The Impact of Race and Gender on Black Women Police," *Social Problems* 41, no. 3 (1994): 383–400.

11. Susan E. Martin, *Officers on the Move: The Status of Women in Policing* (Washington, DC: Police Foundation, 1991).

12. Glen Townes, "Showing Her Mettle," *Hispanic* 6 (1993): 2–3.

13. Rabe-Hemp, "Survival," 262.

14. Rabe-Hemp, "Survival," 263.

15. Thomas Whetstone and Deborah Wilson, "Dilemmas Confronting Female Police Officer Promotional Candidates: Glass Ceiling, Disenfranchisement or Satisfaction?" *International Journal of Police Science and Management* 2 (1995): 128–43.

16. Alissa Worden, "The Attitudes of Women and Men in Policing: Testing Conventional and Contemporary Wisdom," *Criminology* 31 (1993): 203–41.

17. JoAnne Belknap and Jill K. Shelley, "The New Lone Ranger: Policewomen on Patrol," *American Journal of Police* 12 (1993): 47–76.

18. Carol Watson, "Female Officers Fighting Crime—and Sexism: Law Enforcement: Some Policewomen Say Departments Are Slow to Integrate Women and Are Plagued by 'a Lot of Old Male Views,'" *Los Angeles Times*, June 24, 1990, accessed September 2016, http://articles.latimes.com/1990-06-24/local/me-645_1_police-departments/2.

Chapter 9

1. Lisa Belkin, "Woman Named Police Chief," *New York Times*, January 20, 1990, accessed October 2016, http://www.nytimes.com/1990/01/20/us/woman-named-police-chief-of-houston.html.

2. Belkin, "Woman Named Police Chief."

3. David J. Bordua and Albert J. Reiss, "Command, Control, and Charisma: Reflections on Police Bureaucracy," *American Journal of Sociology* 72 (1966): 68–76.

4. Depending on the level of department presented, rank structure varies. Although the large and varied number of federal, state, and local police departments and sheriff's offices have different ranks, a general model, from highest to lowest rank, would be:

chief of police/police commissioner/superintendent/sheriff
deputy chief of police/deputy commissioner/deputy superintendent/undersheriff
inspector/commander/colonel
major/deputy inspector
captain
lieutenant
sergeant
detective/inspector/investigator
officer/deputy sheriff/corporal

5. Michael McLaurin, "How to Run an Assessment Center," *Police Magazine*, March 1, 2005, accessed August 2016, http://www.policemag.com.

6. Kathryn Scarborough, G. Norman Van Tubergen, Larry K. Gaines, and Scott Whitlow, "An Examination of Police Officers' Motivation to Participate in the Promotional Process," *Police Quarterly* 2 (1990): 302–20.

7. Carol Archbold and Dorothy Moses Schulz, "Making Rank: The Lingering Effects of Tokenism on Female Police Officers' Promotion Aspirations," *Police Quarterly* 11 (2008): 50–73.

8. International Association of Chiefs of Police, *The Future of Women in Policing: Mandates for Action* (Washington, DC: IACP, 1998), 6.

9. Cara E. Rabe-Hemp, "Survival in an 'All Boys Club': Policewomen and Their Fight for Acceptance," *Policing* 31 (2008): 259.

10. Rosabeth M. Kanter, *Men and Women of the Corporation* (New York: Basic Books, 1977).

11. Susan Miller, *Gender and Community Policing: Walking the Talk* (Boston: Northeastern University Press, 1999).

12. Jennifer Gossett and Joyce Williams, "Perceived Discrimination among Women in Law Enforcement," *Women and Criminal Justice* 10 (1998): 53–73.

13. Christopher Commission Report, *Report of the Independent Commission on the Los Angeles Police Department* (Los Angeles: Independent Commission on the Los Angeles Police Department, 1991), 81.

14. Susan E. Martin, *Breaking and Entering: Policewomen on Patrol* (Berkeley: University of California Press, 1980).

15. Michael G. Breci, "Female Officers on Patrol: Public Perceptions in the 1990s," *Journal of Criminal Justice* 20 (1997): 153–65; K. Winnand, "Police Women and the People They Serve," *Police Chief* 53 (1986): 62–63.

16. Kristen Leger, "Public Perceptions of Female Police Officer on Patrol," *American Journal of Criminal Justice* 21 (1997): 248.

17. Rabe-Hemp, "Survival," 263.

18. Martin, *Breaking and Entering*; Julie Wexler and D. Logan, "Sources of Stress among Women Police Officers," *Journal of Police Science and Administration* 11 (1983): 46–53.

19. Roslyn Maglione, "Recruiting, Retaining and Promoting Women: The Success of the Charlotte-Mecklenburg Police Department's Women's Network," *The Police Chief*, March 2002, 19–24.

20. Barbara R. Price, "Sexual Integration in American Law Enforcement," in *Police Ethics*, ed. William C. Hefferman (New York: John Jay Press, 1985), 209.

21. Rabe-Hemp, "Survival," 258.

22. National Center for Women and Policing, *Homepage*, accessed October 2016, http://www.womenandpolicing.org/.

23. Corrine Schulze, "Family Leave and Law Enforcement: A Survey of Parents in U.S. Police Departments," *Critical Criminology* 19 (2010): 137–53.

24. Thomas Whetstone and Deborah Wilson, "Dilemmas Confronting Female Police Officer Promotional Candidates: Glass Ceiling, Disenfranchisement or Satisfaction?" *International Journal of Police Science and Management* 2 (1995): 128–43.

25. Archbold and Schulz, "Making Rank."

26. Susan E. Martin and Nancy C. Jurik, *Doing Justice, Doing Gender* (Thousand Oaks, CA: Sage, 1996).

27. Martin, *Officers On the Move.*

28. Rabe-Hemp, "Survival," 266.

29. Rabe-Hemp, "Survival," 263.

30. Julie Williams, *Unbending Gender: Why Work and Family Conflict and What to Do about It* (New York: Oxford University Press, 2000).

Introduction to Section III

1. National Public Radio, "Timeline: America's War on Drugs," *The Forgotten War on Drugs* (special series), April 2, 2007, accessed January 2017, http://www.npr.org/templates/story/story.php?storyId=9252490.

2. Taylor Wofford, "How America's Police Became an Army: The 1033 Program," *Newsweek*, August 13, 2014, accessed January 2017, http://www.newsweek.com/how-americas-police-became-army-1033-program-264537.

3. Human Rights Watch, *United States: Punishment and Prejudice: Racial Disparities in the War on Drugs* (Washington, DC: Human Rights Watch, 2000), 1, accessed December 2016, https://www.hrw.org/reports/2000/usa/.

4. Kara Dansky, *War Comes Home: The Excessive Militarization of American Police* (New York: ACLU, June 2014), accessed December 2016, https://www.aclu.org/report/war-comes-home-excessive-militarization-american-police.

5. Kimberly Kindy, Marc Fisher, Julie Tate, and Jennifer Jenkins, "A Year of Reckoning: Police Fatally Shoot Nearly 1,000," *Washington Post*, December 26, 2015, accessed January 2017, http://www.washingtonpost.com/sf/investigative/2015/12/26/a-year-of-reckoning-police-fatally-shoot-nearly-1000/.

6. Christina Asquith, "Why Aren't U.S. Police Departments Recruiting More Women?" *Atlantic Monthly*, August 30, 2016, accessed January 2017, http://www.the atlantic.com/politics/archive/2016/08/police-departments-women-officers/497963/; Amy Stewart, "Female Police Officers Save Lives," *New York Times*, July 26, 2016, accessed January 2017, http://www.nytimes.com/2016/07/26/opinion/female-police -officers-save-lives.html?_r=0.

7. Brian Reaves, *Local Police Departments, 2013: Personnel, Policies, and Practices* (Washington, DC: Bureau of Justice Statistics, May 2015), http://www.bjs.gov/con tent/pub/pdf/lpd13ppp.pdf.

Chapter 10

1. Cara Rabe-Hemp, "Policewomen and Matrons," in *Encyclopedia of Criminology and Criminal Justice*, January 22, 2014, accessed February 2017, http://onlinelibrary .wiley.com/doi/10.1002/9781118517383.wbeccj119/abstract;jsessionid=0592AD45EF 2172DE111B4459365E3CDE.f04t02.

2. Joseph Balkin, "Why Policemen Don't Like Policewomen," *Journal of Police Science and Administration* 16 (1988): 29–38; Daniel J. Bell, "Policewomen: Myths and Realities," *Journal of Police Science and Administration* 10 (1982): 29–36.

3. Peter Horne, *Women in Law Enforcement* (Springfield, IL: Charles C. Thomas, 1980); Catherine Milton, *Women in Policing* (Washington, DC: The Police Foundation, 1972); Lawrence Sherman, "An Evaluation of Policewomen on Patrol in a Suburban Police Department," *Journal of Police Science and Administration* 3 (1975): 434–38.

4. Cited in Balkin, "Why Policemen Don't Like Policewomen," 32.

5. *Muller v. Oregon*, 208 US 412 (1908), 422–23.

6. Ernestine Friedl, *Women and Men: An Anthropologist's View* (New York: Holt, Rinehart and Winston, 1975).

7. Louann Brizendine, *The Female Brain* (New York: Random House, 2007).

8. Albert Bandura, *Social Learning Theory* (Englewood Cliffs, NJ: Prentice Hall, 1977).

9. Sandra Bem, *The Lenses of Gender: Transforming the Debate on Sexual Equality* (New Haven, CT: Yale University Press, 1993), 111.

10. Anne Fausto-Sterling, *The Myths of Gender: Biological Theories about Women and Men* (New York: Basic Books, 1985).

11. Valerie Bryson, *Feminist Political Theory* (Basingstoke, UK: Macmillan, 1992), 49.

12. International Association of Chiefs of Police, *The Future of Women in Policing: Mandates for Action* (Washington, DC: IACP, 1998).

13. Jason Bacon, "Man Killed in Shootout with Florida Deputy," *USA Today*, March 10, 2016, accessed January 2017, http://www.usatoday.com/story/news/ nation/2016/05/10/man-dead-after-fla-deputy-opens-fire-during-traffic-stop/8417 3180/.

14. Melanie Eversley, "Video Shows Unarmed Black Man Terence Crutcher Shot by Tulsa Officer," *USA Today*, September 20, 2016, accessed January 2017, http://

www.usatoday.com/story/news/2016/09/19/police-involved-shooting-black-man
-tulsa-prompts-investigation/90716058/.

15. Jodi M. Brown and Patrick A. Langan, *Policing and Homicide, 1976–98: Justifiable Homicide of Felons by Police and Murder of Police by Felons* (Washington, DC: Bureau of Justice Statistics, March 1, 2001), accessed January 2017, https://www.bjs.gov/content/pub/pdf/ph98.pdf.

16. John R. Lott, "Does a Helping Hand Put Others at Risk? Affirmative Action, Police Departments, and Crime," *Economic Inquiry* (April 2000): 241.

17. Esther Koenig, "An Overview of Attitudes toward Women in Law Enforcement," *Public Administration Review* 38 (1978): 271.

18. R. G. Talney, "Women in Law Enforcement: An Expanded Role," *Police* 19 (1969): 50.

19. Kimberly Lonsway, Michelle Wood, and Katharine Spillar, "Officer Gender and Excessive Force," *Law and Order* 50 (2002): 60–66.

20. Charlotte, NC; Colorado Springs, CO; Dallas, TX; St. Petersburg, FL; San Diego, CA, Police; and San Diego, CA, Sheriff's Office (N = 7512).

21. Lonsway et al., "Officer Gender," 2.

22. Patricia Remmington, *Policing: The Occupation and Introduction of Female Officers* (Washington, DC: University Press of America, 1982).

Chapter 11

1. Kenneth Kerber, Stephen Andes, and Michelle Mittler, "Citizen Attitudes regarding the Competence of Female Police Officers," *Journal of Police Science and Administration* 5 (1977): 337–47; Barbara R. Price, "Sexual Integration in American Law Enforcement," in *Police Ethics*, ed. William C. Heffferman (New York: John Jay Press, 1985), 209; Alissa Worden, "The Attitudes of Women and Men in Policing: Testing Conventional and Contemporary Wisdom," *Criminology* 31 (1993): 203–41.

2. Venessa Garcia, "'Difference' in the Police Department," *Journal of Contemporary Criminal Justice* 19 (2003): 330–44.

3. Denise Gosselin, *Heavy Hands* (Boston, MA: Pearson, 2014).

4. Gosselin, *Heavy Hands.*

5. Christina Asquith, "Why Aren't U.S. Police Departments Recruiting More Women?" *Atlantic Monthly*, August 30, 2016, accessed January 2017, http://www.theatlantic.com/politics/archive/2016/08/police-departments-women-officers/497963/.

6. Asquith, "Why Aren't U.S. Police Departments Recruiting More Women?"

7. Bojana Balon, "Women in the Police Means a Better Response to Community Needs," United Nations Development Programme, April 18, 2013, accessed January 2017, http://europeandcis.undp.org/blog/2013/04/18/women-in-the-police-means-a-better-response-to-community-needs/.

8. Christina Asquith, "US Spending Millions to Train Women Police Officers Worldwide. What about at Home?" *PRI*, August 15, 2016, accessed January 2017, http://www.pri.org/stories/2016-08-15/us-spending-millions-train-women-police-officers-worldwide-what-about-home.

9. Robert Homant and Daniel Kennedy, "Police Perceptions of Spouse Abuse: A Comparison of Male and Female Officers," *Journal of Criminal Justice* 13 (1985): 29–47.

10. Norma Riccucci, Greg Van Ryzin, and Cecilia Lavena, "Representative Bureaucracy in Policing: Does It Increase Perceived Legitimacy?" *Journal of Public Administration Research and Theory* 24 (2014): 537–51.

11. Amy Dellinger Page, "Judging Women and Defining Crime: Police Officers' Attitudes toward Women and Rape," *Sociological Spectrum* 28 (2008): 389–411.

12. Amie Schuck and Cara E. Rabe-Hemp, "Women Police: The Use of Force by and against Female Officers," *Women & Criminal Justice* 16 (2005): 109.

13. John Volanti, Desta Fekedulegn, Tara Hartley, Luenda Charles, Michael Andrew, Claudia Ma, and Cecil Burchfiel, "Highly Rates and Most Frequent Stressors among Police Officers: Gender Differences," *American Journal of Criminal Justice* 16 (2016): 645–62.

14. Susan E. Martin, "Police Force or Police Service? Gender and Emotional Labor," *Annals of the American Academy of Political and Social Science* 561 (1999): 111–26.

15. D. J. McCarthy, "Gendering 'Soft' Policing: Multi-Agency Working, Female Cops, and the Fluidities of Police Culture/s," *Policing and Society* 23 (2011): 261–83; Marisa Silvestri, "'Doing' Police Leadership: Enter the 'Smart Macho' Leader," *Journal of Policing and Society: An International Journal of Research and Policy* 17 (2007): 38–58.

Chapter 12

1. Karen J. Kruger, "Pregnancy and Policing: Are They Compatible? Pushing the Legal Limits on Behalf of Equal Employment Opportunities," *Wisconsin Women's Law Journal* 61 (2007): 4, accessed January 2017, http://www.fblaw.com/pdf/kruger -pregnancy-policing.pdf.

2. Maryland Chiefs of Police Association, *A Task Analysis Study of Entry-Level Law Enforcement in the State of Maryland* (Columbia, MD: Author, 1995).

3. Eric Marrapodi, "Officers Death Shocks New Orleans," *CNN*, February 1, 2008, accessed January 2017, http://www.cnn.com/2008/US/02/01/slain.police.of ficer/index.html?_s=PM:US.

4. Leslie Moreland, Gregory Leskin, Caroline Rebecca Block, Jacquelyn Campbell, and Matthew J. Friedman, "Intimate Partner Violence and Miscarriage: Examination of the role of Physical and Psychological Abuse and Posttraumatic Stress Disorder," *Journal of Interpersonal Violence* 23 (2008): 652–69; Angela Taft, "Violence against Women in Pregnancy and after Childbirth: Current Knowledge and Issues in Health Care Responses," *Australian Domestic & Family Violence Clearinghouse* 6 (2002): 1–23.

5. Sylvia Abel, Raymond Césaire, Danielle Cales-Quist, Odile Béra, Guy Sobesky, and Andre Cabié, "Occupational Transmission of Human Immunodeficiency Virus and Hepatitis C Virus after a Punch," *Clinical Infectious Diseases* 31 (2000): 1494–95; Dean Scoville, "Protect Yourself from Blood Borne Diseases," *Police: The Law Enforcement*

Magazine, August 8, 2008, accessed January 2017, http://www.policemag.com/blog/patrol-tactics/story/2008/08/protect-yourself-from-blood-borne-diseases.aspx.

6. Abel et al., "Occupational Transmission of Human Immunodeficiency Virus."

7. Harold Weiss and Stephen Strotmeyer, "Characteristics of Pregnant Women in Motor Vehicle Accidents," *Injury Prevention* 8 (2002): 207–10.

8. National Institute for Occupational Safety and Health Administration, *Work Related Roadway Crashes: Challenges and Opportunities for Prevention* (Washington, DC: Centers for Disease Control and Prevention, September 2003), accessed January 2017, http://www.cdc.gov/niosh/docs/2003-119/default.html.

9. Federal Bureau of Investigation, *Law Enforcement Officers Killed and Assaulted, 2005* (Washington, DC: FBI, 2006), accessed January 2017, http://www.fbi.gov/ucr/ucr.htm.

10. Equal Employment Opportunity Commission, *Pregnancy Discrimination*, accessed January 2017, https://www.eeoc.gov/laws/types/pregnancy.cfm.

11. Equal Employment Opportunity Commission, *Pregnancy Discrimination*.

12. Susan E. Martin and Nancy C. Jurik, *Doing Justice, Doing Gender* (Thousand Oaks, CA: Sage, 1996).

13. Deborah Calloway, "Accommodating Pregnancy in the Workplace," *Stetson Law Review* 25 (1995): 1–53; Equal Employment Opportunity Commission, *Pregnancy Discrimination*.

14. Joanna Grossman and Gillian Thomas, "Making Pregnancy Work: Overcoming the Pregnancy Discrimination Act's Capacity-Based Model," *Yale Journal of Law and Feminism* 21 (2009): 1–47.

15. Susan E. Martin, *Officers on the Move: The Status of Women in Policing* (Washington, DC: Police Foundation, 1991).

16. Cara Rabe-Hemp and Gail Humiston, "A Survey of Maternity Policies and Pregnancy Accommodations in the United States," *Police Practice and Research* 16, no. 3 (2014): 239–53.

17. Renee Cowan and Jamie Bochantin, "Pregnancy and Motherhood on the Thin Blue Line: Female Police Officers' Perspectives on Motherhood in a Highly Masculinized Work Environment," *Women and Language* 32 (2009): 22–29; Cara Rabe-Hemp, "Exploring Administrators' Perceptions of Light-Duty Assignment," *Police Quarterly* 14 (2011): 124–41.

18. Cowan, "Pregnancy and Motherhood on the Thin Blue Line"; Martin, *Officers on the Move*; Corrine Schulze, "Institutional Masculinity in US Police Departments: How Maternity Leave Policies (or Lack Thereof) Affect Women in Policing," *Criminal Justice Studies* 23 (2010): 177–93.

19. Schulze, "Institutional Masculinity."

20. *O'Loughlin v. Pinchback*, 579 So.2d 788. (Fla. App. 1 Dist. 1991); *United Automobile Workers v. Johnson Controls, Inc.*, 499 US 187 (1991).

21. *United Automobile Workers v. Johnson Controls, Inc.*, 205.

22. Burhan Abudhaise, M. Atzoubi, Atalla Rabi, and Rahi'H Alwash, "Lead Exposure in Indoor Firing Ranges: Environmental Impact and Health Risk to the Range Users," *International Journal of Occupational Medicine & Environmental Health* 9 (1996): 323–29.

23. Carolyn Gardella, "Lead Exposure in Pregnancy: A Review of the Literature and Argument for Routine Prenatal Screening," *Obstetrical and Gynecological Survey* 56 (2001): 231–38; National Institute for Occupational Safety and Health Administration, *The Effects of Workplace Hazards on Female Reproductive Health* (Washington, DC: Centers for Disease Control and Prevention, 1999), accessed January 2017, http://www.cdc.gov/NIOSH/99-104.html.

24. D. S. Shimm, and M. Passamaneck, *Shooting Noise, Hearing Loss, and Hearing Protection* (Berryville, AR: International Defensive Pistol Association, 2011).

25. *Graham v. Connor*, 490 US 386 (1989).

26. Calloway, "Accommodating Pregnancy in the Workplace."

27. Rabe-Hemp, "Exploring Administrators' Perceptions of Light-Duty Assignment."

28. Carole Moore, "Pregnant Officer Policies," *Law and Order* 51 (2003): 74–78.

29. Cowan, "Pregnancy and Motherhood on the Thin Blue Line."

30. IACP National Law Enforcement Policy Center, "Pregnancy Policy," March 2010, accessed February 2017, http://www.iacp.org/Model-Policies-Alphabetical-Order.

31. Kruger, "Pregnancy and Policing."

32. Kruger, "Pregnancy and Policing."

33. Peter Moss, *International Review of Leave Policies and Related Research* (London, UK: Institute of Education University of London, June 2014), accessed January 2017, http://www.leavenetwork.org/fileadmin/Leavenetwork/Annual_reviews/2014_annual_review_korr.pdf; Rebecca Ray, Janet Gornick, and John Schmitt, *Parental Leave Policies in 21 Countries* (Washington, DC: Center for Economic and Policy Research, June 2009), accessed January 2017, http://www.cepr.net/documents/publications/parental_2008_09.pdf.

34. Moss, *International Review of Leave Policies and Related Research*.

Chapter 13

1. Steven. G. Brandl, and Megan S. Stroshine, "Toward an Understanding of the Physical Hazards of Police Work," *Police Quarterly* 6 (2003): 172–91; Deborah W. Newman and M. Leanne Rucker-Reed, "Police Stress, State-Trait Anxiety, and Stressors among U.S. Marshals," *Journal of Criminal Justice* 32 (2004): 631–41.

2. Susan E. Martin, "Police Force or Police Service? Gender and Emotional Labor," *Annals of American Academy of Political and Social Sciences* 561 (1999): 111–26.

3. Tahera Darensberg, Michael Andrew, Tara Hartley, Cecil Burchfiel, Desta Fekedulegn, and John M. Violanti, "Gender and Age Differences in Posttraumatic Stress Disorder and Depression among Buffalo Police Officers," *Traumatology* 12 (2006): 200–228.

4. Centers for Disease Control and Prevention (CDC), *Worker Health Chartbook, 2004*, DHHS (NIOSH) Publication No. 2004-146 (Washington, DC: Department of Health and Human Services, 2004), accessed February 2017, https://www.cdc.gov/niosh/docs/2004-146/pdfs/2004-146.pdf.

5. Ellen Kirschman, *I Love a Cop* (New York: Guilford Press, 2007), 19.

6. Richard Daft and Dorothy Marcic, *Understanding Management* (Mason, OH: South-Western-Cengage Learning, 2009).

7. Kirschman, *I Love a Cop*, 64.

8. Kirschman, *I Love a Cop*.

9. Merry Morash, Robin Haarr, and Dae Hoon Kwak, "Multi-Level Influences on Police Stress," *Journal of Contemporary Criminal Justice* 22 (2006): 26–43.

10. Jennifer Lawless and Richard Fox, *Men Rule: The Continued Under-Representation of Women in U.S. Politics* (Washington, DC: Women in Politics Institute, 2012).

11. Robin Haarr and Merry Morash, "Gender, Race, and Strategies of Coping with Occupational Stress in Policing," *Justice Quarterly* 16 (1999): 303–36.

12. William McCarty, Jihong Solomon Zhao, and Brett E. Garland, "Occupational Stress and Burnout between Male and Female Police Officers: Are There Any Gender Differences?" *Policing: An International Journal of Police Strategies and Management* 30 (2007): 672–91.

13. Arlie Russell Hoschschild, *The Second Shift* (New York: Viking Penguin, 1989).

14. Thomas Whetstone and Deborah Wilson, "Dilemmas Confronting Female Police Officer Promotional Candidates: Glass Ceiling, Disenfranchisement or Satisfaction?" *International Journal of Police Science and Management* 2 (1995): 128–43.

15. Carol Archbold and Kimberly Hassell, "Paying the Marriage Tax: An Examination of the Barriers to the Promotion of Female Police Officers," *Policing: An International Journal of Police Strategies and Management* 32, no. 1 (2009): 56–74.

16. Mark Pogrebin, Mary Dodge, and Harold Chatham, "Reflections of African-American Women on Their Careers in Urban Policing: Their Experiences of Racial and Sexual Discrimination," *International Journal of the Sociology of Law* 28 (2000): 311–26.

17. Susan E. Martin, *Breaking and Entering: Policewomen on Patrol* (Berkeley: University of California Press, 1980), 97.

18. Kathryn Loving, "10 Ways Law Enforcement Ruined Me as a Woman," *PoliceOne*, September 2, 2016, accessed February 2017, https://www.policeone.com/women-officers/articles/217721006-10-ways-law-enforcement-ruined-me-as-a-woman/.

19. Philip E. Carlan and Lisa S. Nored, "An Examination of Officer Stress: Should Police Departments Implement Mandatory Counseling?" *Journal of Police and Criminal Psychology* 23 (2008): 8–15.

20. Jeff Watson, "Mental Health and Peer Support in Law Enforcement," *Cops Alive.com*, February 16, 2012, accessed February 2017, http://www.copsalive.com/mental-health-peer-support-in-law-enforcement/.

21. Watson, "Mental Health."

22. Joseph Harpold and Samuel Feenster, "Negative Influences of Police Stress," *FBI Law Enforcement Bulletin* 71 (2002): 1–7.

23. Jihong Solomon Zhao, Ni He, and Nicholas Lovrich, "Predicting Five Dimensions of Police Officer Stress: Looking More Deeply into Organizational Settings for Sources of Police Stress," *Police Quarterly* 5 (2002): 43–62.

24. Christina Maslach, Wilmar Schaufeli, and Michael Leiter, "Job Burnout," *Annual Review of Psychology* 53 (2001): 397–422.

25. Leigh Goodmark, "Hands Up at Home: Militarized Masculinity and Police Officers Who Commit Intimate Partner Violence," *Brigham Young University Law Review*, March 9, 2015: 1183–1246.

26. National Coalition against Domestic Violence, *What Is Domestic Violence?* accessed February 2017, http://www.ncadv.org/learn-more/what-is-domestic-violence.

27. Karen Oehme, Elizabeth A. Donnelly, and Annelise Martin, "Alcohol Abuse, PTSD, and Officer-Committed Domestic Violence," *Policing* 6 (2012): 418–30.

28. Egbert Zavala, Lisa A. Melander, and Don L. Kurtz, "The Importance of Social Learning and Critical Incident Stressors on Police Officer's Perpetration of Intimate Partner Violence," *Victims & Offenders* 10 (2015): 51–73.

29. Kirschman, *I Love a Cop*, 159.

30. Lynn Langston, *Women in Law Enforcement, 1987–2008* (Washington, DC: US Department of Justice, 2010).

31. Ellen Galinsky, Kersten Aumann, and James T. Bond, *Times Are Changing: Gender and Generation at Work and at Home*, Families and Work Institute, 2009, accessed February 2017, http://familiesandwork.org/site/research/reports/Times _Are_Changing.pdf.

32. Galinksy et al., *Times Are Changing*.

33. Michael Balsamo, "Growing Number of Women Leading US Police Departments," *AP News*, February 4, 2017, accessed February 2017, http://abcnews.go.com/ US/wireStory/growing-number-women-leading-us-police-departments-45269005.

Conclusion

1. Barack Obama, "Dallas Police Memorial Service" (comments presented at the Dallas Shooting Memorial Service, Dallas, Texas, July 12, 2016), accessed December 2016, http://time.com/4403543/president-obama-dallas-shooting-memorial-service speech-transcript/.

2. Lindsay Hixson, Bradford B. Hepler, and Myoung Ouk Kim, *The White Population: 2010, 2010 Census Briefs* (Washington, DC: US Census Bureau, 2011), accessed December 2016, https://www.census.gov/prod/cen2010/briefs/c2010br-05.pdf.

3. Stephen M. Hennessy, "Achieving Cultural Competency," *Police Chief* 60 (August 1993): 46–54.

4. President's Task Force on 21st Century Policing, *Final Report of the President's Task Force on 21st Century Policing* (Washington, DC: Office of Community Oriented Policing Services, 2015), 16.

5. Kimberly Lonsway, Michelle Wood, and Katharine Spillar, "Officer Gender and Excessive Force," *Law and Order* 50 (2002): 60–66; Cara E. Rabe-Hemp, "Female Officers and the Ethic of Care: Does Officer Gender Impact Police Behaviors?" *Journal of Criminal Justice* 36 (2008), 426–34; Cara E. Rabe-Hemp and Amie Schuck, "Violence against Police Officers: Are Female Officers at Greater Risk?" *Police Quarterly* 10 (2007): 411–28; Amie Schuck and Cara E. Rabe-Hemp, "Women Police: The Use of Force by and against Female Officers," *Women & Criminal Justice* 16 (2005): 91–117.

6. Kim Lersch, "Exploring Gender Differences in Citizen Allegations of Police Misconduct: An Analysis of a Municipal Police Department," *Women and Criminal Justice* 9 (1998): 69–79; Amie Schuck and Cara Rabe-Hemp, "Citizen Complaints and Gender Diversity in Police Organizations," *Police and Society* 26 (2016): 859–74.

7. Daniel Lockwood and Ariane Prohaska, "Police Officer Gender and Attitudes toward Intimate Partner Violence: How Policy Can Eliminate Stereotypes," *International Journal of Criminal Justice Sciences* 10 (2015): 77–90; Kimberly Lonsway and Joanne M. Archambault, "The 'Justice Gap' for Sexual Assault Cases: Future Directions for Research and Reform," *Violence against Women* 18 (2012): 145–68; Kenneth Meier and Jill Nicholson-Crotty, "Gender, Representative Bureaucracy, and Law Enforcement: The Case of Sexual Assault," *Public Administration Review* 66 (2006): 850–60; Cassie Spohn and Katharine Tellis, "The Criminal Justice System's Response to Sexual Violence," *Violence against Women* 18 (2012): 169–92.

8. Amie Schuck, "Gender Differences in Policing: Testing Hypotheses from the Performance and Disruption Perspectives," *Feminist Criminology* 9 (2014): 160–85.

9. Marie-Elene Roberge and Rolf Van Dick, "Recognizing the Benefits of Diversity: When and How Does Diversity Increase Group Performance," *Human Resource Management Review* 20 (2010): 295–308.

10. Deborah J. Campbell and Karen J. Kruger, "Chief's Counsel: IACP Policy Assists Agencies to Define Pregnancy Policies," *Police Chief* 77 (2010): 12–14; Cara Rabe-Hemp and Gail Humiston, "A Survey of Maternity Policies and Pregnancy Accommodations in the United States," *Police Practice and Research* 16 (2015): 239–53; Ellen Scrivner, "Recruitment and Hiring: Challenge or Opportunity for Change?" (RAND Center for Quality Policing Recruitment and Retention Summit, Arlington, VA, 2008), accessed December 2016, http://www.cops.usdoj.gov/pdf/conference/rand/Scrivner-Recruitmentpresentation.pdf; Marisa Silvestri, "'Doing' Police Leadership: Enter the 'New Smart Macho,'" *Policing & Society* 17 (2007): 38–58; Jeremy Wilson and Clifford Grammich, *Police Recruitment and Retention in the Contemporary Urban Environment: A National Discussion of Personnel Experiences and Promising Practices from the Front Lines* (CF-261-DOJ) (Santa Monica, CA: RAND Corporation, 2009), accessed December 2016, http://www.rand.org/pubs/conf_ proceedings/CF261.

11. Brian Reaves, *Local Police Departments, 2013: Personnel, Policies, and Practices* (Washington, DC: Bureau of Justice Statistics, May 2015), http://www.bjs.gov/content/pub/pdf/lpd13ppp.pdf.

12. Salomon A. Guajardo, "New York City Police Department Downsizing and Its Impact on Female Officer Employment," *Journal of Ethnicity in Criminal Justice* 13 (2015): 255–82.

13. Reaves, *Local Police Departments, 2013*.

14. National Center for Women and Policing, *Equality Denied* (Washington, DC: Feminist Majority, 2001).

15. Michael Birzer and Delores Craig, "Gender Differences in Police Physical Ability Test Performance," *American Journal of Police* 15 (1996): 93–108.

16. Marc Levy, "U.S. Sues Pa. State Police, Saying Physical Fitness Test Discriminates against Women," *Pennlive.com*, July 30, 2014, http://www.pennlive.com/midstate/index.ssf/2014/07/us_sues_pa_state_police_saying.html.

17. Anthony Raganella and Michael D. White, "Race, Gender, and Motivation for Becoming a Police Officer: Implications for Building a Representative Police Department," *Journal of Criminal Justice* 32 (2004): 501–13.

18. Jody Kasper, "Proven Steps for Recruiting Women," *Law and Order*, December 2006, accessed December 2016, http://www.hendonpub.com/resources/article_ar chive/results/details?id=3443.

19. National Center for Women and Policing, *Equality Denied*.

20. William G. Doerner, "Officer Retention Patterns: An Affirmative Action Concern for Police Agencies?" *American Journal of Police* 14 (1995): 198.

21. Gary Cordner and AnnMarie Cordner, "Stuck on a Plateau? Obstacles to Recruitment, Selection and Retention of Women Police," *Police Quarterly* 14 (2011): 207–26.

22. Cara E. Rabe-Hemp, "Survival in an 'All Boys Club': Policewomen and Their Fight for Acceptance," *Policing: An International Journal of Police Strategies and Management* 31 (2008): 251–70; Chaiyavej Somvadee and Merry Morash, "Dynamics of Sexual Harassment for Policewomen Working alongside Men," *Policing: An International Journal of Police Strategies and Management* 31(2008): 485–98.

23. Michael Balsamo, "Growing Number of Women Leading US Police Departments," *AP News*, February 4, 2017, accessed February 2017, https://www.yahoo.com/news/growing-number-women-leading-us-police-departments-174047302.html.

24. Kevin Johnson, "Women Move into Law Enforcement's Highest Ranks," *USA Today*, December 2, 2015, accessed December 2016, http://www.usatoday.com/story/news/nation/2013/08/13/women-law-enforcement-police-dea-secret-ser vice/2635407/.

25. Jodi Lane, Nicole E. Rader, Billy Henson, Bonnie S. Fisher, and David C. May, *Fear of Crime in the United States: Causes, Consequences, and Contradictions* (Durham, NC: Carolina Academic Press, 2014).

Bibliography

Abel, Sylvia, Raymond Césaire, Danielle Cales-Quist, Odile Béra, Guy Sobesky, and Andre Cabié, "Occupational Transmission of Human Immunodeficiency Virus and Hepatitis C Virus after a Punch." *Clinical Infectious Diseases* 31 (2000): 1494–95.

Abudhaise, Burhan, M. Atzoubi, Atalla Rabi, and Rahi'H Alwash. "Lead Exposure in Indoor Firing Ranges: Environmental Impact and Health Risk to the Range Users." *International Journal of Occupational Medicine & Environmental Health* 9 (1996): 323–29.

Archbold, Carol, and Kimberly Hassell. "Paying the Marriage Tax: An Examination of the Barriers to the Promotion of Female Police Officers." *Policing: An International Journal of Police Strategies and Management* 32, no. 1 (2009): 56–74.

Archbold, Carol, and Dorothy Moses Schulz. "Making Rank: The Lingering Effects of Tokenism on Female Police Officers' Promotion Aspirations." *Police Quarterly* 11 (2008): 50–73.

Armat, Virginia. "Policewomen in Action." *Saturday Evening Post*, July 1975.

Asquith, Christina. "US Spending Millions to Train Women Police Officers Worldwide. What about at Home?" Public Radio International, August 15, 2016. Accessed January 2017. http://www.pri.org/stories/2016-08-15/us-spending-millions-train-women-police-officers-worldwide-what-about-home.

Asquith, Christina. "Why Aren't U.S. Police Departments Recruiting More Women?" *Atlantic Monthly*, August 30, 2016. Accessed January 2017. http://www.theatlantic.com/politics/archive/2016/08/police-departments-women-officers/497963/.

Bacon, Jason. "Man Killed in Shootout with Florida Deputy." *USA Today*, March 10, 2016. Accessed January 2017. http://www.usatoday.com/story/news/nation/2016/05/10/man-dead-after-fla-deputy-opens-fire-during-traffic-stop/84173180/.

Balkin, Joseph. "Why Policemen Don't Like Policewomen." *Journal of Police Science and Administration* 16 (1988): 29–38.

Balon, Bojana. "Women in the Police Means a Better Response to Community Needs." United Nations Development Programme, April 18, 2013. Accessed January 2017. http://europeandcis.undp.org/blog/2013/04/18/women-in-the-police -means-a-better-response-to-community-needs/.

Balsamo, Michael, "Growing Number of Women Leading US Police Departments." *AP News*, February 4, 2017. Accessed February 2017. https://www.yahoo. com/news/growing-number-women-leading-us-police-departments-174047302 .html.

Balz, Dan. "24 States Face Orders to Relieve Overcrowding." *Washington Post*, June 16, 1983. Accessed August 15, 2016. https://www.washingtonpost.com/archive/ politics/1981/06/16/24-states-face-orders-to-relieve-overcrowding/e8bd2eb8 -33c9-4684-a255-21eece40939d/.

Bandura, Albert. *Social Learning Theory*. Englewood Cliffs, NJ: Prentice Hall, 1977.

Bartlett, Harold W., and Arthur Rosenblum. *Policewomen Effectiveness*. Denver, CO: Denver Civil Service Commission, 1977.

Belkin, Lisa. "Woman Named Police Chief." *New York Times*, January 20, 1990. Accessed October 2016. http://www.nytimes.com/1990/01/20/us/woman-named-police-chief-of-houston.html.

Belknap, JoAnne, and Jill K. Shelley. "The New Lone Ranger: Policewomen on Patrol." *American Journal of Police* 12 (1993): 47–76.

Bell, Daniel J. "Policewomen: Myth and Reality." *Journal of Police Science and Administration* 10 (1982): 112–20.

Belton Texas Police Department. "Police Officer Agility Test." Accessed August 15, 2016. http://www.beltontexas.gov/DocumentCenter/Home/View/428.

Bem, Sandra. *The Lenses of Gender: Transforming the Debate on Sexual Equality*. New Haven, CT: Yale University Press, 1993.

Biography. "Rodney King (1965–2012)." Accessed October 26, 2016. http://www .biography.com/people/rodney-king-9542141#acquittal-and-resulting-riots.

Birzer, Michael, and Delores Craig. "Gender Differences in Police Physical Ability Test Performance." *American Journal of Police* 15 (1996): 93–108.

Bloch, Peter, and Daniel Anderson. *Policewomen on Patrol*. Washington, DC: Police Foundation, 1974.

Bonifacio, Philip. *The Psychosocial Effects of Police Work: A Psychodynamic Approach*. New York: Plenum Press, 1991.

Bordua, David J., and Albert J. Reiss. "Command, Control, and Charisma: Reflections on Police Bureaucracy." *American Journal of Sociology* 72 (1966): 68–76.

Bouza, Anthony V. *The Police Mystique: An Insider's Look at the Cops, Crime, and the Criminal Justice System*. New York: Plenum Press, 1990.

Brandl, Steven G., and Megan S. Stroshine. "Toward an Understanding of the Physical Hazards of Police Work." *Police Quarterly* 6 (2003): 172–91.

Breci, Michael G. "Female Officers on Patrol: Public Perceptions in the 1990s." *Journal of Criminal Justice* 20 (1997): 153–65.

Brizendine, Louann. *The Female Brain*. New York: Random House, 2007.

Brown, Jodi M., and Patrick A. Langan. *Policing and Homicide, 1976–98: Justifiable Homicide of Felons by Police and Murder of Police by Felons.* Washington, DC: Bureau of Justice Statistics, March 1, 2001. Accessed January 2017. https://www.bjs.gov/content/pub/pdf/ph98.pdf.

Bryson, Valerie. *Feminist Political Theory.* Basingstoke, UK: Macmillian, 1992.

Bureau of Justice Statistics. *State and Local Law Enforcement Statistics, 1999.* Washington, DC: NIJ, 2000. Accessed October 2016. http://www.nrc.uscg.mil/insum2005/facilityfire1.html.

California Highway Patrol. *Women Traffic Officer Project: Final Report.* Sacramento: California Highway Patrol, 1976.

Calloway, Deborah. "Accommodating Pregnancy in the Workplace." *Stetson Law Review* 25 (1995): 1–53.

Campbell, Deborah J., and Karen J. Kruger. "Chief's Counsel: IACP Policy Assists Agencies to Define Pregnancy Policies." *The Police Chief* 77 (2010): 12–14.

Carlan, Philip E., and Lisa S. Nored. "An Examination of Officer Stress: Should Police Departments Implement Mandatory Counseling?" *Journal of Police and Criminal Psychology* 23 (2008): 8–15.

Centers for Disease Control and Prevention (CDC). *Worker Health Chart Book, 2004.* Washington, DC: DHHS (NIOSH), 2004. Accessed February 2017. https://www.cdc.gov/niosh/docs/2004-146/pdfs/2004-146.pdf.

Chicago Tribune. "The Only Woman Detective on the Chicago Police Force." October 28, 1906. Accessed August 15, 2016. http://archives.chicagotribune.com/1906/10/28/page/59/article/the-only-woman-detective-on-the-chicago-foree.

Christopher Commission Report. *Report of the Independent Commission on the Los Angeles Police Department.* Los Angeles: Independent Commission on the Los Angeles Police Department, 1991.

Clark, Dan W., and Elizabeth K. White. "Clinicians, Cops and Suicide." In *Police Suicide: Tactics for Prevention,* edited by Dell L. Hackett and John M. Volanti, 16–36. Springfield, IL: Charles C. Thomas Publishers, 2003.

Colcker, David. "Fanchon Blake Dies at 93; Lawsuit Broke LAPD's Glass Ceiling for Women." *Los Angeles Times,* May 2, 2015. Accessed September 2016. http://www.latimes.com/local/obituaries/la-me-fanchon-blake-20150503-story.html.

COPS. *Community Policing Dispatch,* January 2008. Accessed October 26, 2016. https://cops.usdoj.gov/html/dispatch/january_2008/nugget.html.

Cops. "Season 3, Episode 24, Pittsburgh, PA2." Accessed August 15, 2016. http://www.pogdesign.co.uk/cat/Cops/Season-3/Episode-24.

Cordner, Gary, and AnnMarie Cordner. "Stuck on a Plateau? Obstacles to Recruitment, Selection and Retention of Women Police." *Police Quarterly* 14 (2011): 207–26.

Courier-Journal (Louisville, Kentucky). "Incident at the Airport." January 21, 1973.

Cowan, Renee, and Jamie Bochantin. "Pregnancy and Motherhood on the Thin Blue Line: Female Police Officers' Perspectives on Motherhood in a Highly Masculinized Work Environment." *Women and Language* 32 (2009): 22–29.

Daft, Richard, and Dorothy Marcic. *Understanding Management.* Mason, OH: South-Western-Cengage Learning, 2009.

Dansky, Kara. *War Comes Home: The Excessive Militarization of American Police.* New York: ACLU, June 2014. Accessed December 2016. https://www.aclu.org/report/war-comes-home-excessive-militarization-american-police.

Darensberg, Tahera, Michael Andrew, Tara Hartley, Cecil Burchfiel, Desta Fekedulegn, and John M. Violanti. "Gender and Age Differences in Posttraumatic Stress Disorder and Depression among Buffalo Police Officers." *Traumatology* 12 (2006): 200–228.

Diamond, Diane. "More Female Officers, Please." *Diane Diamond* (blog). http://dianedimond.net/more-female-police-officers-please/.

Dilulio, John J., Jr. "The Coming of the Super-Predators." *Weekly Standard*, November 27, 1995.

Doerner, William G. "Officer Retention Patterns: An Affirmative Action Concern for Police Agencies?" *American Journal of Police* 14 (1995): 198.

Dothard v. Rawlinson, 433 US 321, 1977.

Dreifus, Claudia. "People Are Always Asking Me What I Am Trying to Prove." *Police Magazine* 3 (1980): 19–25.

Equal Employment Opportunity Commission. *Pregnancy Discrimination.* Washington, DC, 2007. Accessed January 2017. http://www.eeoc.gov/types/pregnancy.html.

Eversley, Melanie. "Video Shows Unarmed Black Man Terence Crutcher Shot by Tulsa Officer." *USA Today*, September 20, 2016. Accessed January 2017. http://www.usatoday.com/story/news/2016/09/19/police-involved-shooting-black-man-tulsa-prompts-investigation/90716058/.

Fausto-Sterling, Anne. *The Myths of Gender: Biological Theories about Women and Men.* New York: Basic Books, 1985.

Federal Bureau of Investigation. "About *Law Enforcement Officers Killed and Assaulted.*" Washington, DC: FBI, 2010. Accessed August 15, 2016. http://cdn.ca9.uscourts.gov/datastore/library/2013/02/26/Mattos_LEOK.pdf.

Federal Bureau of Investigation. *Law Enforcement Officers Killed and Assaulted, 2005.* Washington, DC: FBI, 2006. Accessed January 2017. http://www.fbi.gov/ucr/ucr.htm.

Federal Bureau of Investigation. *Law Enforcement Officers Killed in the Line of Duty.* Washington, DC: FBI, 1971.

Fleming, Alice. *New on the Beat.* New York: Coward, McCann, and Geoghegan, 1975.

Franklin, Courtney A. "Male Peer Support and Police Culture: Understanding the Resistance and Opposition of Women in Policing." *Women and Criminal Justice* 16 (2007): 1–25.

Fridell, Lorie A., and Anthony Pate. *Death on Patrol: Felonious Homicides of American Police Officers*, Final Report. NCJ 159609. Washington, DC: Police Foundation, 1995.

Friedl, Ernestine. *Women and Men: An Anthropologist's View.* New York: Holt, Rinehart and Winston, 1975.

Fry, Lincoln. "A Preliminary Examination of the Factors Related to Turnover of Women in Law Enforcement." *Journal of Police Science and Administration* 11 (1983): 149–55.

Galinsky, Ellen, Kersten Aumann, and James T. Bond. *Times Are Changing: Gender and Generation at Work and at Home.* Families and Work Institute, 2009. Accessed February 2017. http://familiesandwork.org/site/research/reports/Times_Are_Changing.pdf.

Garcia, Venessa. "'Difference' in the Police Department." *Journal of Contemporary Criminal Justice* 19 (2003): 330–44.

Gardella, Carolyn. "Lead Exposure in Pregnancy: A Review of the Literature and Argument for Routine Prenatal Screening." *Obstetrical and Gynecological Survey* 56 (2001): 231–38.

Garrett, Laurie. "Murder by Teens Has Soared Since '85." *New York Newsday*, February 18, 1995.

Good Housekeeping. "Good Housekeeping Finds Out What a Policewoman Does." 113 (1941): 26–28.

Goodmark, Leigh. "Hands Up at Home: Militarized Masculinity and Police Officers Who Commit Intimate Partner Violence." *Brigham Young University Law Review*, March 9, 2015: 1183–246.

Gosselin, Denise. *Heavy Hands*. Boston: Pearson, 2014.

Gossett, Jennifer, and Joyce Williams. "Perceived Discrimination among Women in Law Enforcement." *Women and Criminal Justice* 10 (1998): 53–73.

Graham v. Connor, 490 US 386, 1989.

Green, Robert. "Police as Social Service Workers?" *Journal of Sociology & Social Welfare* 3 (1976). Accessed March 2017. http://scholarworks.wmich.edu/jssw/vol3/iss6/9.

Griggs v. Duke Power Company, 401 US 424, 1971.

Grossman, Joanna, and Gillian Thomas. "Making Pregnancy Work: Overcoming the Pregnancy Discrimination Act's Capacity-Based Model." *Yale Journal of Law and Feminism* 21 (2009): 1–47.

Guajardo, Salomon A. "New York City Police Department Downsizing and Its Impact on Female Officer Employment." *Journal of Ethnicity in Criminal Justice* 13 (2015): 255–82.

Haarr, Robin N. "Factors Affecting the Decision of Police Recruits to 'Drop Out' of Police Work." *Police Quarterly* 8 (2005): 431–53.

Haarr, Robin, and Merry Morash. "Gender, Race, and Strategies of Coping with Occupational Stress in Policing." *Justice Quarterly* 16 (1999): 303–36.

Hamilton, Mary. *Policewoman: Her Service and Ideals*. New York: Frederick A. Stokes, 1924.

Harless v. Duck, 619F2d 611, 1980.

Harpold, Joseph, and Samuel Feenster. "Negative Influences of Police Stress." *FBI Law Enforcement Bulletin* 71 (2002): 1–7.

Hennessy, Stephen M. "Achieving Cultural Competency." *Police Chief* 60 (August 1993): 46–54.

Herrington, Nancy L. "Female Cops." In *Critical Issues in Policing*, edited by Roger Dunham and Geoffrey Alpert. Prospect Heights, IL: Waveland Press, 1992.

Hixson, Lindsay, Bradford B. Hepler, and Myoung Ouk Kim. *The White Population: 2010 Census Briefs*. Washington, DC: US Census Bureau, 2011. Accessed December 2016. https://www.census.gov/prod/cen2010/briefs/c2010br-05.pdf.

Homant, Robert, and Daniel Kennedy. "Police Perceptions of Spouse Abuse: A Comparison of Male and Female Officers." *Journal of Criminal Justice* 13 (1985): 29–47.

Horne, Peter. "Policewomen: Their First Century and the New Era." *Police Chief* 73, no. 9 (2006): 23–32. Accessed August 15, 2016. http://policechiefmagazine.org/magazine/index.cfm?fuseaction=display_arch&article_id=1000&issue_id=92006.

Horne, Peter. *Women in Law Enforcement*. Second edition. Springfield, IL: Charles C. Thomas, 1980.

Hoschschild, Arlie Russell. *The Second Shift*. New York: Viking Penguin, 1989.

Human Rights Watch. *United States: Punishment and Prejudice: Racial Disparities in the War on Drugs*. Washington, DC: Human Rights Watch, 2000. Accessed December 2016. https://www.hrw.org/reports/2000/usa/.

Hunt, Jennifer. "The Logic of Sexism among Police." *Women and Criminal Justice* 1, no. 2 (1990): 3–30.

IACP National Law Enforcement Policy Center. "Pregnancy Policy." March 2010. Accessed February 2017. http://www.iacp.org/Model-Policies-Alphabetical-Order.

Illinois Law Enforcement Training and Standards Board. *Peace Officer Wellness Evaluation Report (POWER)*. 2016. Accessed August 15, 2016. http://www.nemrt .com/downloads/POWERTEST.pdf.

Indianapolis News. "Women on Patrol?" September 16, 1968.

International Association of Chiefs of Police. *The Future of Women in Policing: Mandates for Action*. Washington, DC: IACP, 1998.

International Association of Chiefs of Police. "National Law Enforcement Policy Center, Pregnancy Policy." March 2010. Alexandria, VA: IACP. Accessed February 2017. http://www.iacp.org/Model-Policies-Alphabetical-Order.

Johnson, Carrie. "20 Years Later, Parts of Major Crime Bill Viewed as Terrible Mistake." *Morning Edition*, National Public Radio, September 14, 2014. Accessed September 12, 2016. http://www.npr.org/2014/09/12/347736999/20-years-later -major-crime-bill-viewed-as-terrible-mistake.

Johnson, Kevin. "Women Move into Law Enforcement's Highest Ranks." *USA Today*, December 2, 2015. Accessed December 2016. http://www.usatoday.com/story/news/ nation/2013/08/13/women-law-enforcement-police-dea-secret-service/2635407/.

Journal of the House of Representatives for the State of Indiana. "As to the Affairs of the South Prison." April 14, 1869.

"Jury Awards $900,000 to Black Female Officer in Detroit Police Case." *Jet* 72 (April 27, 1987).

Kanter, Rosabeth M. *Men and Women of the Corporation*. New York: Basic Books, 1977.

Kasper, Jody. "Proven Steps for Recruiting Women." *Law and Order*, December 2006. Accessed December 2016. http://www.hendonpub.com/resources/article_archive/ results/details?id=3443.

Kappeler, Victor E., Richard D. Sluder, and Geoffrey P. Alpert. *Breeding Deviant Conformity from Forces of Deviance: The Dark Side of Policing*. Long Grove, IL: Waveland Press, 1998.

Kelling, George L., and Mark H. Moore. *The Evolving Strategy of Policing*. Washington, DC: The National Institute of Justice, November 1988.

Kerber, Kenneth, Stephen Andes, and Michelle Mittler. "Citizen Attitudes Regarding the Competence of Female Police Officers." *Journal of Police Science and Administration* 5 (1977): 337–47.

Kilborn, Peter. "Minorities in Blue—a Special Report: New York Police Force Lagging in Recruitment of Black Officers." *New York Times*, July 17, 1994. Accessed September 2016. http://www.nytimes.com/1994/07/17/nyregion/minorities-blue-special -report-new-york-police-force-lagging-recruitment-black.html?pagewanted=all.

Kindy, Kimberly, Marc Fisher, Julie Tate, and Jennifer Jenkins. "A Year of Reckoning: Police Fatally Shoot Nearly 1,000." *Washington Post*, December 26, 2015. Accessed January 2017. http://www.washingtonpost.com/sf/investigative/2015/12/26/a-year-of-reckoning-police-fatally-shoot-nearly-1000/.

Kirschman, Ellen. *I Love a Cop*. New York: Guilford Press, 2007.

Koenig, Esther. "An Overview of Attitudes toward Women in Law Enforcement." *Public Administration Review* 38 (1978): 267–75.

Kruger, Karen J. "Pregnancy and Policing: Are They Compatible? Pushing the Legal Limits on Behalf of Equal Employment Opportunities." *Wisconsin Women's Law Journal* 61 (2007). Accessed January 2017. http://www.fblaw.com/pdf/kruger-pregnancy-policing.pdf.

Lane, Jodi, Nicole E. Rader, Billy Henson, Bonnie S. Fisher, and David C. May. *Fear of Crime in the United States: Causes, Consequences, and Contradictions*. Durham, NC: Carolina Academic Press, 2014.

Langston, Lynn. *Women in Law Enforcement, 1987–2008*. Washington, DC: US Department of Justice, 2010.

Langworthy, Robert, Tad Hughes, and Beth Sanders. *Law Enforcement Recruitment, Selection, and Training: A Survey of Major Police Departments in the US*. Highland Heights, KY: Academy of Criminal Justice Sciences—Police Section, 1995.

Lawless, Jennifer, and Richard Fox. *Men Rule: The Continued Under-Representation of Women in U.S. Politics*. Washington, DC: Women in Politics Institute, 2012.

Leger, Kristen. "Public Perceptions of Female Police Officer on Patrol." *American Journal of Criminal Justice* 21 (1997): 231–49.

Lersch, Kim. "Exploring Gender Differences in Citizen Allegations of Police Misconduct: An Analysis of a Municipal Police Department." *Women and Criminal Justice* 9 (1998): 69–79.

Levy, Marc. "U.S. Sues Pa. State Police, Saying Physical Fitness Test Discriminates against Women." *Pennlive.com*, July 30, 2014. Accessed December 2016. http://www.pennlive.com/midstate/index.ssf/2014/07/us_sues_pa_state_police_saying.html.

Lockwood, Daniel, and Ariane Prohaska. "Police Officer Gender and Attitudes toward Intimate Partner Violence: How Policy Can Eliminate Stereotypes." *International Journal of Criminal Justice Sciences* 10 (2015): 77–90.

Lonsway, Kimberly, and Joanne M. Archambault. "The 'Justice Gap' for Sexual Assault Cases Future Directions for Research and Reform." *Violence against Women* 18 (2012): 145–68.

Lonsway, Kimberly, Michelle Wood, and Katharine Spillar. "Officer Gender and Excessive Force." *Law and Order* 50 (2002): 60–66.

Lord, Lesli K. "A Comparison of Male and Female Peace Officers' Stereotypic Perceptions of Women and Women Peace Officers." *Journal of Police Science and Administration* 14 (1986): 231–49.

Los Angeles Police Department. *Annual Report, Police Department, City of Los Angeles, California, for the Fiscal Year Ending June 30, 1914*. Los Angeles: Los Angeles Police Department, 1914.

Los Angeles Times. "First Woman Policeman." September 14, 1910.

Los Angeles Times. "Want Naughty Plays Stopped." March 15, 1911, I15.

Lott, John R. "Does a Helping Hand Put Others at Risk? Affirmative Action, Police Departments, and Crime." *Economic Inquiry*, April 2000, 239–77.

Loving, Kathryn. "10 Ways Law Enforcement Ruined Me as a Woman." *PoliceOne*, September 2, 2016. Accessed February 2017. https://www.policeone.com/women-officers/articles/217721006-10-ways-law-enforcement-ruined-me-as-a-woman/.

Lunneborg, Patricia. *Women Police Officer: Current Career Profile*. Springfield, IL: Charles C. Thomas, 1989.

Maglione, Roslyn. "Recruiting, Retaining and Promoting Women: The Success of the Charlotte-Mecklenburg Police Department's Women's Network." *Police Chief*, March 2002, 19–24.

Marrapodi, Eric. "Officers Death Shocks New Orleans." *CNN*, February 1, 2008. Accessed January 2017. http://www.cnn.com/2008/US/02/01/slain.police.officer/index.html?_s=PM:US.

Martin, Susan E. *Breaking and Entering: Policewomen on Patrol*. Berkeley: University of California Press, 1980.

Martin, Susan E. "The Changing Status of Women Officers." In *The Changing Roles of Women in the Criminal Justice System*, edited by Imogene L. Moyer. Second edition. Prospect Heights, IL: Waveland, 1992.

Martin, Susan E. *On the Move: The Status of Women in Policing*. Washington, DC: Police Foundation, 1990.

Martin, Susan E. "Outsider within the Stationhouse: The Impact of Race and Gender on Black Women Police." *Social Problems* 4 (1994): 383–400.

Martin, Susan E. "Police Force or Police Service? Gender and Emotional Labor." *The Annals of the American Academy of Political and Social Science* 561 (1999): 111–26.

Martin, Susan E., and Nancy C. Jurik. *Doing Justice, Doing Gender: Women in Legal and Criminal Justice Occupations*. Thousand Oaks, CA: Sage, 2007.

Maryland Chiefs of Police Association. *A Task Analysis Study of Entry-Level Law Enforcement in the State of Maryland*. Columbia, MD: Author, 1995.

Maslach, Christina, Wilmar Schaufeli, and Michael Leiter. "Job Burnout." *Annual Review of Psychology* 53 (2001): 397–422.

McCarthy, D. J. "Gendering 'Soft' Policing: Multi-Agency Working, Female Cops, and the Fluidities of Police Culture/s." *Policing and Society* 23 (2011): 261–83.

McCarty, William, Jihong Solomon Zhao, and Brett E. Garland. "Occupational Stress and Burnout between Male and Female Police Officers: Are There Any Gender Differences?" *Policing: An International Journal of Police Strategies and Management* 30 (2007): 672–91.

McElroy, Jackie. "Officer Gail Cobb." Accessed August 15, 2016. http://www.mcjackie.com/cobb.html.

McKay, Hollie. "Angie Dickinson 'Felt Exploited' in '*Police Woman*' but Says Women's Roles in Crimes Dramas Have 'Evolved.'" *Fox News Entertainment*, June 23, 2014. Accessed August 15, 2016. http://www.foxnews.com/entertainment/2014/06/23/angie-dickinson-felt-exploited-in-police-woman-but-says-womens-roles-in-crimes.html.

McLaurin, Michael. "How to Run an Assessment Center." *Police Magazine*, March 1, 2005. Accessed August 2016. http://www.policemag.com.

Meier, Kenneth, and Jill Nicholson-Crotty. "Gender, Representative Bureaucracy, and Law Enforcement: The Case of Sexual Assault." *Public Administration Review* 66 (2006): 850–60.

Melchionne, Theresa M. "Report of Committee 'A' Organization and Administrative Considerations." In *Proceedings of Workshop for Policewomen*, edited by Nelson Watson and Robert Walker. Washington, DC: International Association of Chiefs of Police, 1966.

Miller, Laurence. "Practical Strategies for Preventing Officer Suicide." *Law and Order* 3 (2006): 90–92.

Miller, Susan. *Gender and Community Policing: Walking the Talk*. Boston: Northeastern University Press, 1999.

Milton, Catherine, Ava Abramowitz, Laura Crites, Margaret Gates, Ellen Mintz, and Georgette Sandler. *Women in Policing: A Manual*. Washington, DC: Police Foundation, 1974.

Milton, Catherin H. *Women in Policing*. Washington, DC: Police Foundation, 1972.

Moore, Carole. "Pregnant Officer Policies." *Law and Order* 51 (2003): 74–78.

Morash, Merry, Robin Haarr, and Dae Hoon Kwak. "Multi-Level Influences on Police Stress." *Journal of Contemporary Criminal Justice* 22 (2006): 26–43.

Moreland, Leslie, Gregory Leskin, Caroline Rebecca Block, Jacquelyn Campbell, and Matthew J. Friedman. "Intimate Partner Violence and Miscarriage: Examination of the Role of Physical and Psychological Abuse and Posttraumatic Stress Disorder." *Journal of Interpersonal Violence* 23 (2008): 652–69.

Morn, Frank. *Forgotten Reformer: Robert McClaughry and Criminal Justice Reform in Nineteenth-Century America*. Lanham, MD: University Press of America, 2010.

Moss, Peter. *International Review of Leave Policies and Related Research*. London: Institute of Education, University of London, June 2014. Accessed January 2017. http://www.leavenetwork.org/fileadmin/Leavenetwork/Annual_reviews/2014_annual_review_korr.pdf.

Muller v. Oregon, 208 US 412, 422-423, 1908.

National Center for Women and Policing. *Equality Denied*. Washington, DC: Feminist Majority, 2001.

National Center for Women and Policing. *Homepage*. Accessed October 2016. http://www.womenandpolicing.org/.

National Coalition against Domestic Violence. *What Is Domestic Violence?* Accessed February 2017. http://www.ncadv.org/learn-more/what-is-domestic-violence.

National Institute for Occupational Safety and Health Administration. *The Effects of Workplace Hazards on Female Reproductive Health*. Washington, DC: Centers for Disease Control and Prevention, 1999. Accessed January 2017. http://www.cdc.gov/NIOSH/99-104.html.

National Institute for Occupational Safety and Health Administration. *Work Related Roadway Crashes: Challenges and Opportunities for Prevention*. Washington, DC: Centers for Disease Control and Prevention, September 2003. Accessed January 2017. http://www.cdc.gov/niosh/docs/2003-119/default.html.

National Public Radio. "Timeline: America's War on Drugs." *The Forgotten War on Drugs* (special series), April 2, 2007. Accessed January 2017. http://www.npr.org/templates/story/story.php?storyId=9252490.

Nelson, Josephine. "On the Policewoman's Beat." *Independent Woman*, May 1936. Accessed August 15, 2016. www.sameshield.com/press/sspress112.html.

Newman, Deborah W., and M. Leanne Rucker-Reed. "Police Stress, State-Trait Anxiety, and Stressors among U.S. Marshals." *Journal of Criminal Justice* 32 (2004): 631–41.

New York City Police Department. *New York City Police Department Annual Firearms Discharge Report, 2012.* Accessed August 15, 2016. http://www.nyc.gov/html/nypd/downloads/pdf/analysis_and_planning/nypd_annual_firearms_discharge_report_2012.pdf.

New York Times. "Police Matron's Job Is Not a Sinecure—What with Preventing Suicides and Lodging Vagrants Her Life's a Busy One." February 16, 1908. Accessed August 15, 2016. http://query.nytimes.com/mem/archivefree/pdf?res=9802E7D7173EE233A25755C1A9649C946997D6CF.

Obama, Barack. "Dallas Police Memorial Service." Comments presented at the Dallas Shooting Memorial Service, Dallas, Texas, July 12, 2016. Accessed December 2016. http://time.com/4403543/president-obama-dallas-shooting-memorial-service-speech-transcript/.

Oehme, Karen, Elizabeth A. Donnelly, and Annelise Martin. "Alcohol Abuse, PTSD, and Officer-Committed Domestic Violence." *Policing* 6 (2012): 418–30.

Office of the Attorney General. *The New York City Police Department's "Stop and Frisk" Practices: A Report to the People of New York from the Office of the Attorney General.* Albany: Office of the New York State Attorney General, December 1999.

O'Loughlin v. Pinchback, 579 So.2d 788 (Fla. App. 1 Dist. 1991).

Oregonian. "Portland to Ban Public Dances." November 1912, 15.

Owens, Marie. "Enforcement of the Child Labor Laws." *Chicago Daily Tribune*, July 28, 1901. Accessed August 15, 2016. https://www.newspapers.com/newspage/28521967/.

Owings, Chloe. *Women Police.* Montclair, NJ: Patterson Smith, 1969.

Page, Amy Dellinger. "Judging Women and Defining Crime: Police Officers' Attitudes toward Women and Rape." *Sociological Spectrum* 28 (2008): 389–411.

Philadelphia Police Department. *Preference Points*, 2012. Accessed September 2016. www.phillypolice.com/careers/preference-points.

Pike, Diane L. "Women in Police Academy Training: Some Aspects of Organizational Response." In *The Changing Roles of Women in the Criminal Justice System: Offenders, Victims, and Professionals*, edited by Imogene L. Moyer. Prospect Heights, IL: Waveland Press, 1985.

Pogrebin, Mark, Mary Dodge, and Harold Chatham. "Reflections of African-American Women on Their Careers in Urban Policing: Their Experiences of Racial and Sexual Discrimination." *International Journal of the Sociology of Law* 28 (2000): 311–26.

Polisar, Joseph, and Donna Milgram. "Recruiting, Integrating, and Retaining Women Police Officers: Strategies That Work." *Police Chief* 65 (October 1998): 42–52.

President's Task Force on 21st Century Policing. *Final Report of the President's Task Force on 21st Century Policing.* Washington, DC: Office of Community Oriented Policing Services, 2015.

Price, Barbara R. "Sexual Integration in American Law Enforcement." In *Police Ethics*, edited by William C. Hefferman. New York: John Jay Press, 1985.

Prokos, Anastasia, and Irene Padavic. "'There Oughtta Be a Law against Bitches': Masculinity Lessons in Police Academy Training." *Gender, Work & Organization* 9 (2002): 439–59.

President's Commission of Law Enforcement and Administration of Justice. *The Challenge of Crime in a Free Society*. Washington, DC: US Government Printing Office, 1967.

Rabe-Hemp, Cara. "Exploring Administrators' Perceptions of Light-Duty Assignment." *Police Quarterly* 14 (2011): 124–41.

Rabe-Hemp, Cara E. "Female Officers and the Ethic of Care: Does Officer Gender Impact Police Behaviors?" *Journal of Criminal Justice* 36 (2008): 426–34.

Rabe-Hemp, Cara. "Policewomen and Matrons." In *Encyclopedia of Criminology and Criminal Justice*, January 22, 2014. Accessed February 2017. http://onlinelibrary. wiley.com/doi/10.1002/9781118517383.wbeccj119/abstract;jsessionid=0592AD45 EF2172DE111B4459365E3CDE.f04t02.

Rabe-Hemp, Cara E. "Survival in an 'All Boys Club': Policewomen and Their Fight for Acceptance." *Policing* 31 (2008): 251–70.

Rabe-Hemp, Cara, and Gail Humiston. "A Survey of Maternity Policies and Pregnancy Accommodations in the United States." *Police Practice and Research* 16, no. 3 (2014): 239–53.

Rabe-Hemp, Cara E., and Amie Schuck. "Violence against Police Officers: Are Female Officers at Greater Risk?" *Police Quarterly* 10 (2007): 411–28.

Rafter, Nicole Hahn. *Partial Justice: Women, Prisons and Social Control*. New Brunswick, NJ: Transaction, 1990.

Raganella, Anthony, and Michael D. White. "Race, Gender, and Motivation for Becoming a Police Officer: Implications for Building a Representative Police Department." *Journal of Criminal Justice* 32 (2004): 501–13.

Ray, Rebecca, Janet Gornick, and John Schmitt. *Parental Leave Policies in 21 Countries*. Washington, DC: Center for Economic and Policy Research, June 2009. Accessed January 2017. http://www.cepr.net/documents/publications/paren tal_2008_09.pdf.

Reaves, Brian. "Campus Law Enforcement, 2011–12, NCJ 248028." Bureau of Justice Statistics, January 2015. Accessed March 13, 2017. https://www.bjs.gov/index.cfm? ty=pbdetail&iid=5216.

Reaves, Brian. *Local Police Departments, 2013: Personnel, Policies, and Practices*. Washington, DC: Bureau of Justice Statistics, May 2015. Accessed August 15, 2016. http://www.bjs.gov/content/pub/pdf/lpd13ppp.pdf.

Remmington, Patricia W. *Policing: The Occupation and Introduction of Female Officers*. Washington, DC: University Press of America, 1982.

Remmington, Patricia W. "Women in the Police: Integration or Separation." *Qualitative Sociology* 6 (1983): 118–35.

Reuters. "Obama Marks 1972 Law Lifting Education Barriers to Girls." June 23, 2010. Accessed August 15, 2016. http://www.reuters.com/article/us-usa-obama-sports-gender-idUSBRE85M0I720120623.

Riccucci, Norma, Greg Van Ryzin, and Cecilia Lavena. "Representative Bureaucracy in Policing: Does It Increase Perceived Legitimacy?" *Journal of Public Administration Research and Theory* 24 (2014): 537–51.

Riordan, Catherine A., Tamara Gross, and Cathlin C. Maloney. "Self-Monitoring, Gender, and the Personal Consequences of Impression Management." *American Behavioral Scientist* 37 (1994): 715–25.

Roberge, Marie-Elene, and Rolf Van Dick. "Recognizing the Benefits of Diversity: When and How Does Diversity Increase Group Performance." *Human Resource Management Review* 20 (2010): 295–308.

Rohrbaugh, Joanna Bunker. "Women in the Workplace." In *Crisis in American Institutions*, edited by Jerome H. Skolnick and Elliott Currie. Boston: Little, Brown, 1976.

Rothman, Sheila. *Women's Proper Place: A History of Changing Ideals and Practices 1870 to Present.* New York: Basic Books, 1978.

Sass, Tim R., and Jennifer L. Troyer. "Affirmative Action, Political Representation, Unions, and Female Police Employment." *Journal of Labor Research* 20 (1999): 571–87.

Saturday Evening Post. "Some Cops Have Lovely Legs." December 24, 1949.

Scarborough, Kathryn, G. Norman Van Tubergen, Larry K. Gaines, and Scott Whitlow. "An Examination of Police Officers' Motivation to Participate in the Promotional Process." *Police Quarterly* 2 (1990): 302–20.

Schuck, Amie. "Gender Differences in Policing: Testing Hypotheses from the Performance and Disruption Perspectives." *Feminist Criminology* 9 (2014): 160–85.

Schuck, Amie, and Cara E. Rabe-Hemp. "Women Police: The Use of Force by and against Female Officers." *Women & Criminal Justice* 16 (2005): 91–117.

Schuck, Amie, and Cara Rabe-Hemp. "Citizen Complaints and Gender Diversity in Police Organizations." *Police and Society* 26 (2014): 859–74.

Schulz, Dorothy Moses. *From Social Worker to Crimefighter: Women in United States Municipal Policing.* Westport, CT: Praeger, 1995.

Schulze, Corrine. "Family Leave and Law Enforcement: A Survey of Parents in U.S. Police Departments." *Critical Criminology* 19 (2010): 137–53.

Scoville, Dean. "Protect Yourself from Blood Borne Diseases." *Police: The Law Enforcement Magazine*, August 8, 2008. Accessed January 2017. http://www.policemag.com/blog/patrol-tactics/story/2008/08/protect-yourself-from-blood-borne-diseases.aspx.

Scrivner, Ellen. *Innovations in Police and Hiring in the Spirit of Service Recruitment Hiring.* Washington, DC: US Department of Justice, Office of Community Oriented Policing Service, 2001. Accessed September 2016. http://ric-zai-inc.com/Publications/cops-p090-pub.pdf.

Scrivner, Ellen. "Recruitment and Hiring: Challenge or Opportunity for Change?" RAND Center for Quality Policing Recruitment and Retention Summit, Arlington, VA, 2008. Accessed December 2016. http://www.cops.usdoj.gov/pdf/conference/rand/ScrivnerRecruitmentpresentation.pdf.

Sherman, Lawrence. "An Evaluation of Policewomen on Patrol in a Suburban Police Department." *Journal of Police Science and Administration* 3 (1975): 434–38.

Sherman, Lawrence. "Causes of Police Behavior: The Current Police State of Quantitative Research." *Journal of Crime and Delinquency* 17 (1980): 69–100.

Shimm, D. S., and M. Passamaneck. *Shooting Noise, Hearing Loss, and Hearing Protection*. Berryville, AR: International Defensive Pistol Association, 2001.

Shpritzer, Felicia. "A Case for the Promotion of Policewomen in the City of New York." *Police* 5 (July/August 1961): 50–57.

Sichel, Joyce L., Lucy N. Friedman, Janet C. Quint, and M. E. Smith. *Women on Patrol: A Pilot Study of Police Performance in New York City*. Washington, DC: National Institute of Law Enforcement and Criminal Justice, 1978.

Silvestri, Marisa. "'Doing' Police Leadership: Enter the 'Smart Macho' Leader." *Journal of Policing and Society: An International Journal of Research and Policy* 17 (2007): 38–58.

Simple Justice. "Culture Shock." https://blog.simplejustice.us/2016/08/15/culture-shock/.

Smith, Bertha H. "The Policewoman." *Good Housekeeping* 52 (March 1911): 296–98.

Smith v. the City of East Cleveland, 363 F. Supp. 1131, 1973.

Somvadee, Chaiyavej, and Merry Morash. "Dynamics of Sexual Harassment for Policewomen Working alongside Men." *Policing: An International Journal of Police Strategies and Management* 31 (2008): 485–98.

Sparrow, Malcolm, Mark Moore, and David Kennedy. *Beyond 911: A New Era for Policing*. New York: Basic Books, 1990.

Spohn, Cassie, and Katharine Tellis. "The Criminal Justice System's Response to Sexual Violence." *Violence against Women* 18 (2012): 169–92.

Snow, Robert. *Policewomen Who Made History*. Lanham, MD: Rowman & Littlefield, 2010.

Stewart, Amy. "Female Police Officers Save Lives." *New York Times*, July 26, 2016. Accessed January 2017. http://www.nytimes.com/2016/07/26/opinion/female-police-officers-save-lives.html?_r=0.

Taft, Angela. "Violence against Women in Pregnancy and after Childbirth: Current Knowledge and Issues in Health Care Responses." *Australian Domestic & Family Violence Clearinghouse* 6 (2002): 1–23.

Talney, R. G. "Women in Law Enforcement: An Expanded Role." *Police* 19 (1969): 50.

Tate, Teresa T. "Police Suicide, What Can Be Done?" *Tears of a Cop*. Accessed August 15, 2016. www.tearsofacop.com/police/articles/tate.html.

Title VII of the 1964 Civil Rights Act, 42 USC 2000a, 2a, 1972.

Thomas v. City of Evanston, 881 F.2d 382, 1985.

Thompson, Heather A. "Why Mass Incarceration Matters: Rethinking Crisis, Decline, and Transformation in Postwar American History." *Journal of American History* 97 (2010): 705–36.

Townes, Glen. "Showing Her Mettle." *Hispanic* 6 (1993): 2–3.

Trostle, Lawrence C. "LAPD Successful in Recruiting Minorities and Women." *Alaska Justice Forum* 7 (Fall 1990): 1, 6–8. Accessed September 2016. http://justice.uaa.alaska.edu/forum/07/3fall1990/a_lapd.html.

United Automobile Workers v. Johnson Controls, Inc., 499 US 187, 1991.

United States Department of Labor. "Facts Over Time." 2014. Accessed October 2016. www.dol.gov/wb/stats/facts_over_time.htm.

United States Department of Labor. "Traditional and Nontraditional Occupations." 2014. Accessed August 2016. https://www.dol.gov/wb/stats/Nontraditional%20 Occupations.pdf.

United States Department of Labor, Occupational Safety, and Health Administration. "Critical Incident Stress Guide." Accessed August 15, 2016. www.osha.gov/SLTC/ emergencypreparedness/guides/critical.html.

Van Brocklin, Val. "Why Aren't There More Women in Police Work? Is the Profession Holding Us Back, or Do We Lack the Ambition?" *PoliceOne*, October 23, 2013. Accessed September 2016. https://www.policeone.com/women-officers/ articles/6539439-Why-arent-there-more-women-in-policework/.

Volanti, John, Desta Fekedulegn, Tara Hartley, Luenda Charles, Michael Andrew, Claudia Ma, and Cecil Burchfiel. "Highly Rates and Most Frequent Stressors among Police Officers: Gender Differences." *American Journal of Criminal Justice* 16 (2016): 645–62.

Vollmer, August. "Meet the Lady Cop." *Survey Graphic*, March 15, 1930.

Walker, Samuel. *Sense and Nonsense about Crime, Drugs, and Communities*. Stamford, CT: Cengage Learning, 2015.

Watson, Carol. "Female Officers Fighting Crime—and Sexism: Law Enforcement: Some Policewomen Say Departments Are Slow to Integrate Women and Are Plagued by 'a Lot of Old Male Views.'" *Los Angeles Times*, June 24, 1990. Accessed September 2016. http://articles.latimes.com/1990-06-24/local/me-645_1_police-departments/2.

Watson, Jeff. "Mental Health and Peer Support in Law Enforcement." *CopsAlive.com*, February 16, 2012. Accessed February 2017. http://www.copsalive.com/mental -health-peer-support-in-law-enforcement/.

Wehrle-Einhorn, Juanita. "Gender, Stress, and Self in the Work-Family Role System." PhD diss., University of Kansas, 1980.

Weisheit, Ralph. "Women in the State Police: Concerns of Male and Female Officers." *Journal of Police Science and Administration* 15 (1987): 137–44.

Weiss, Harold, and Stephen Strotmeyer. "Characteristics of Pregnant Women in Motor Vehicle Accidents." *Injury Prevention* 8 (2002): 207–10.

Wells, Alice Stebbins. "Personal History of Los Angeles's First Policewoman." *Los Angeles Police Association's Bulletin* (October 1940): 5.

West, Marty L. "Sexual Harassment Complaints: A Growing Concern for Police Management." *Journal of California Law Enforcement* 20 (1985): 55–58.

Wexler, Julie, and D. Logan. "Sources of Stress among Women Police Officers." *Journal of Police Science and Administration* 11 (1983): 46–53.

Whetstone, Thomas, and Deborah Wilson. "Dilemmas Confronting Female Police Officer Promotional Candidates: Glass Ceiling, Disenfranchisement or Satisfaction?" *International Journal of Police Science and Management* 2 (1995): 128–43.

Wilbanks, William. *True Heroines: Police Women Killed in the Line of Duty throughout the United States*. Paducah, KY: Turner Publishing Company, 2000.

Wilson, James Q., and George L. Kelling. "Broken Windows: The Police and Neighborhood Safety." *Atlantic Monthly*, March 1982, 1–11.

Wilson, Jeremy, and Clifford Grammich. *Police Recruitment and Retention in the Contemporary Urban Environment: A National Discussion of Personnel Experiences and Promising Practices from the Front Lines.* CF-261-DOJ. Santa Monica, CA: RAND Corporation, 2009. Accessed December 2016. http://www.rand.org/pubs/conf_ proceedings/CF261.

Williams, Julie. "Mentoring for Law Enforcement." *Law Enforcement Bulletin*, March 2000, 19–25.

Williams, Julie. *Unbending Gender: Why Work and Family Conflict and What to Do about It.* New York: Oxford University Press, 2000.

Wines, Enoch, and Theodore Dwight. *Report on the Prisons and Reformatories of the United States and Canada.* Albany, NY: Van Benthuysen and Sons, 1867.

Winnand, K. "Police Women and the People They Serve." *Police Chief* 53 (1986): 62–63.

Wofford, Taylor. "How America's Police Became an Army: The 1033 Program." *Newsweek*, August 13, 2014. Accessed January 2017. http://www.newsweek.com/how-americas-police-became-army-1033-program-264537.

Worden, Alissa. "The Attitudes of Women and Men in Policing: Testing Conventional and Contemporary Wisdom." *Criminology* 31 (1993): 203–41.

Zavala, Egbert, Lisa A. Melander, and Don L. Kurtz. "The Importance of Social Learning and Critical Incident Stressors on Police Officer's Perpetration of Intimate Partner Violence." *Victims & Offenders* 10 (2015): 51–73.

Zhao, Jihong Solomon, Ni He, and Nicholas Lovrich. "Predicting Five Dimensions of Police Officer Stress: Looking More Deeply into Organizational Settings for Sources of Police Stress." *Police Quarterly* 5 (2002): 43–62.

Index

About the Author

Cara Rabe-Hemp graduated from the University of Illinois at Chicago with a PhD in criminal justice in 2005. Inspired by the brave women who wear the police uniform every day, Rabe-Hemp has published extensively in the area of gender and policing, appearing in the top criminology/criminal justice journals for her area of scholarship and bridging the gap between theory and practice. She currently teaches at Illinois State University.